Picture This!

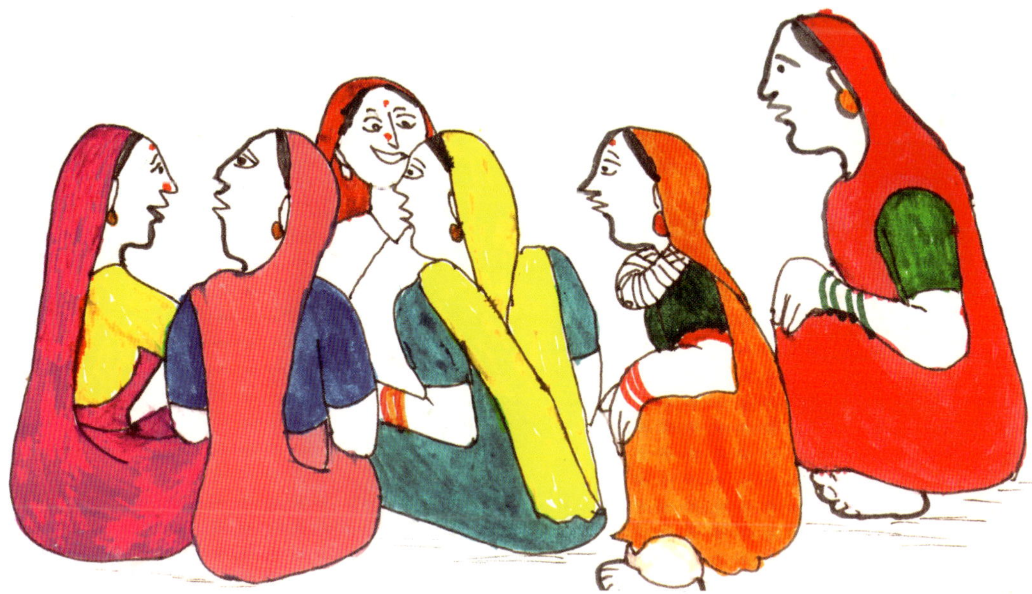

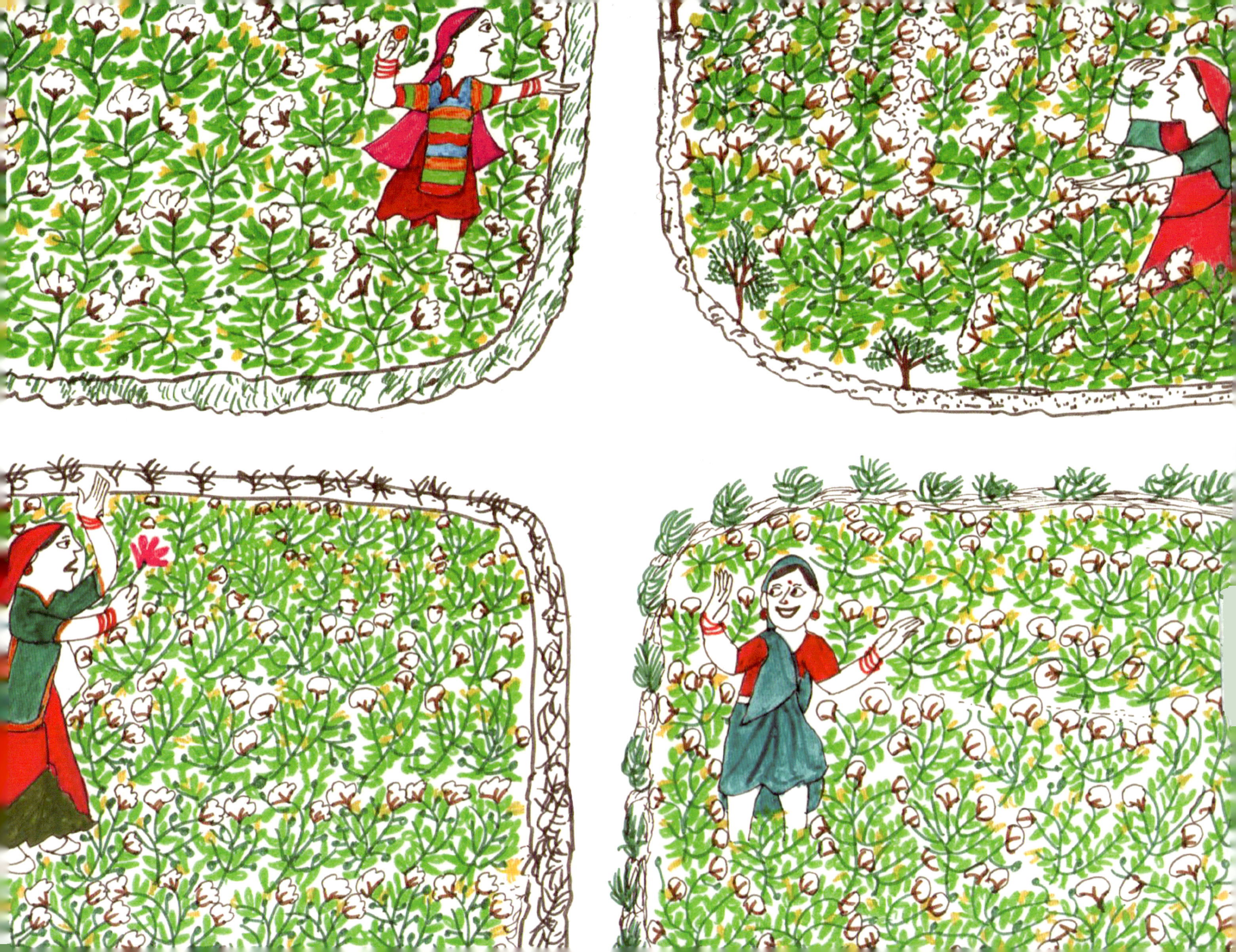

Picture This!

Painting the Women's Movement

ILLUSTRATIONS BY RADHABEN GARVA

ACCOMPANYING TEXT BY SUSHMA IYENGAR

AFTERWORD BY KALPANA SHARMA

zubaan

ZUBAAN
an imprint of Kali for Women
128 B Shahpur Jat, 1st floor
New Delhi 110 049
EMAIL contact@zubaanbooks.com
WEBSITE www.zubaanbooks.com

First published by Zubaan 2013

10 9 8 7 6 5 4 3 2 1

ISBN 978 93 81017 68 5

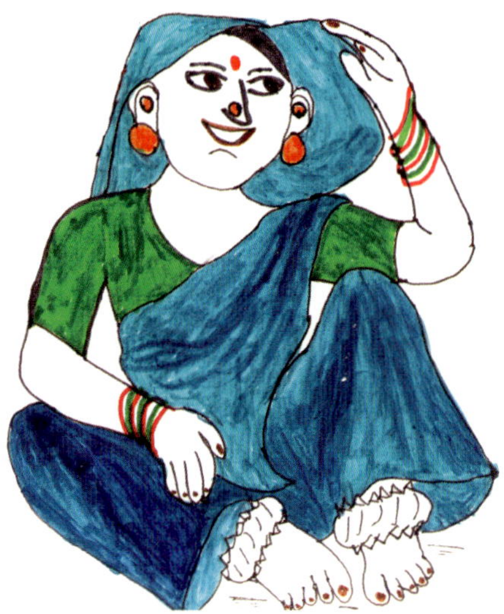

Zubaan is an independent feminist publishing house based in New Delhi, with a strong academic and general list. It was set up as an imprint of the well known feminist house, Kali for Women and carries forward Kali's tradition of publishing world quality books to high editorial and production standards. *Zubaan* means tongue, voice, language, speech in Hindustani. Zubaan is a non-profit publisher, working in the areas of the humanities and social sciences, as well as in fiction, general non-fiction and books for young adults that celebrate difference, diversity and equality, especially for and about the children of India and South Asia under its imprint Young Zubaan.

Designed by Sunandini Banerjee, Seagull Books, Calcutta

Printed and bound in India by Replika Press Pvt. Ltd.

Acknowledgments

Kutch Mahila Vikas Sangathan (KMVS) and Zubaan have collaborated to bring you an unusual book that provides a visual insight into the rural women's movement through the art and times of Radhaben Garva, a leading member of KMVS, and an illustrator.

A quarter century ago, even as the rural women's movement was making its mark in India, support from Swiss Agency for Development Cooperation (SDC) to the women's movement in Kutch was helping give flesh and blood to some of the stories you find in Radhaben's drawings. SDC support to a programme entitled Local Governance Initiative South Asia (LoGIn) – which aimed to capitalize on and document experiences supported by SDC in the past – was instrumental in the development and production of this book. We would like to especially thank Preeta Lall whose motivation and commitment to the idea ensured its publication.

Radhaben's story may never have come to you, had it not been for the perseverance and enthusiasm of the Zubaan team, and of Urvashi Butalia in particular, whose conviction that this was a book worth publishing was infectious, and enabled KMVS to move forward. She hounded and herded us with humour and patiently guided the book through its design, drafts and publication.

A number of individuals have poured their time, expertise and creative energies into shaping this wonderful book. Sushma Iyengar, one of the founders of KMVS, conceived, designed and steered the development of the book, while also embellishing Radhaben's visual story with words. Kalpana Sharma, senior journalist, spent time with KMVS to understand the collective's work, she waded through many discussions and documents to provide Radhaben's drawings a context through her insightful essay; Sunandini Banerjee, book designer extraordinary, who strung together Radhaben's drawings into a beautiful visual tale and designed this book; Chinmayi Shroff, a young designer of handmade books, sifted through more than a thousand drawings with Radhaben, and gave this book its first design contours, and created the design potential through which the eventual book became possible; Kruti Patel of KMVS who coordinated everyone and everything with easy efficiency and a permanent smile.

In many known and invisible ways, many others have contributed – KMVS members, the governing board, friends, fellow travellers of KMVS, and other rural women's collectives in India – who have over the years created a vibrant pool of experiences into which Radhaben's imagination would take an occasional dip! This book is indebted to Nanduba Jadeja, Hakima Theba, Devalben, Niyamat, Javjiba, Naama Meghwal, Alka's Jani, and Lata Sachde who accompanied Radhaben throughout its compilation, and chose the drawings that told their stories the best.

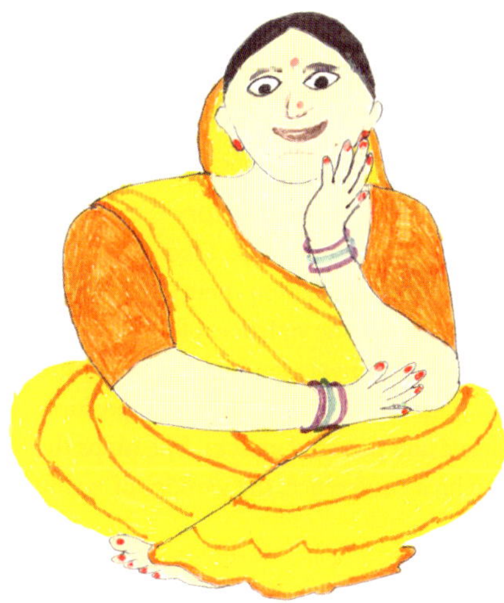

Radhaben's Poem

I set out to expand my world,
And discover its laughter and its pain,
I set out to find the woman within me,
And found instead an artist, speaking to
This woman within me,
Yes, I set out to expand my world.

Translated from Kutchi

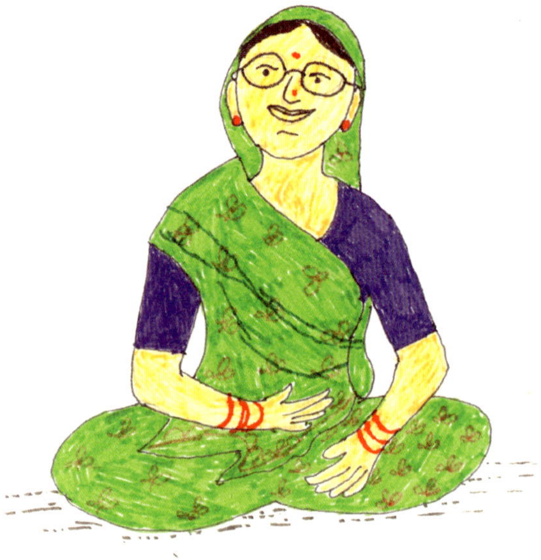

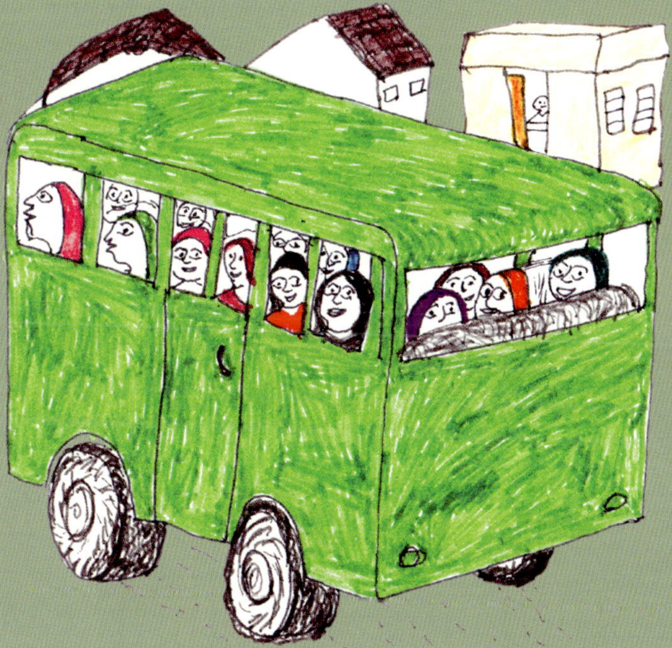

BEGINNINGS

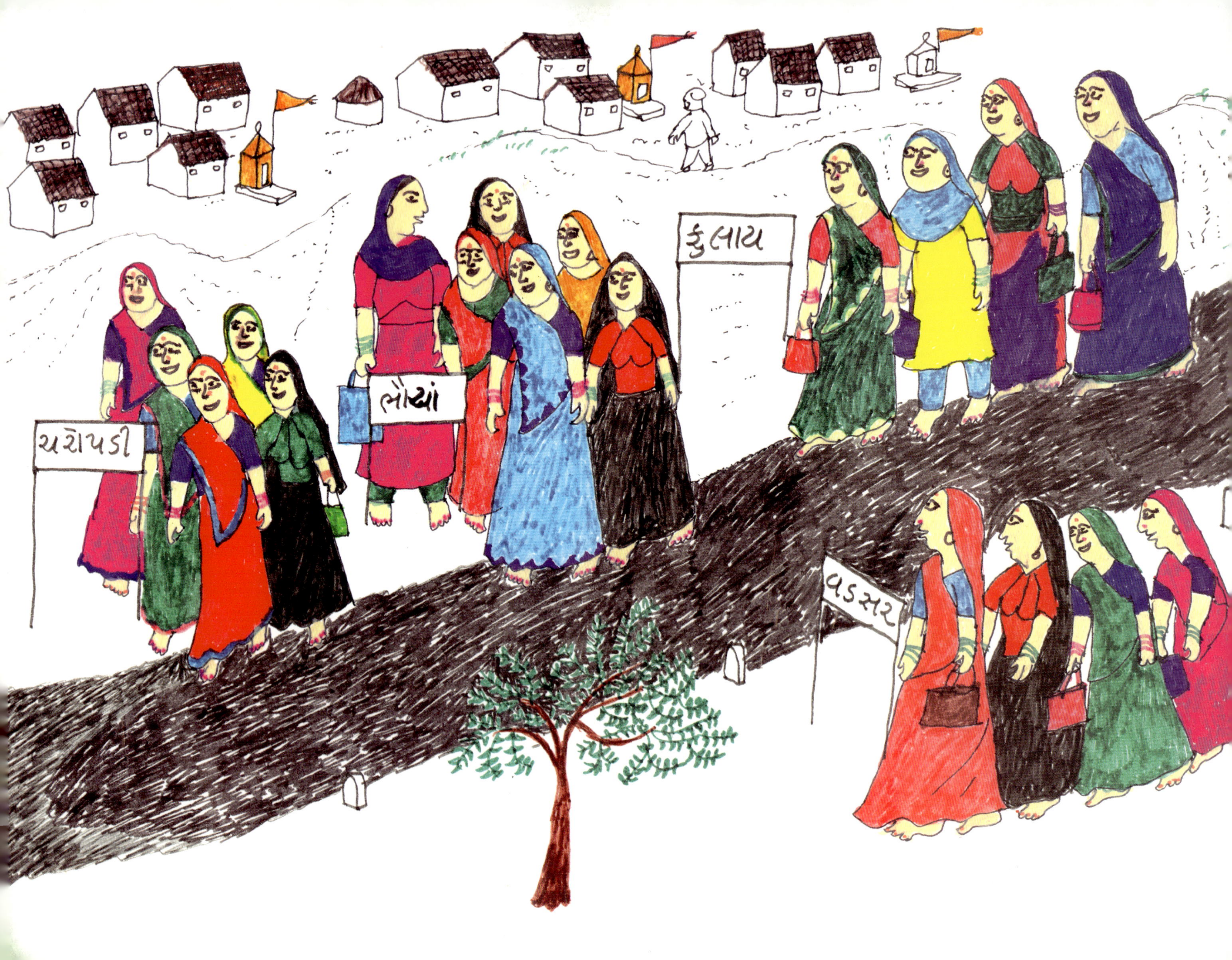
ચરોપડી
ભૌયાં
ફુલાય
વડસર

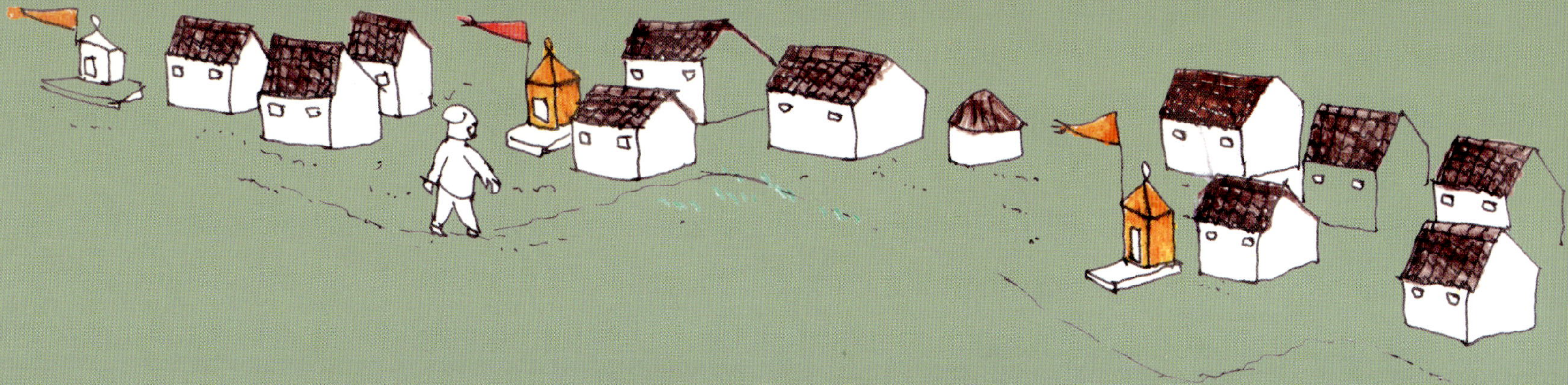

My story, our story, begins 24 years ago.

For many of us, when it began, it was like being caught in a gathering storm with the women who landed in our courtyards one day. They came with their questions, their programmes, their ideas – they cracked our silences and made our spirits soar with their dreams, their songs and their laughter.

And we listened with our questions, our fears and our anxieties.

None of it made sense then. But then, how could it?

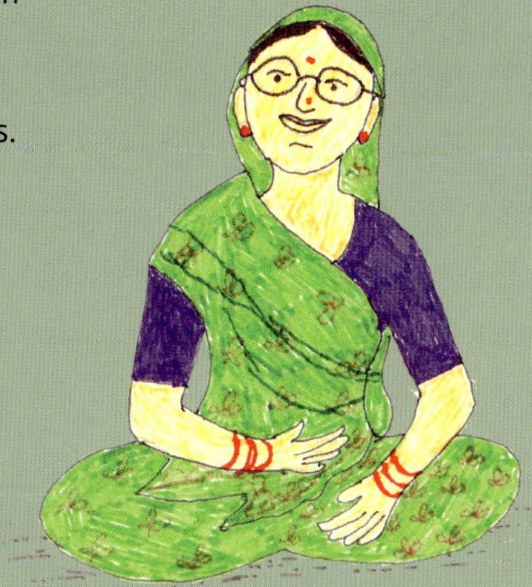

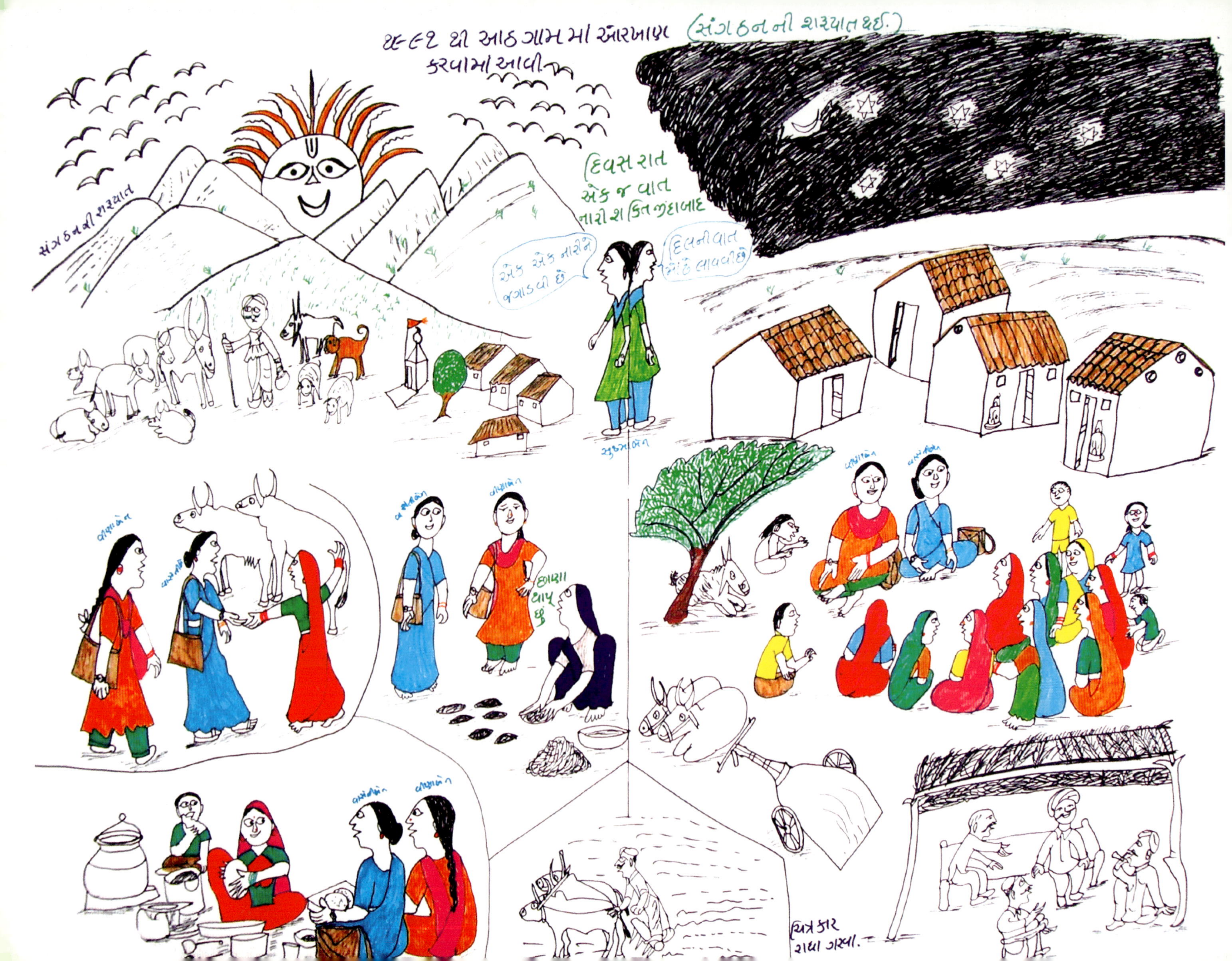

૯૯-૯૨ થી આઠ ગામ મા ઓળખાણ કરવામા આવી.
(સંગઠન ની શરૂઆત થઈ.)
સંગઠનની શરૂઆત
દિવસ રાત
એક જ વાત
નારી શકિત ઝિંદાબાદ
એક એક નારીને જગાડવી છે
દિલની વાત મોઢે લાવવી છે
છાણા થાપુ છું
ચિત્રકાર રાધા ગરવા.

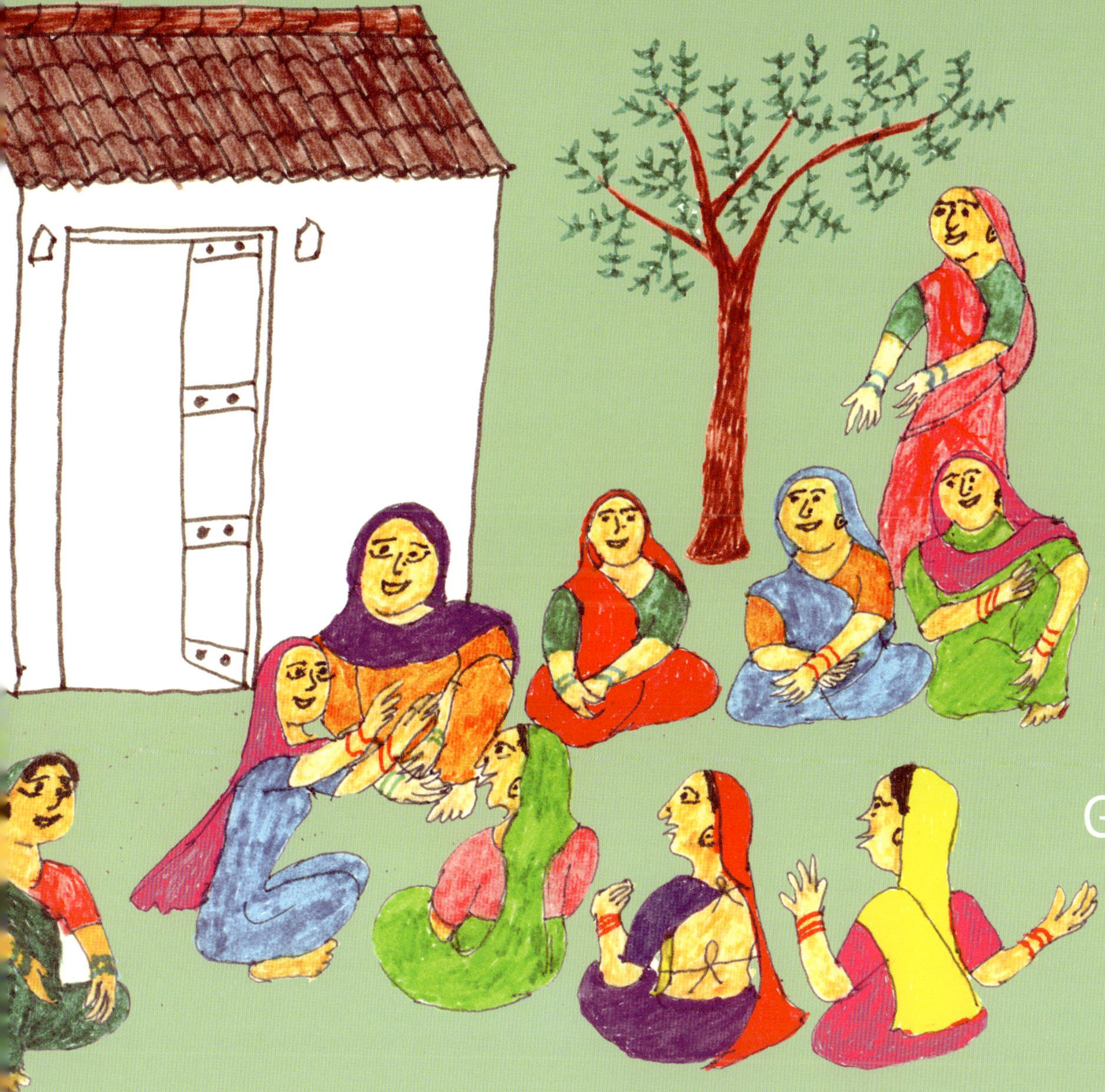

LIFE BEFORE THE GATHERING STORM

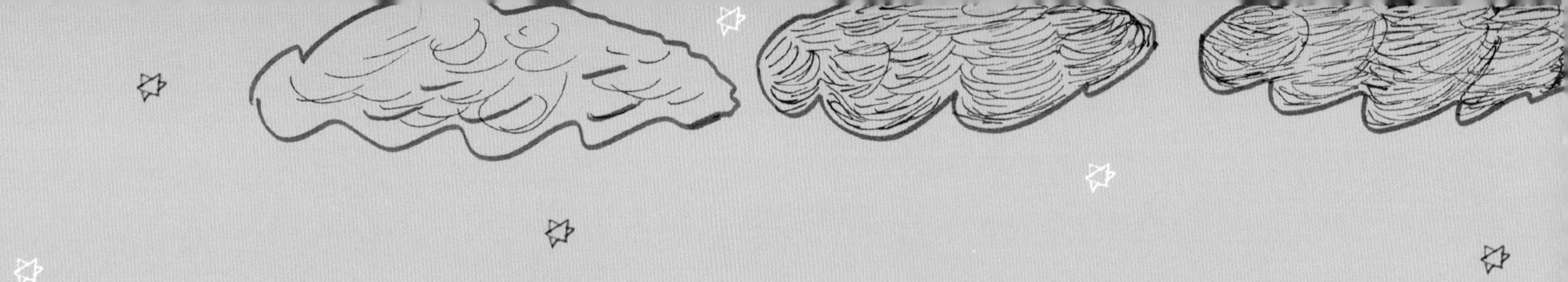

Our lives till then were simple:
made up of babies, pots, worksites and idle men.

They wound themselves around the path leading to our village well and back to our homes, only unwinding at night with our embroidered quilts which mirrored the colourful secrets that lay at the tip of our needles and in the patterns that followed them.

Into this world they came, the women from cities, towns and villages around us, with their dreams of change, dreams that resonated with ours.

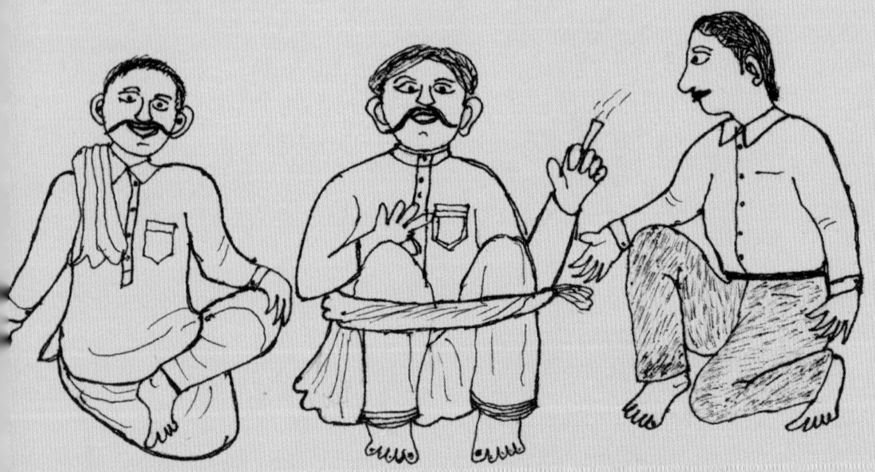

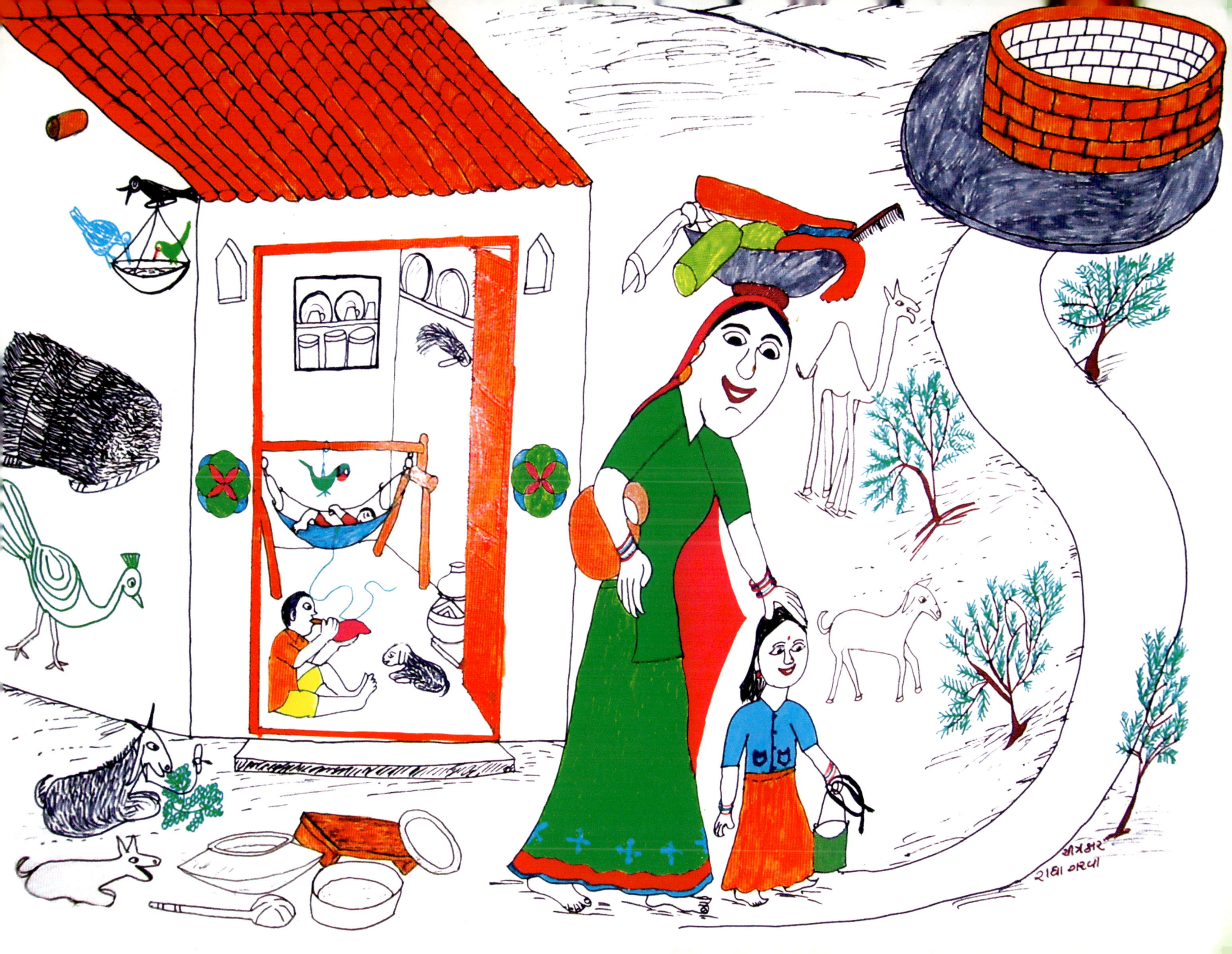
ચીત્રકાર
રાધા ગરવા

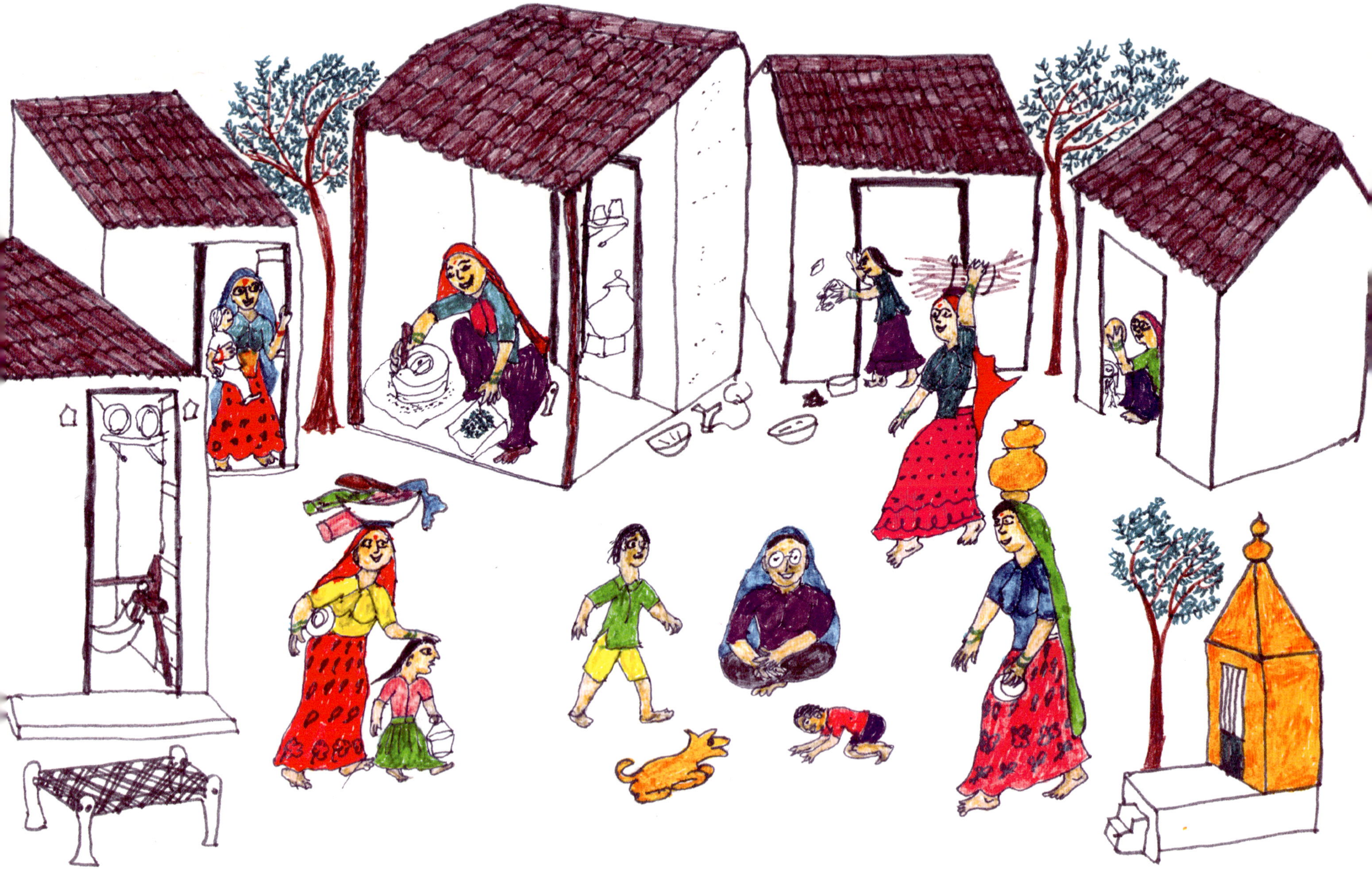

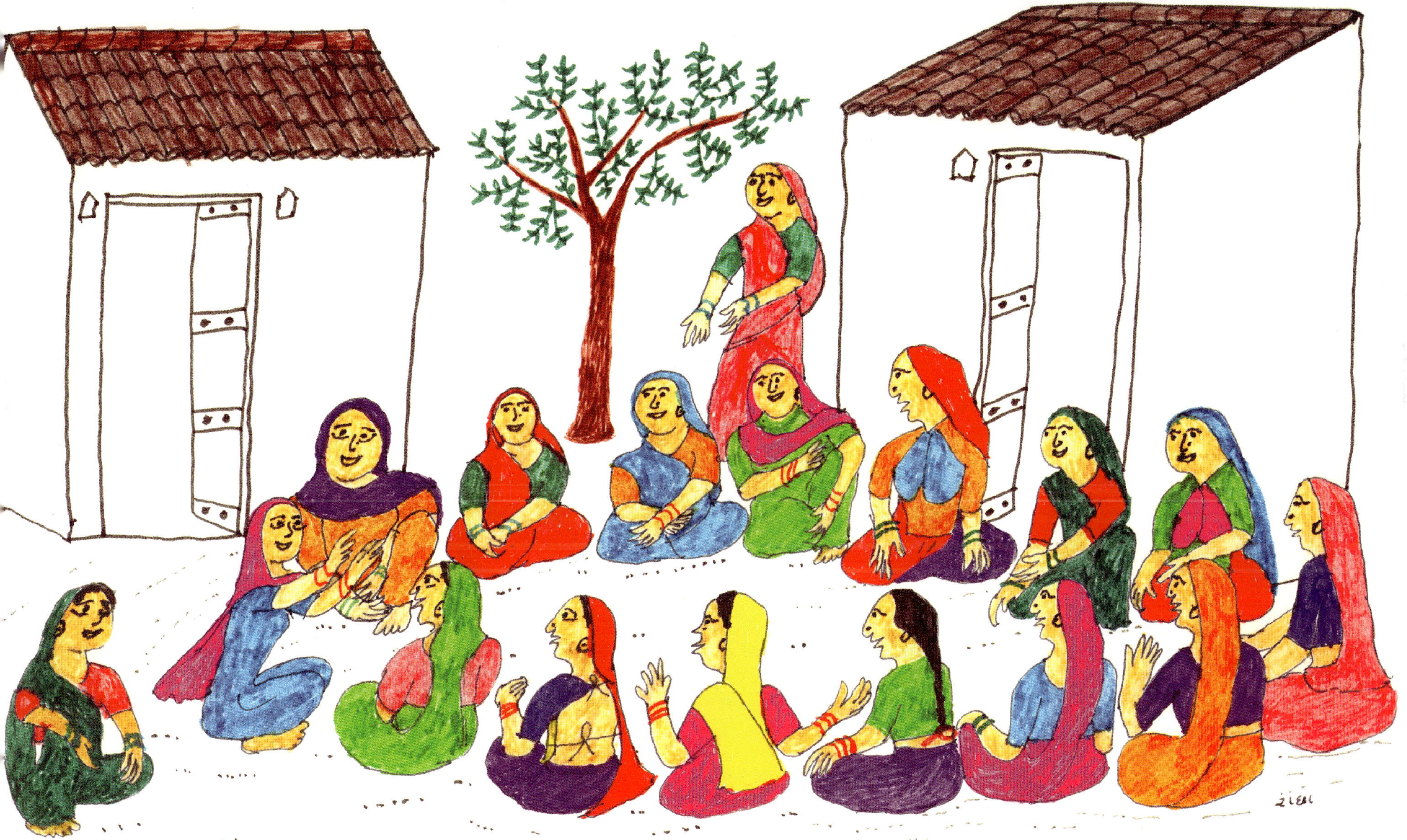

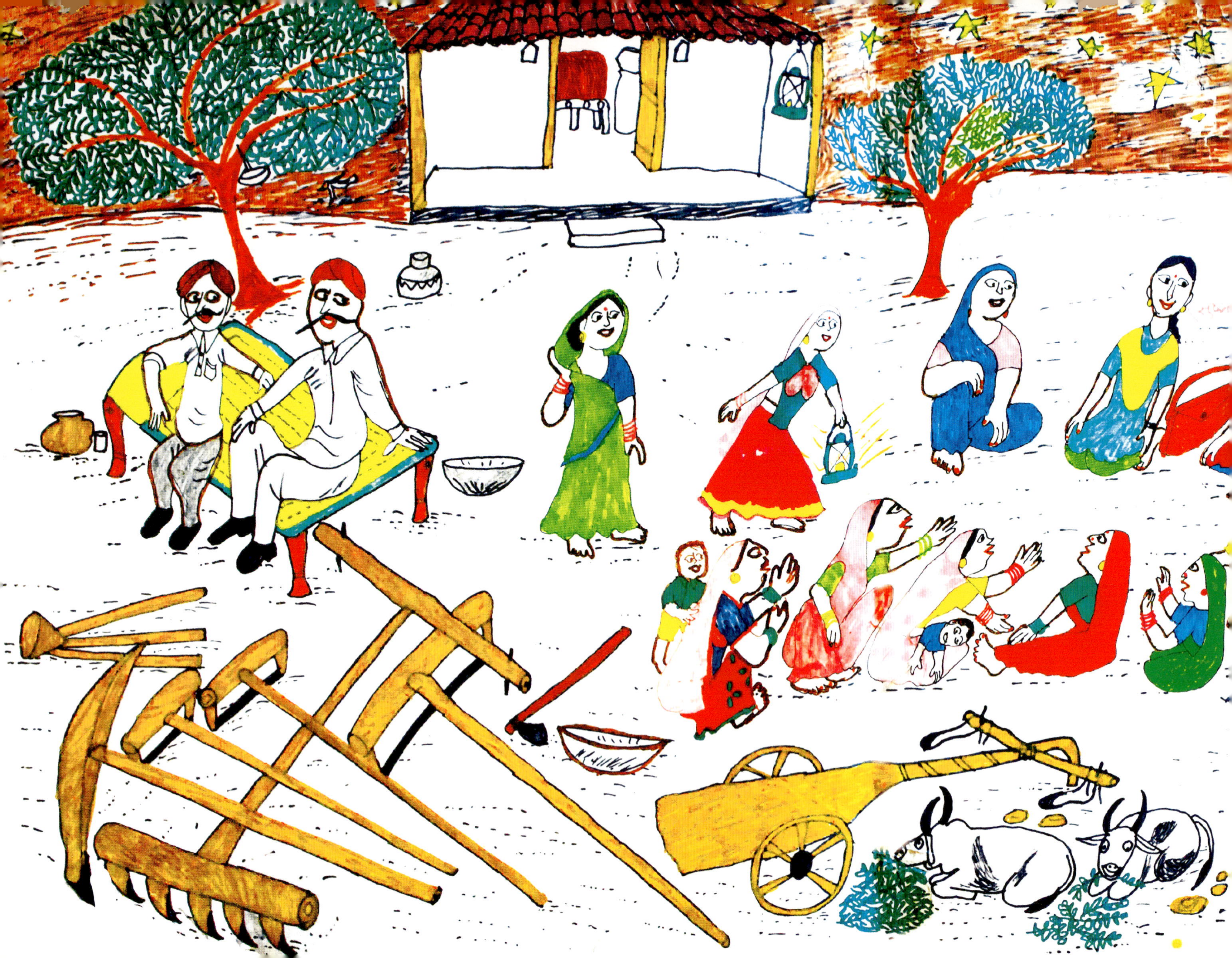

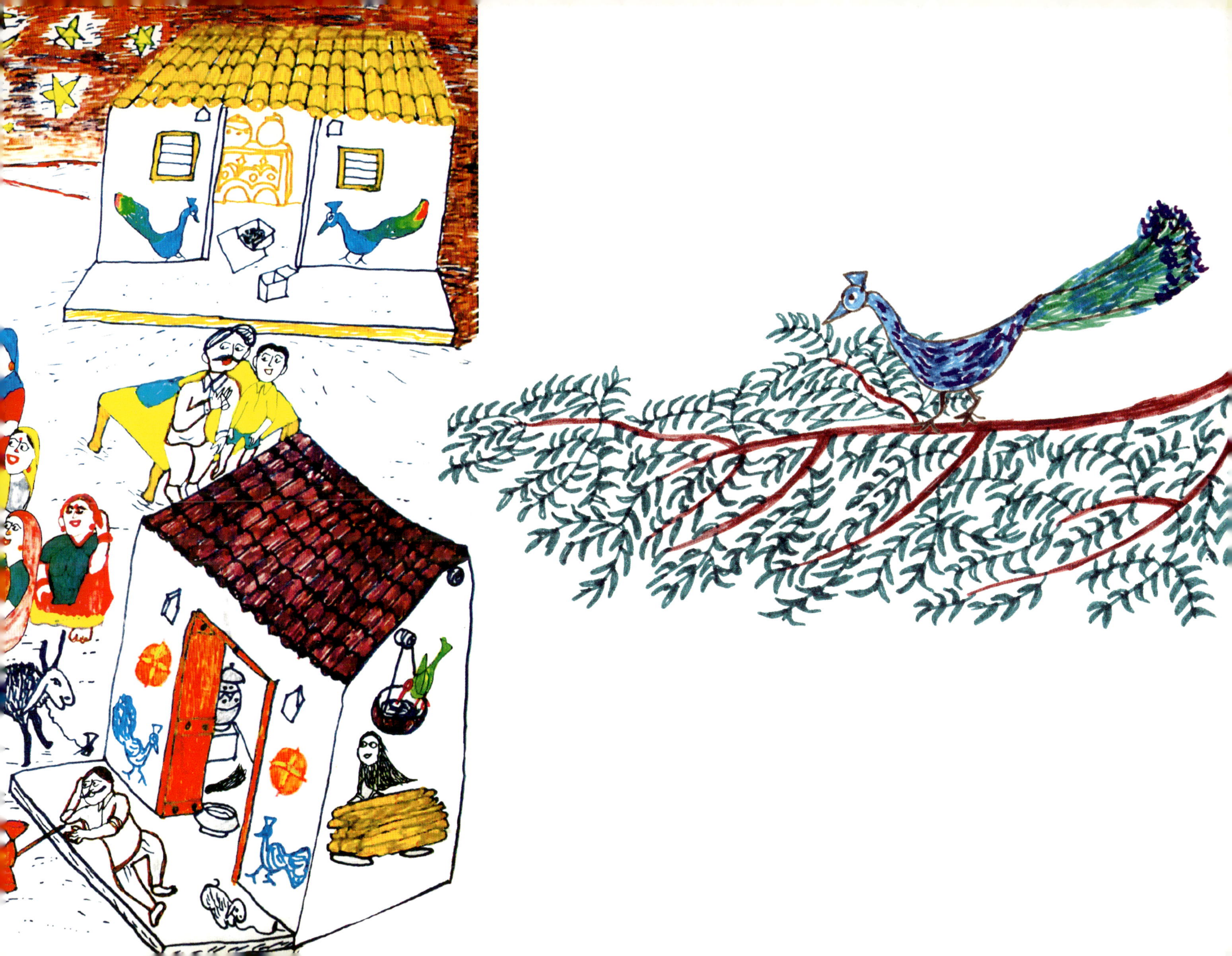

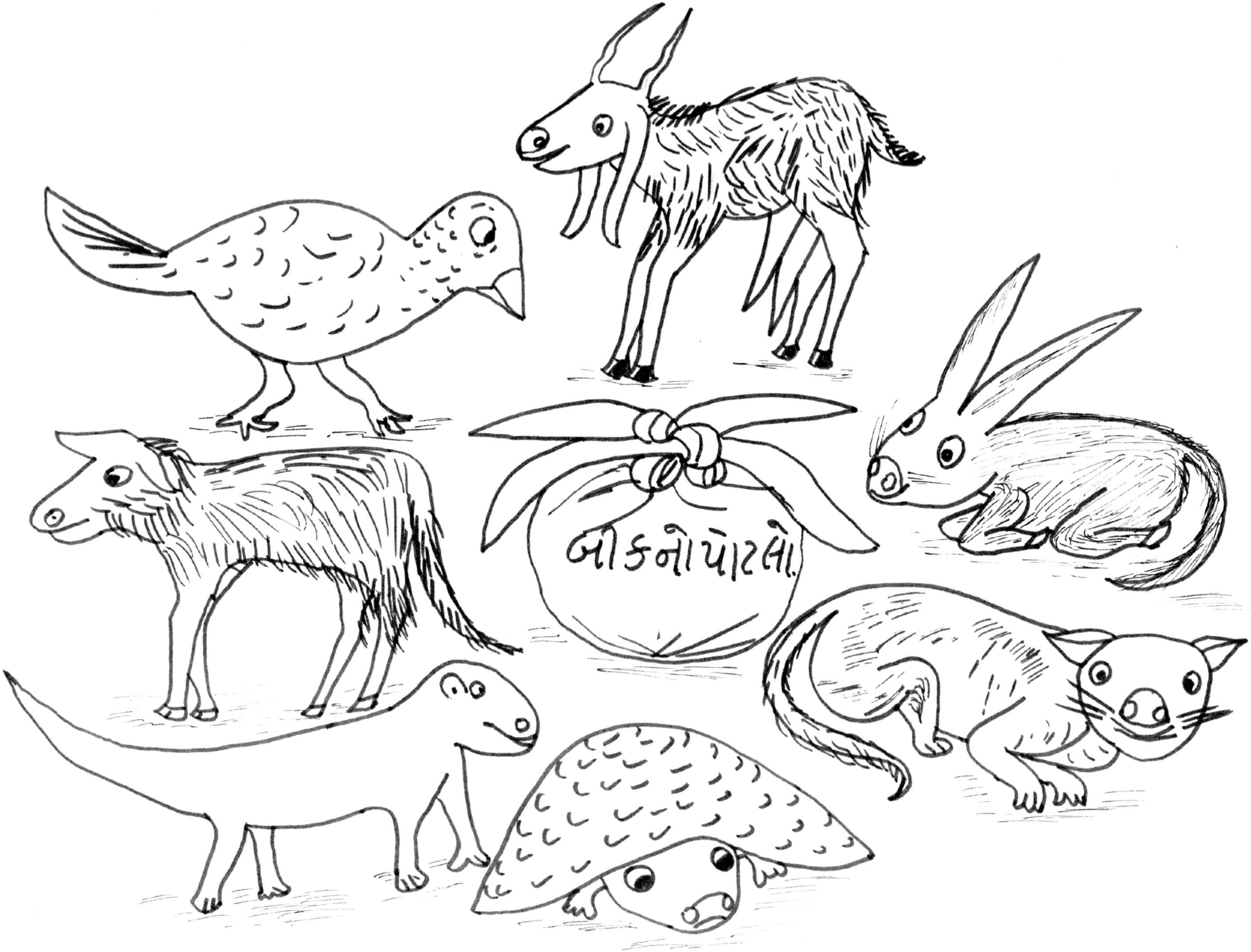
બીકનો પોટલો.

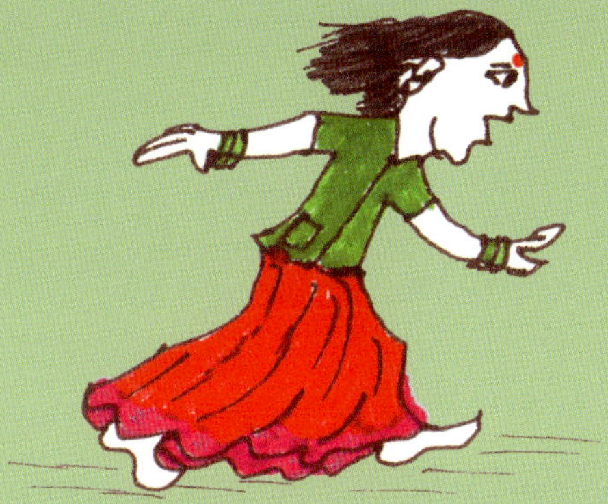

As children, it was when electricity came to our villages that we began to fear the dark. As girls, it was fear itself that we began to fear. We allowed fear to creep into our hearts even before we learnt to play. She became our most intimate friend, our little bundle of fear . . . with her we crept, scampered, lurked. We hid our dreams, our lives, even from ourselves.'

We feared to speak, and yet were truthful. We feared to travel, but braved the long migrations in search of water and fodder; we feared talking about our ailments but we nursed our cattle when they fell ill; we were scared to complain about the rotten grain we got in the ration shop, but we safeguarded the knowledge of conserving seeds which filled our granaries.

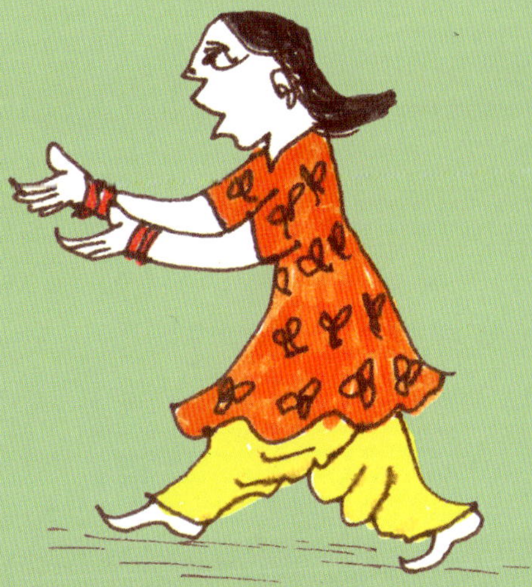

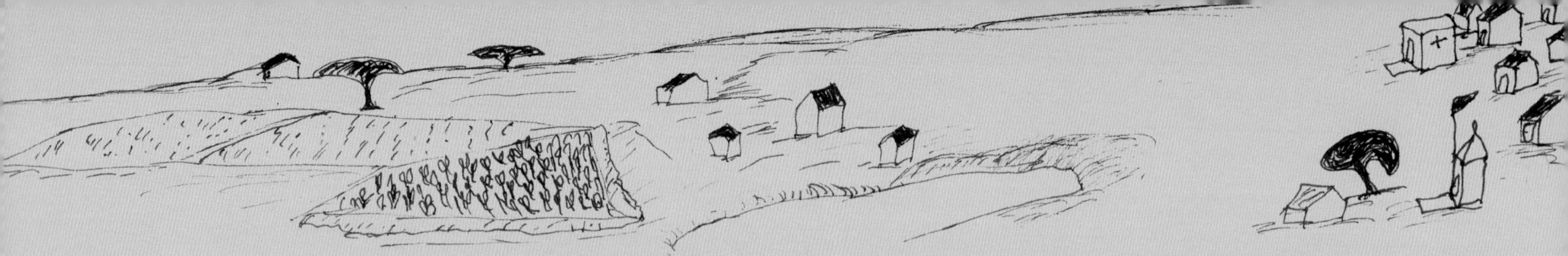

And then, together, as we began to organize, our hours, days, and weeks rolled with the excitement of transgressing the limits laid out for us, and the anxiety of doing so.

Were we going 'too far'? Should we not stop?

But by then, we were consumed by our 'meetings', many many meetings where the slightest shadows of our men, any man, would be wiped away with guile and delight! And we would swing between who we were, who our families wanted us to be, and who we potentially could be.

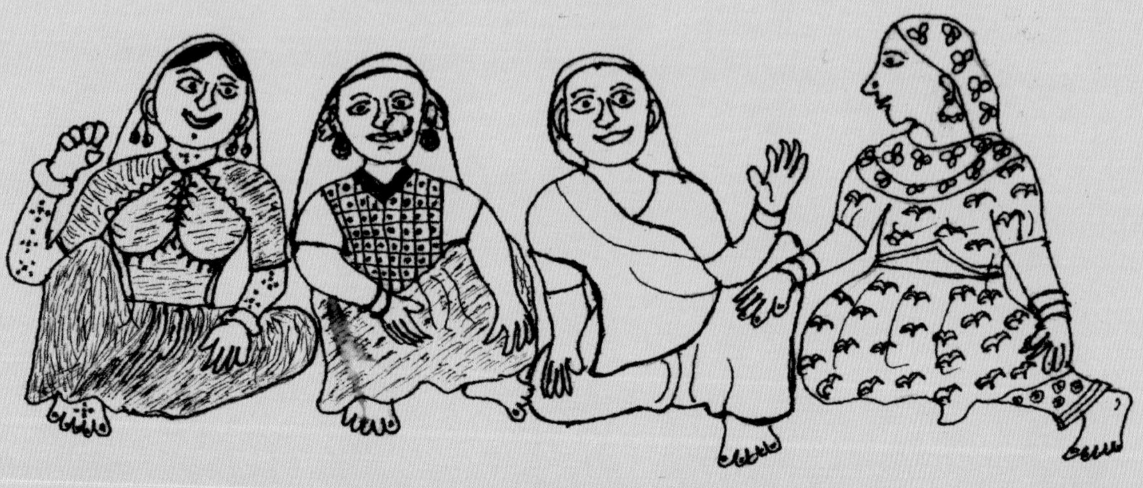

CONFRONTATION AND CONFLICT

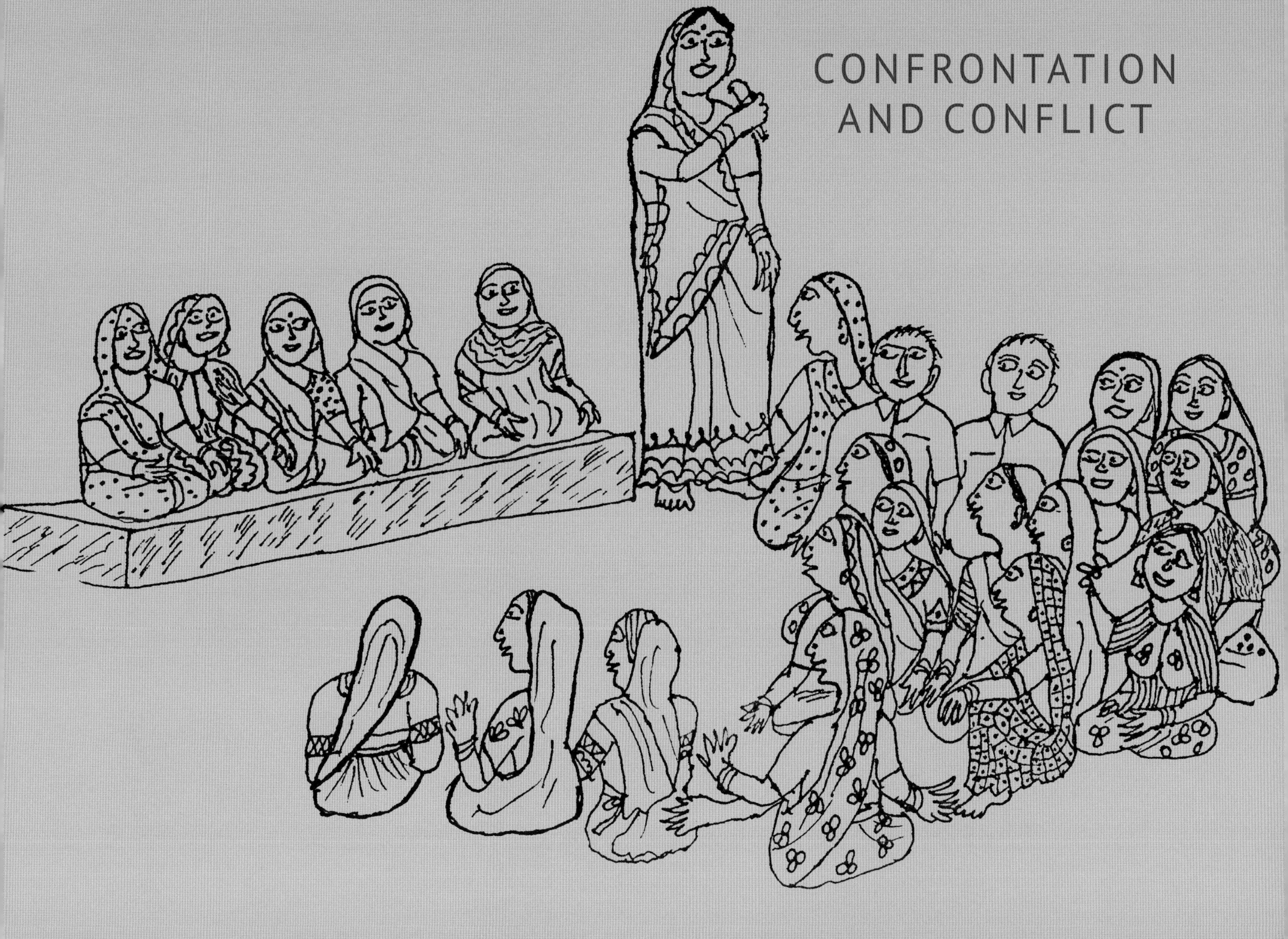

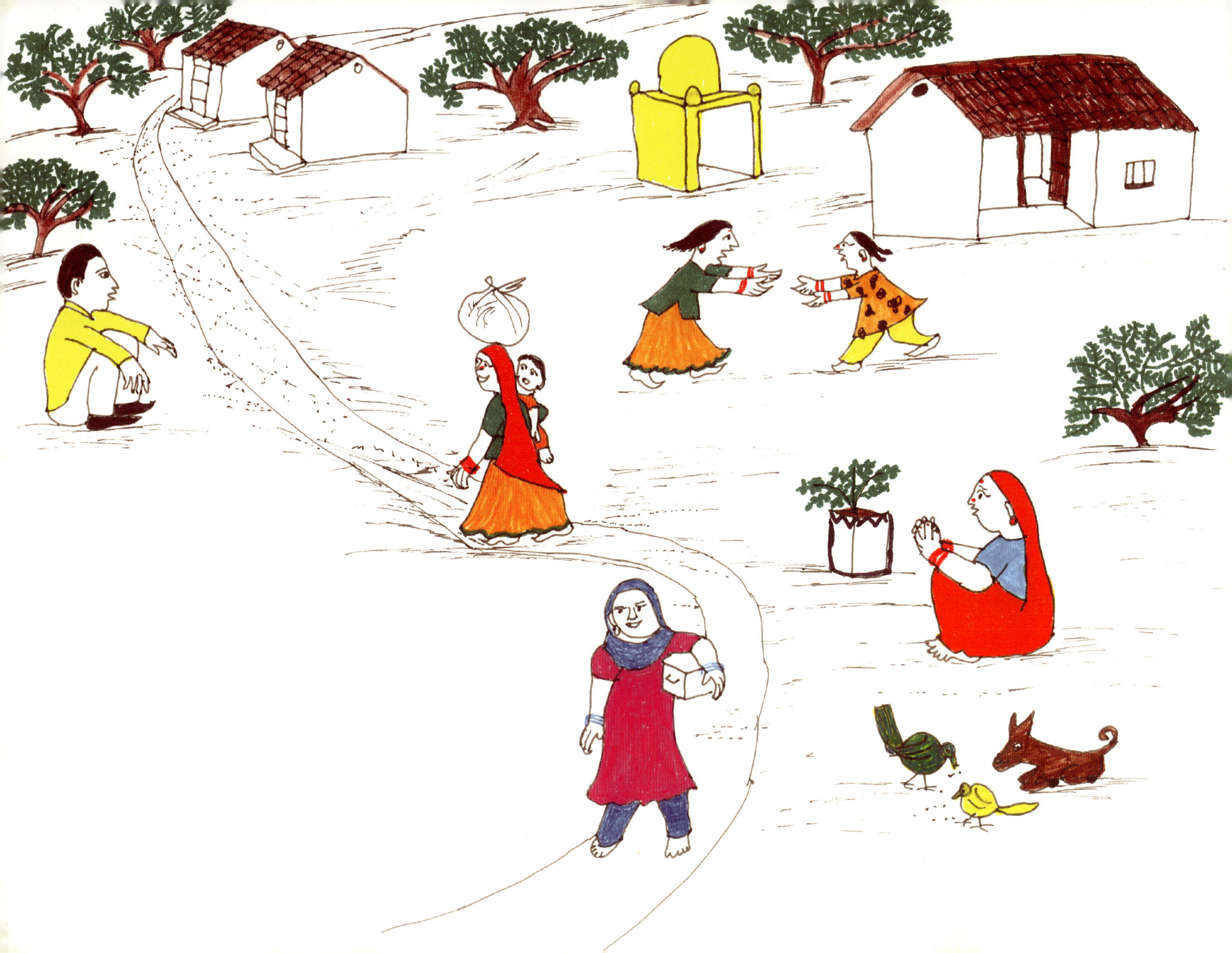

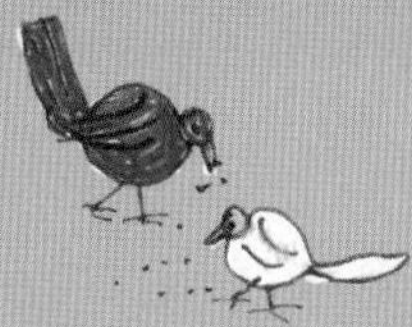

In a life that seemed irreversible, we could suddenly sense the possibility of a curve in our otherwise straight path to nowhere.

We still saw the same world but we now looked at it differently. Had we acquired fresh antennae?

Fear was giving way to anger and acceptance to awareness.

We had begun to shed our familiar notions of what we could do or should not do.

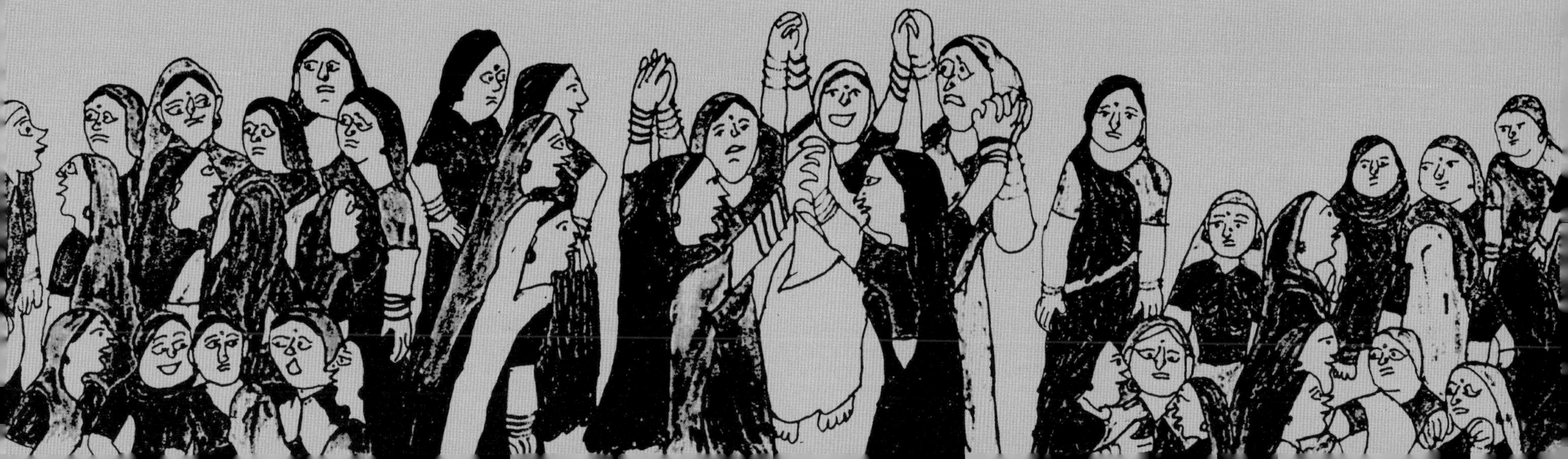

No longer were our routine discords, our despair, our complete indignity at the erratic supply of water — no longer were these acceptable to us.

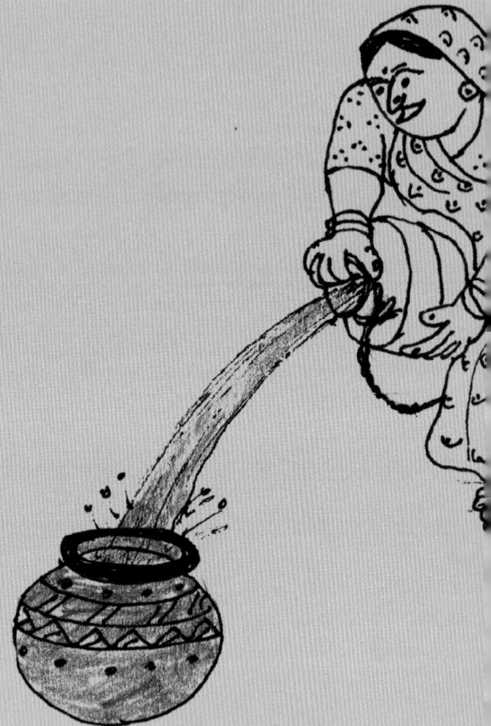

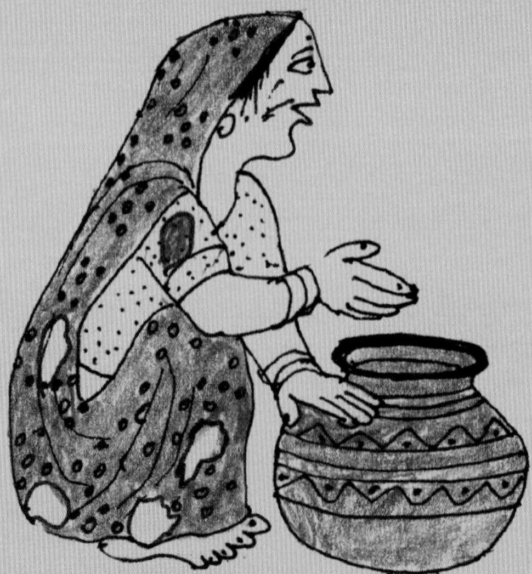

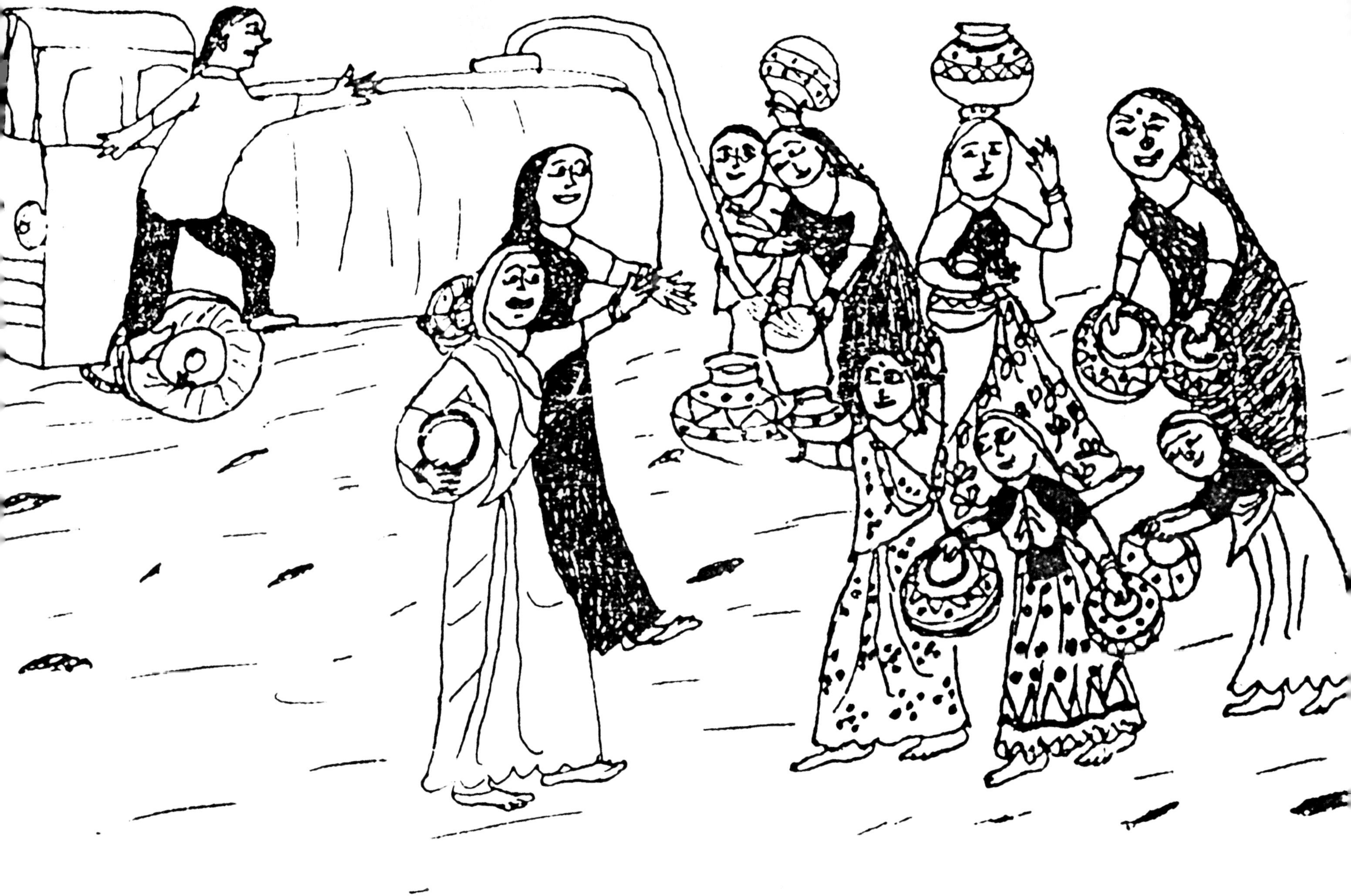

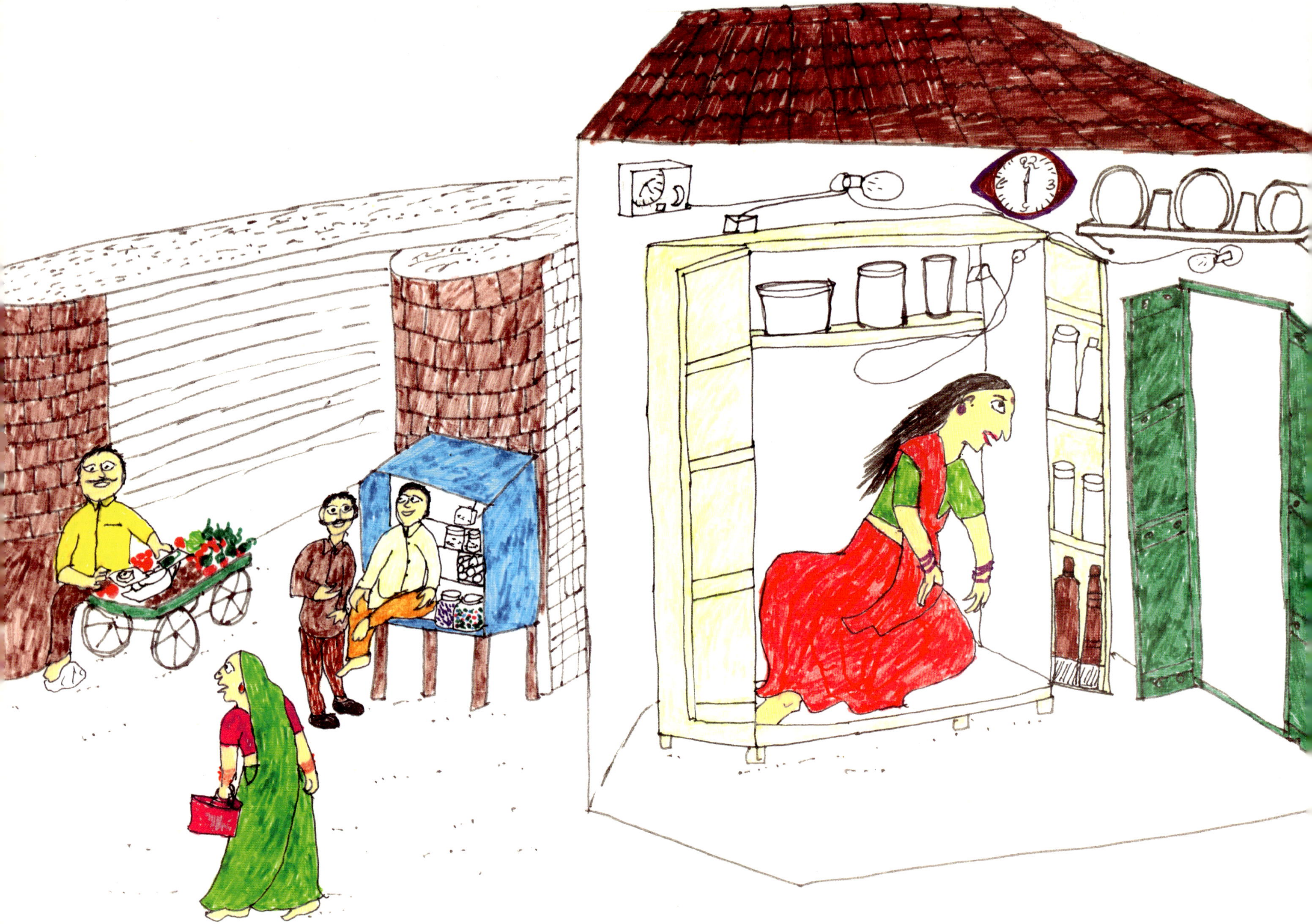

We now understood, for example, that our ex-sarpanch's daughter-in-law, whose body was found inside a newly bought refrigerator, was not a victim of an electric shock. For us, her story was a grotesque introduction to that phenomenon called 'unnatural deaths'.

Now we knew.

And wanted to act.

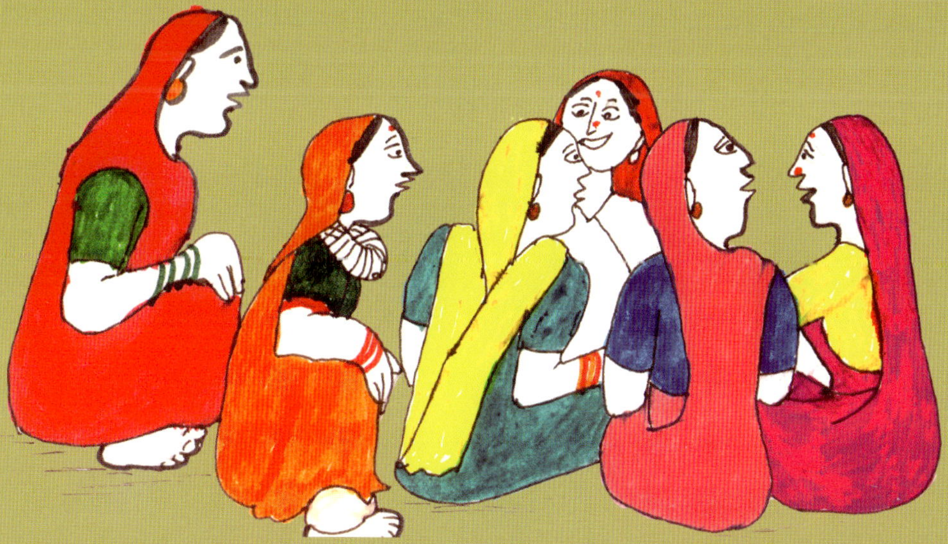

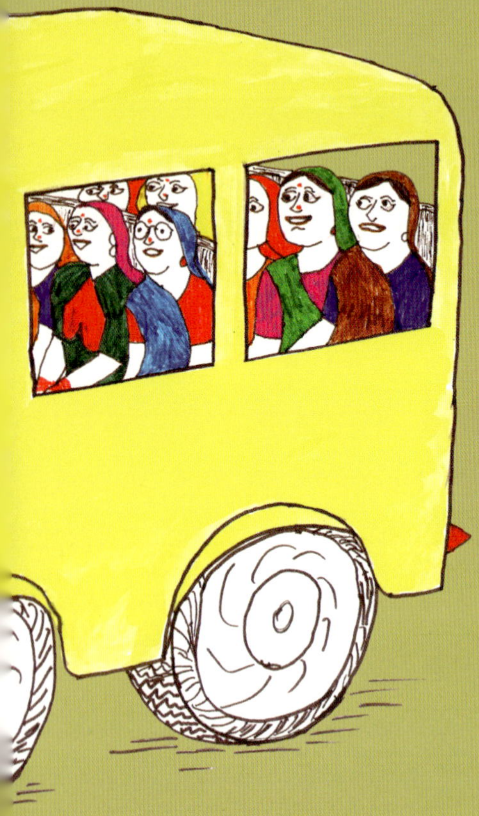

Act we did, when Malji, the sullen sheep rearer, a dalit in our village, was found thrashing Sarli, his young bride, near the bus stand.

Some of us who regularly met the same fate ourselves in the 'quiet' of our homes, picked her up, got into the bus, and left our village for the first time to travel 150 km to Sarli's parental home. There, we filed a police complaint, and returned to our upper caste homes the next morning!

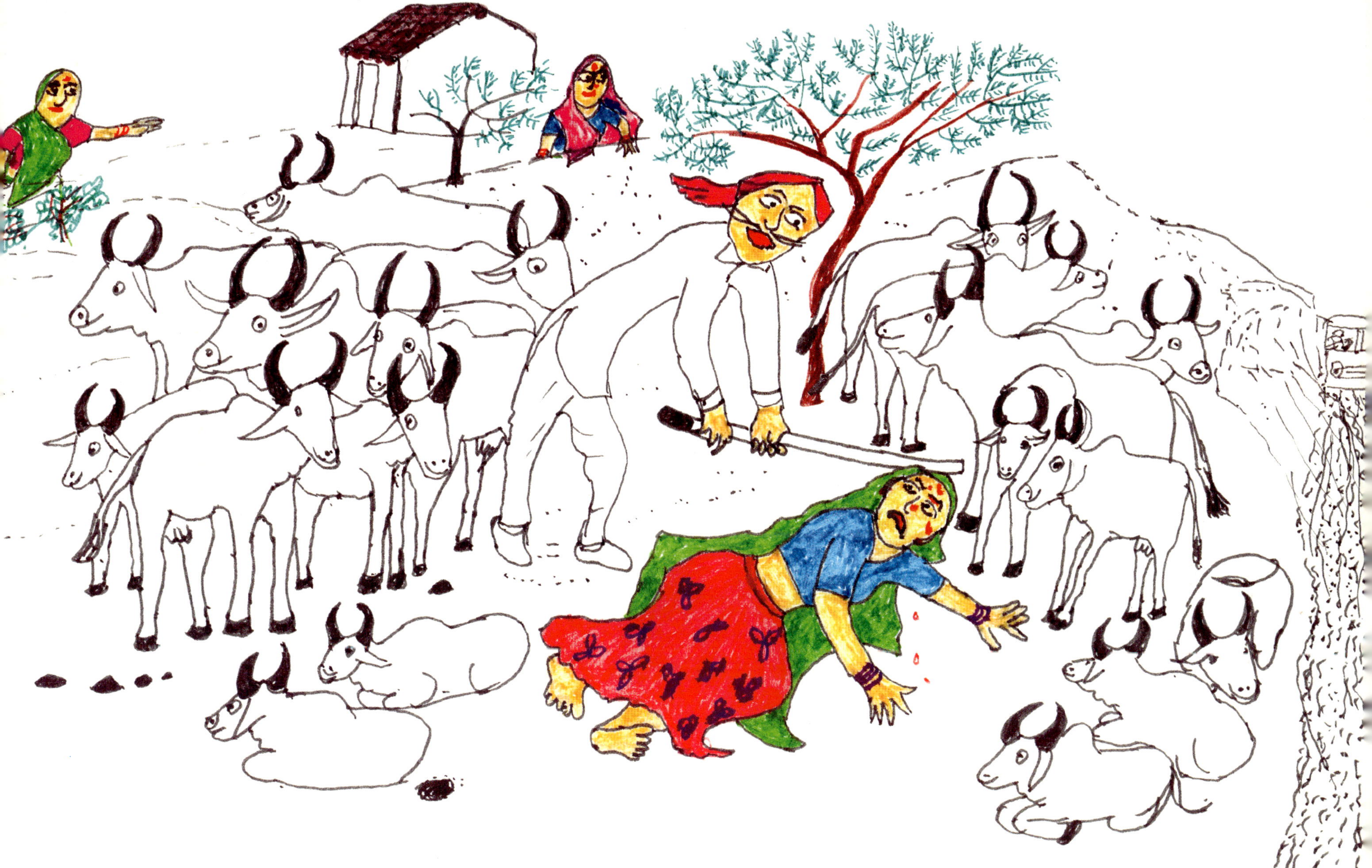

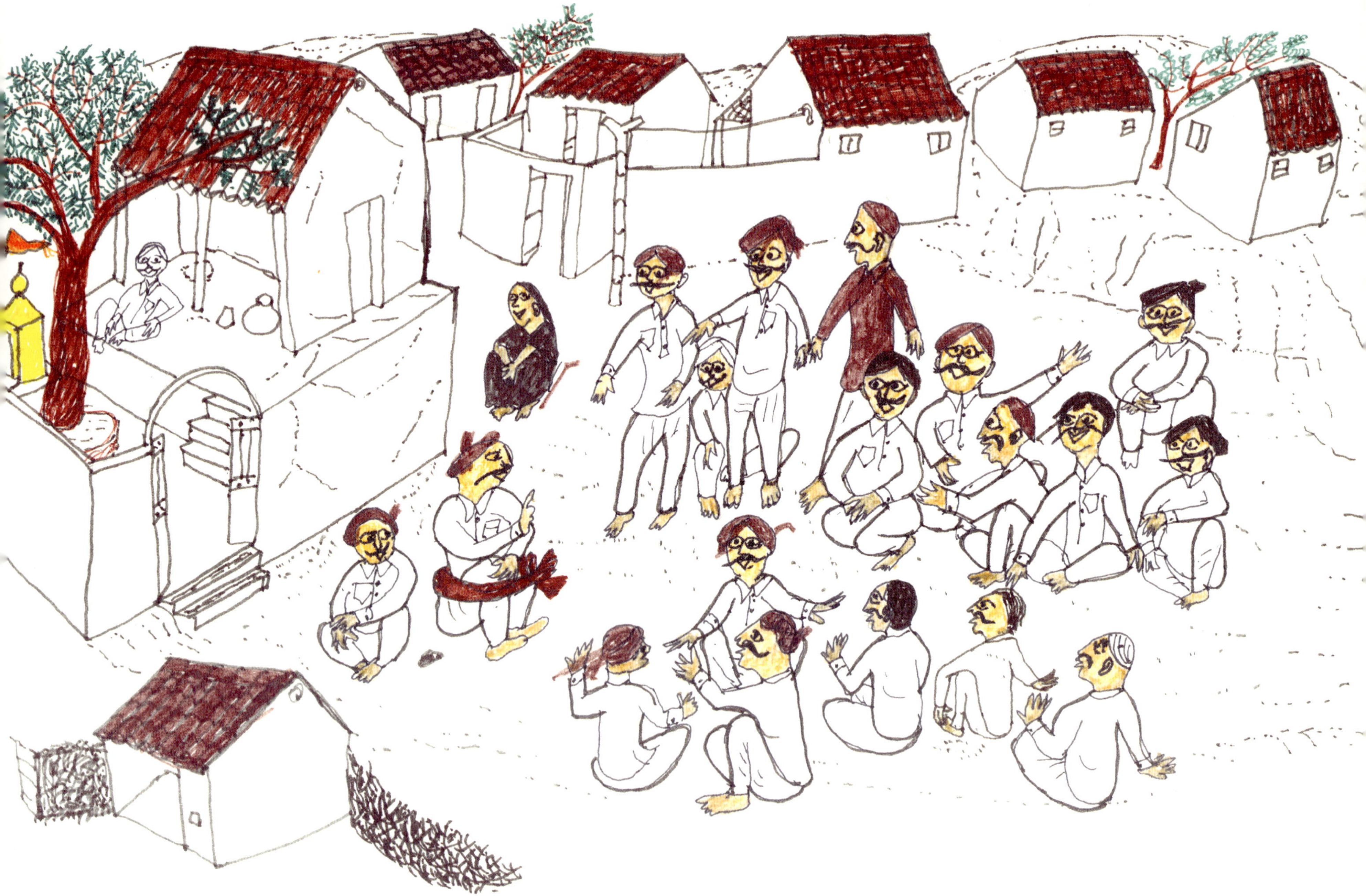

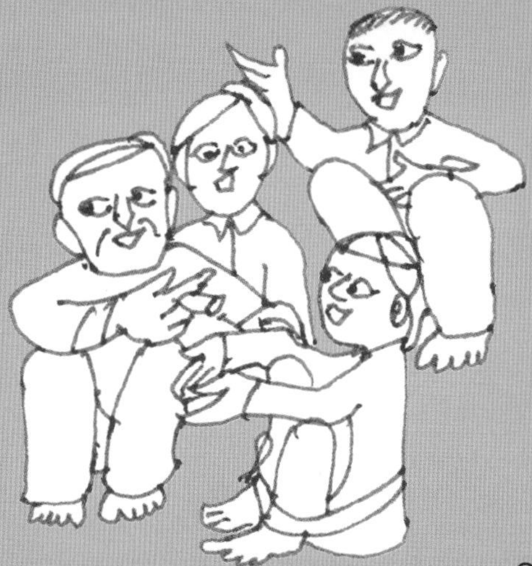

Horrified and furious, the panchayat congregated.

How had we dared to break the rules?

To defy the 'laws' laid down for us?

Our breach had broken a dam it seemed! And amidst this deluge, they huffed and they puffed while we lurked in corners to overhear.

We were barred, they said, from stepping out of our homes. From attending meetings. It did not last of course! But we were not sure then what had angered them more – our identification with a dalit woman, or their identification with Malji, the husband!

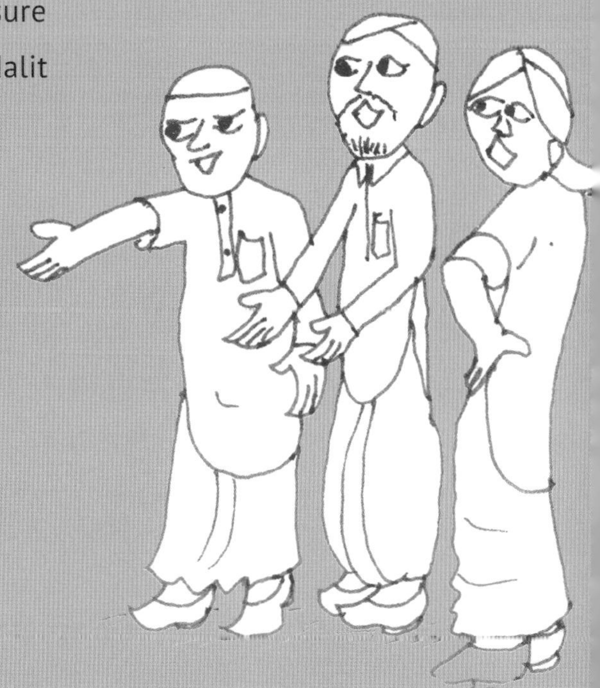

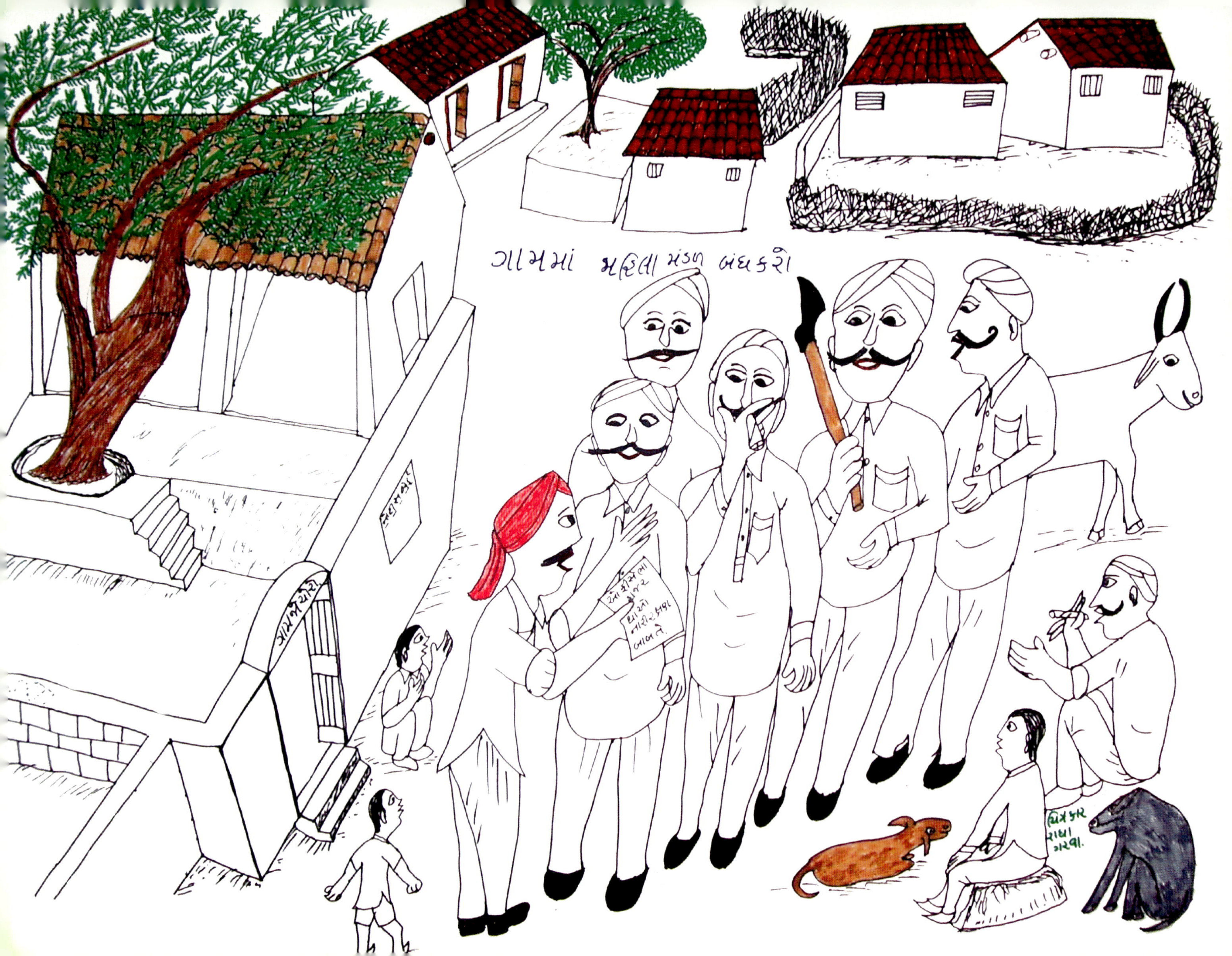
ગામમાં મહિલા મંડળ બંધ કરો
ચિત્રકાર
રાધા
ગરવા.

STEPPING OUT

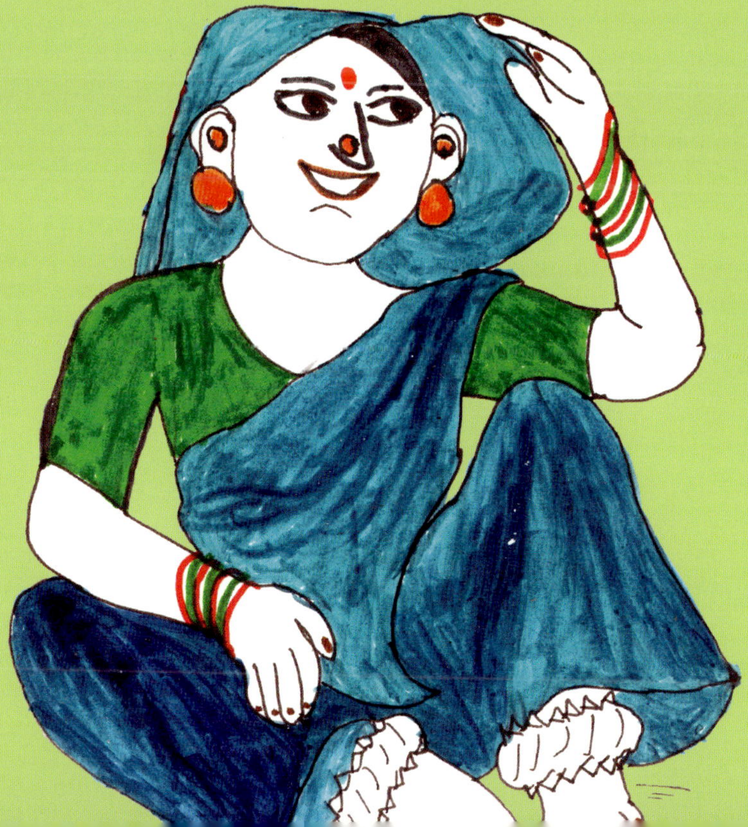

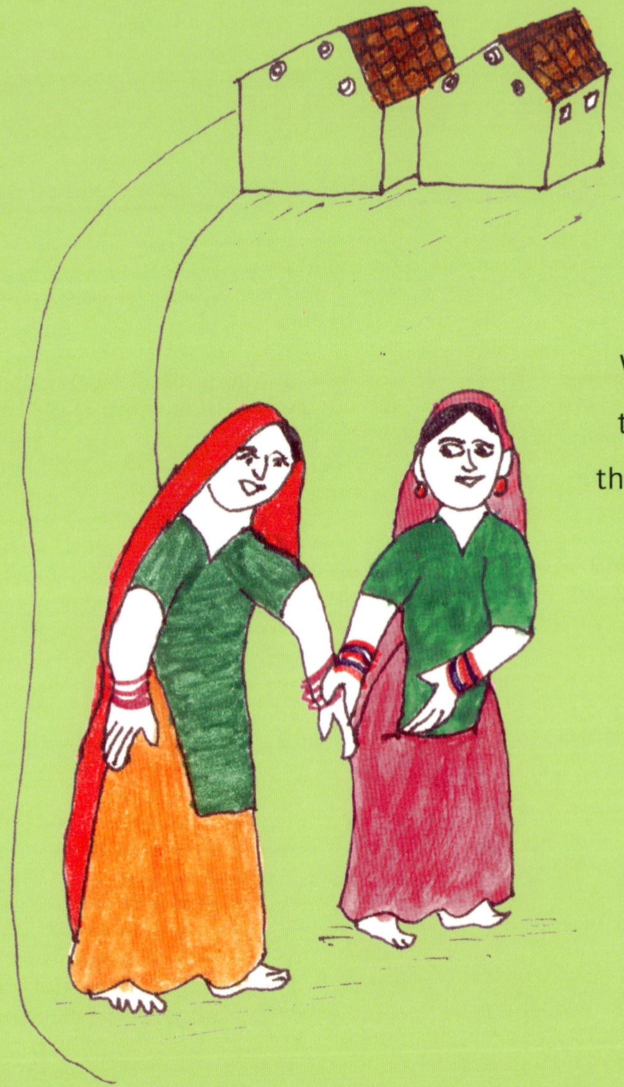

We entered a new world with the incessant noise of telephones, the wild careening of autos, of speeding through the night in trains, our stomachs squeezed in a twirl of anxiety.

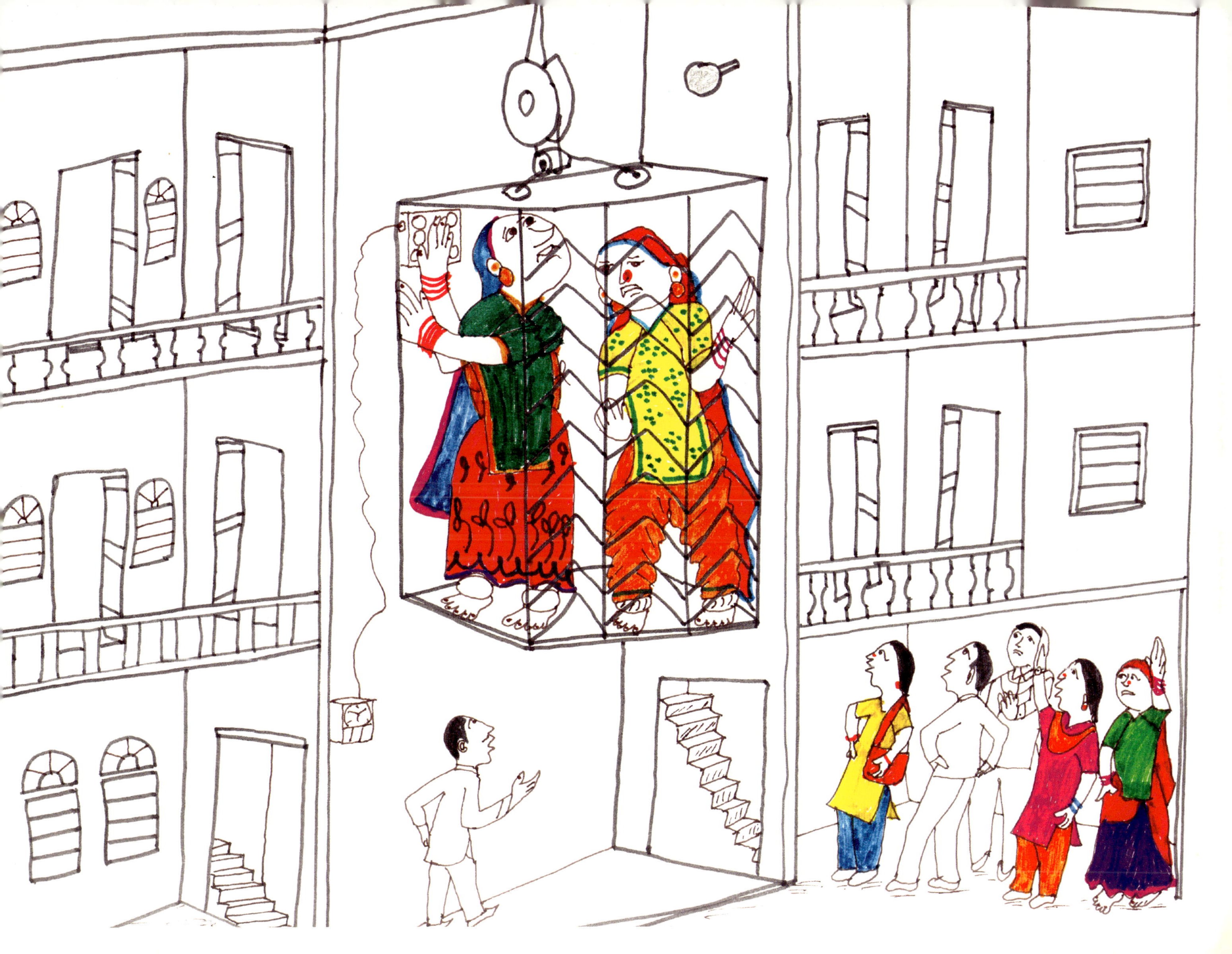

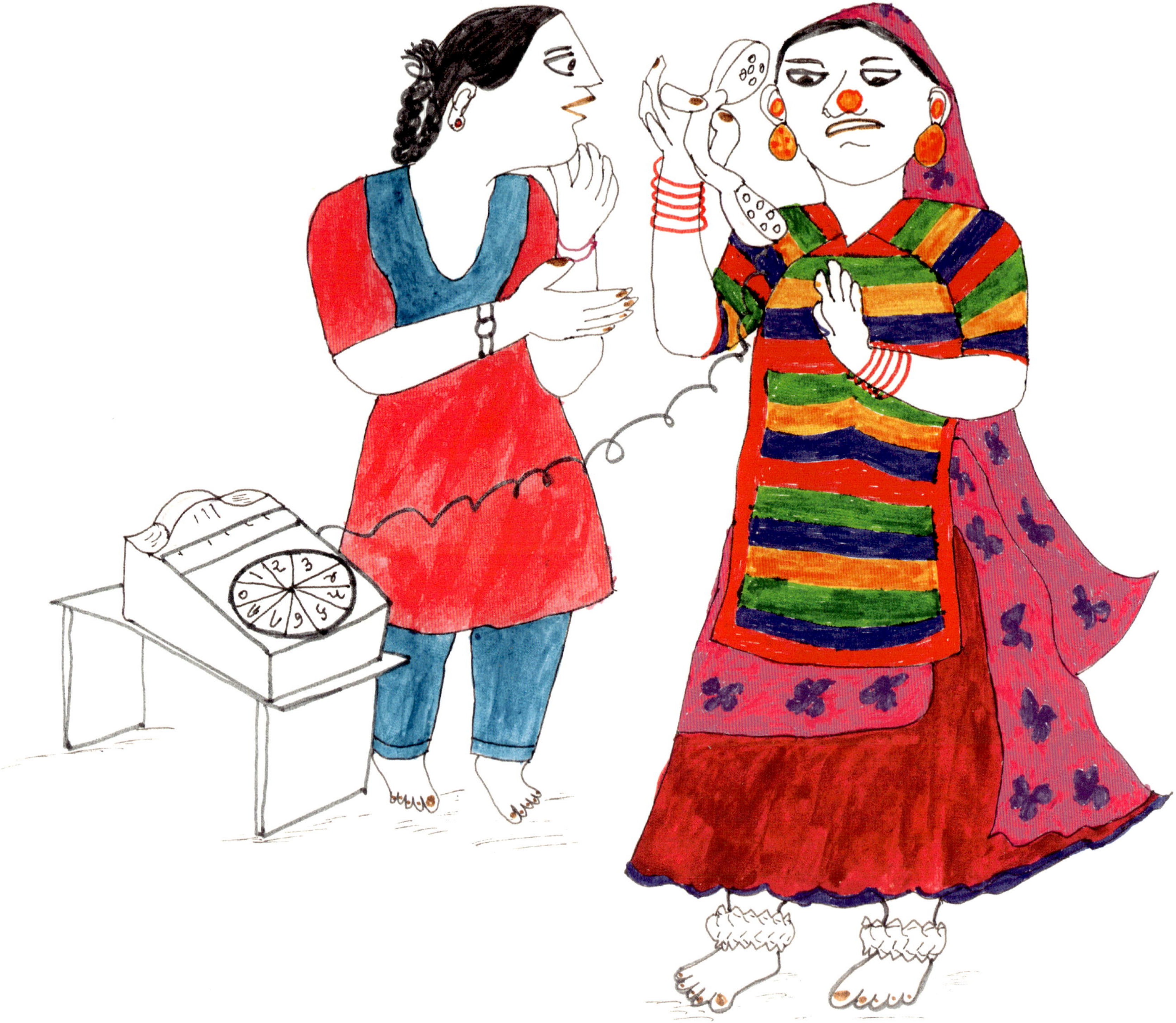

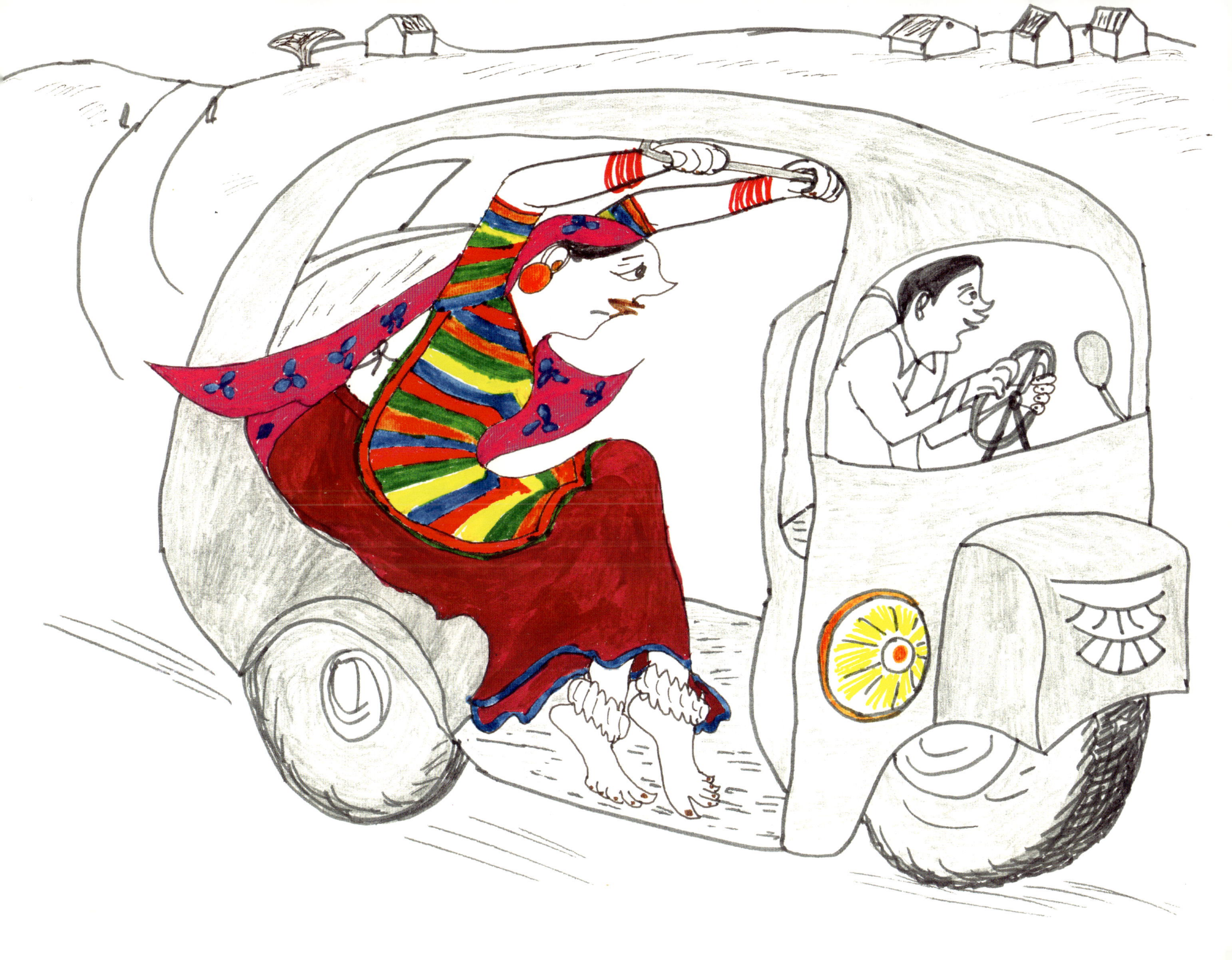

We died a million times during these sojourns, but soared toward a more inspired life each time we returned.

We were dizzy with excitement as we grappled with a world unpacked.

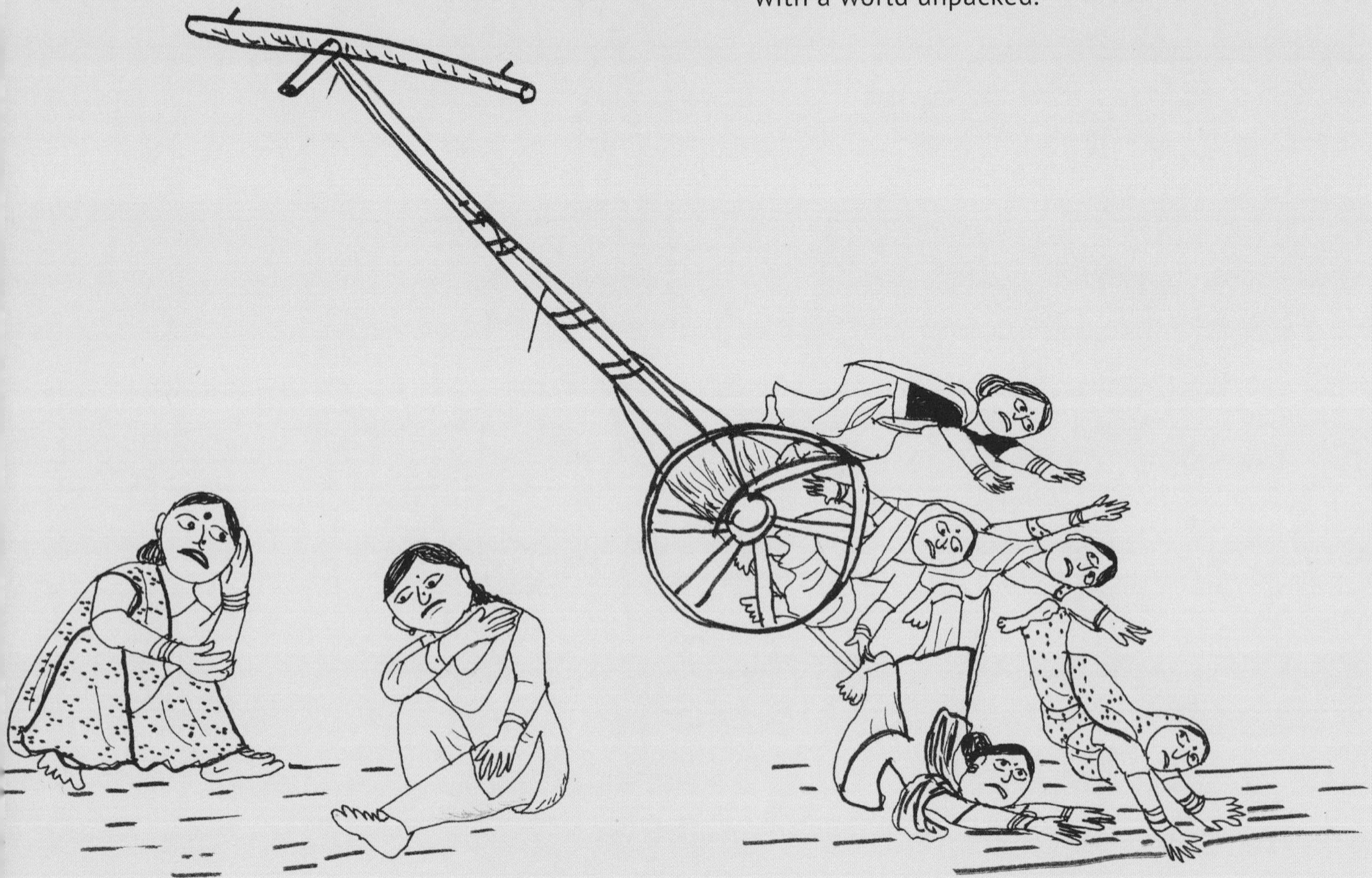

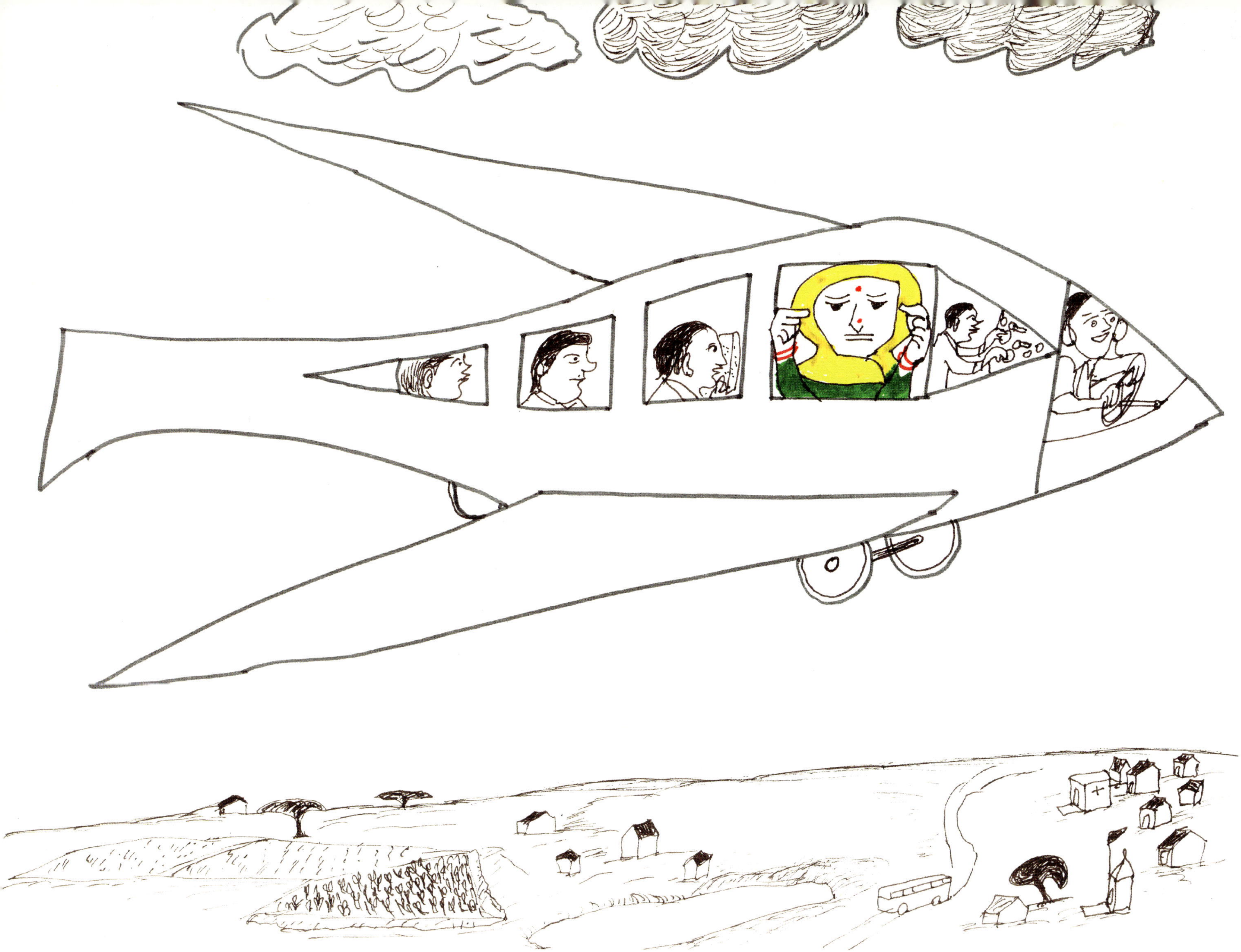

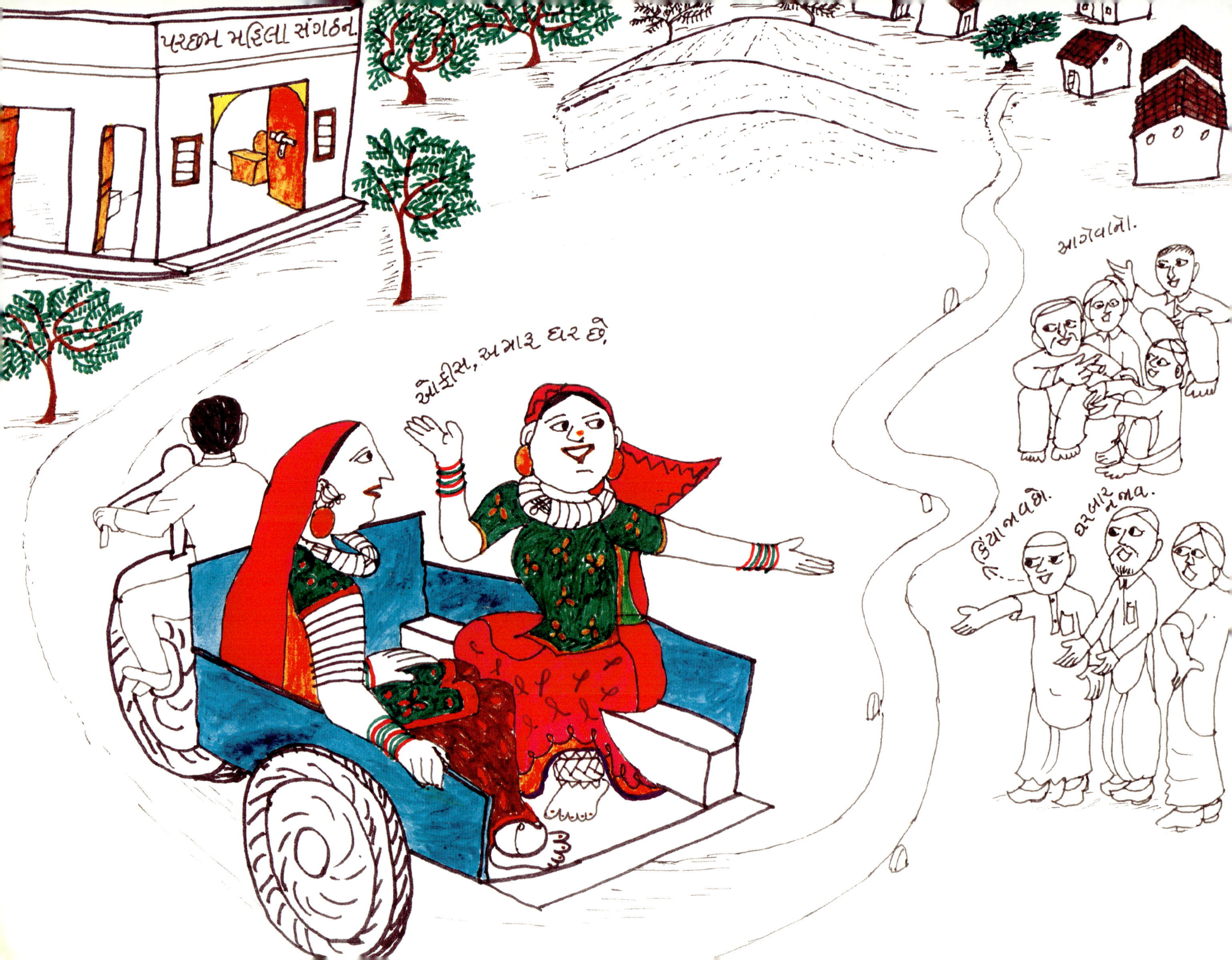
પરછમ મહિલા સંગઠન.
ઓફીસ, અમારૂ ઘર છે.
આગેવાનો.

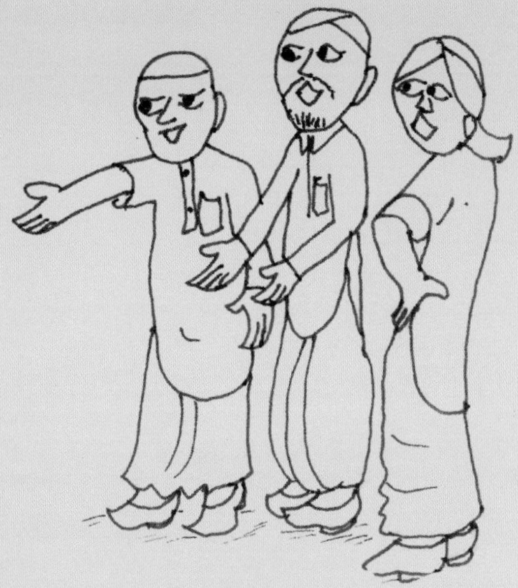

Wherever we went, we stared, and were stared at – for now we were claiming spaces that were not considered ours.

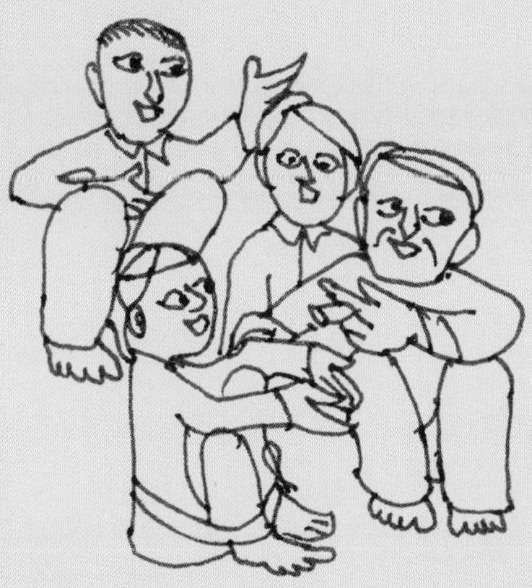

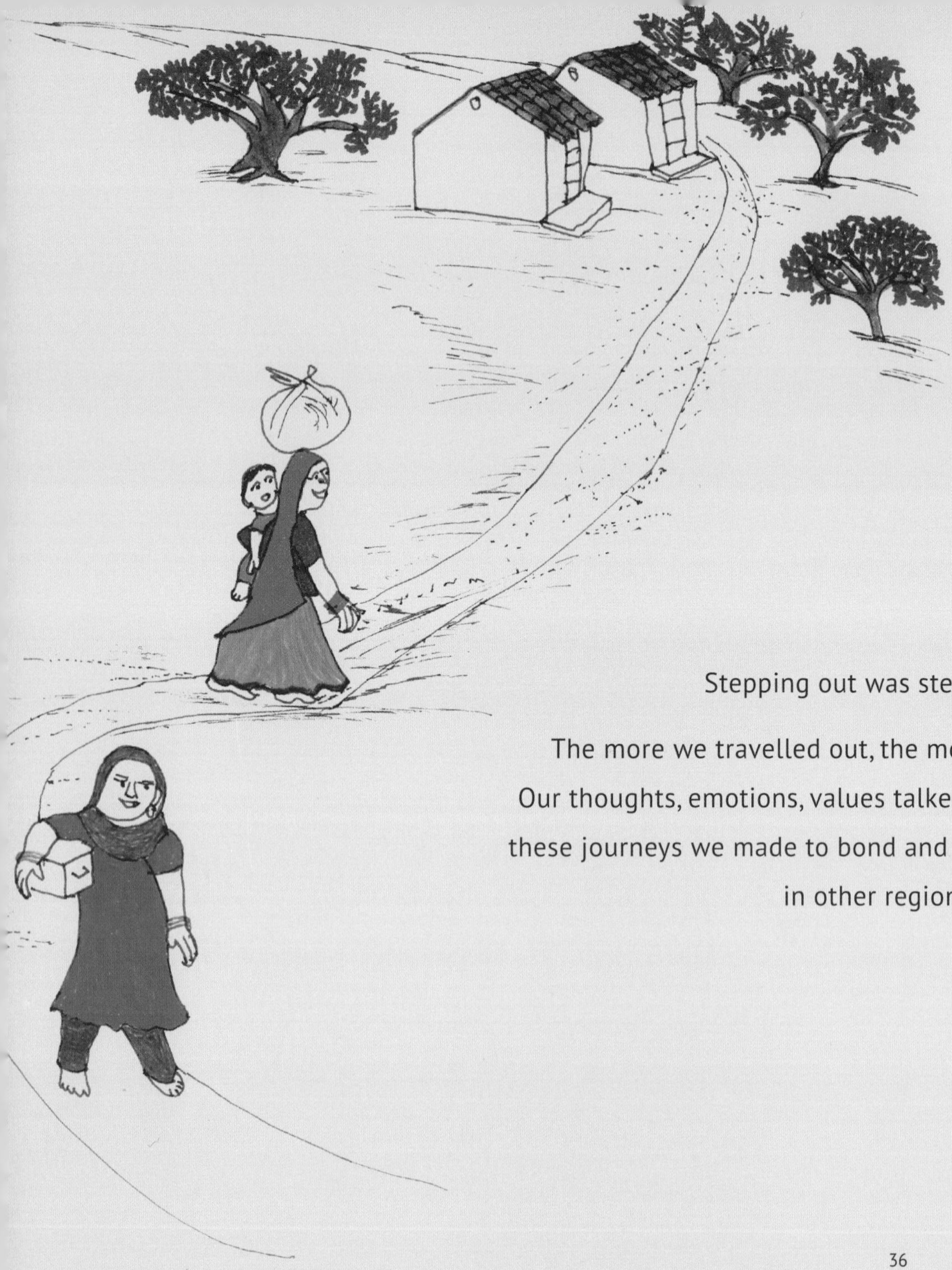

Stepping out was stepping in.

The more we travelled out, the more we met ourselves.
Our thoughts, emotions, values talked to us with ease during
these journeys we made to bond and learn from other women,
in other regions.

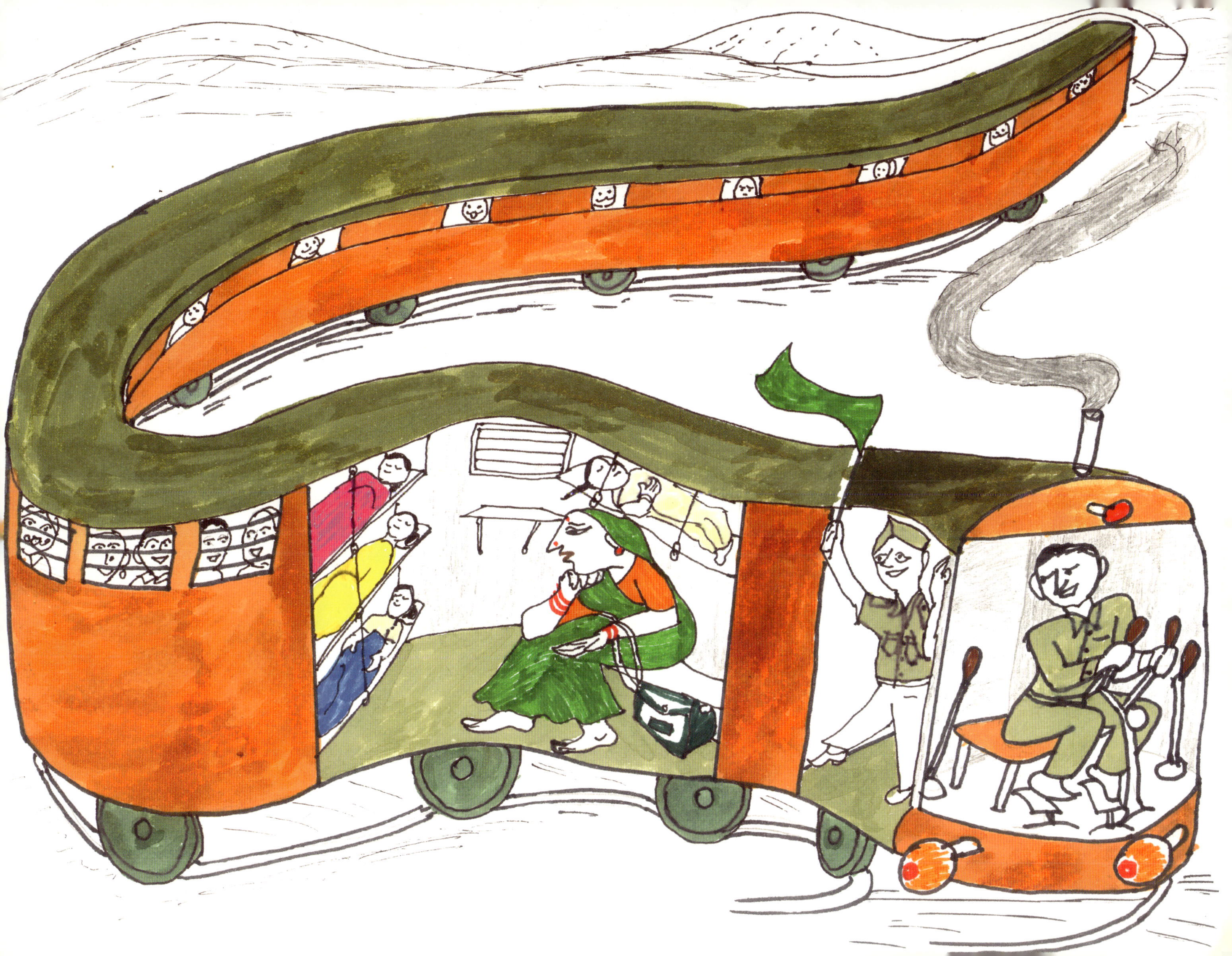

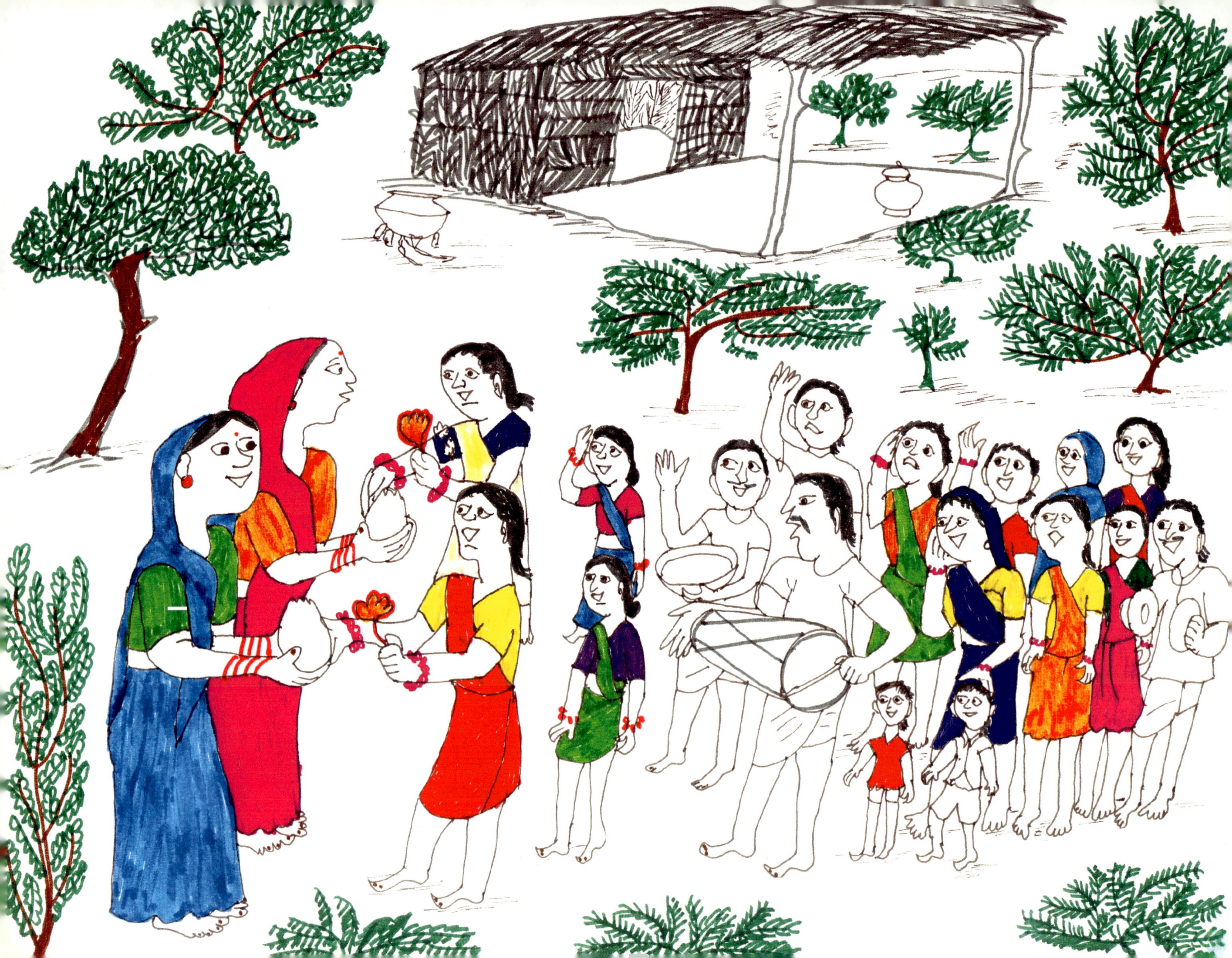

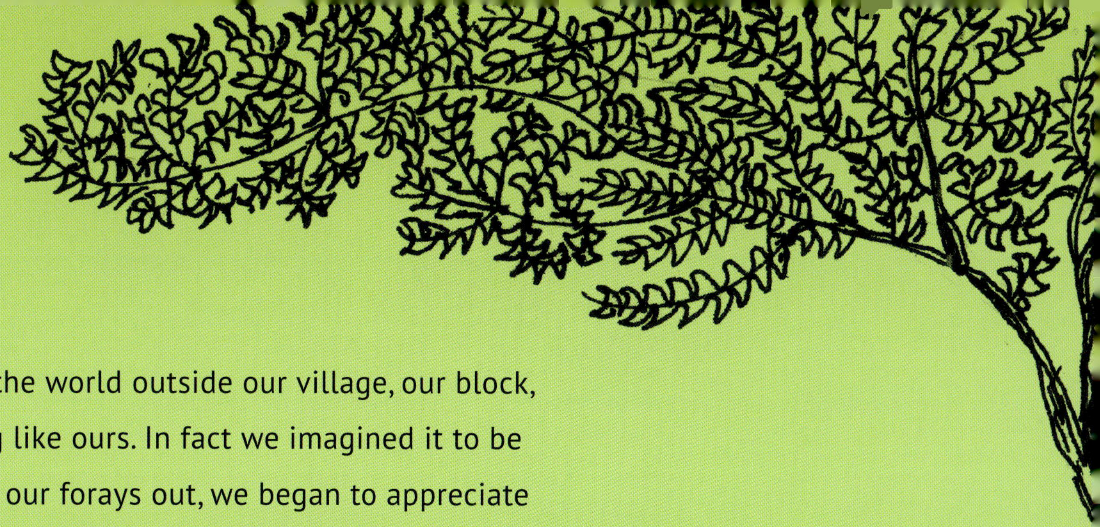

We had always imagined the world outside our village, our block, our district, to be nothing like ours. In fact we imagined it to be far better than ours! With our forays out, we began to appreciate 'difference' without being intimidated by it.

But also, we were shocked with how similar our lives as women were, everywhere.

And then our notions of who was poor, and who wasn't began to change. When we saw those worse off than us, we felt we had to lead the change.

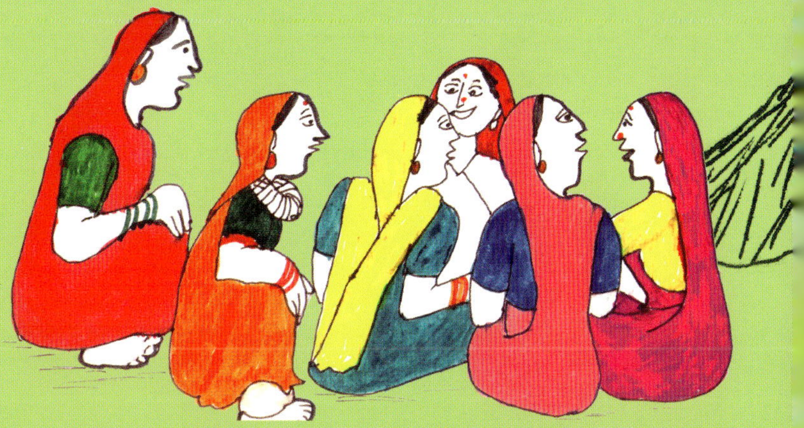

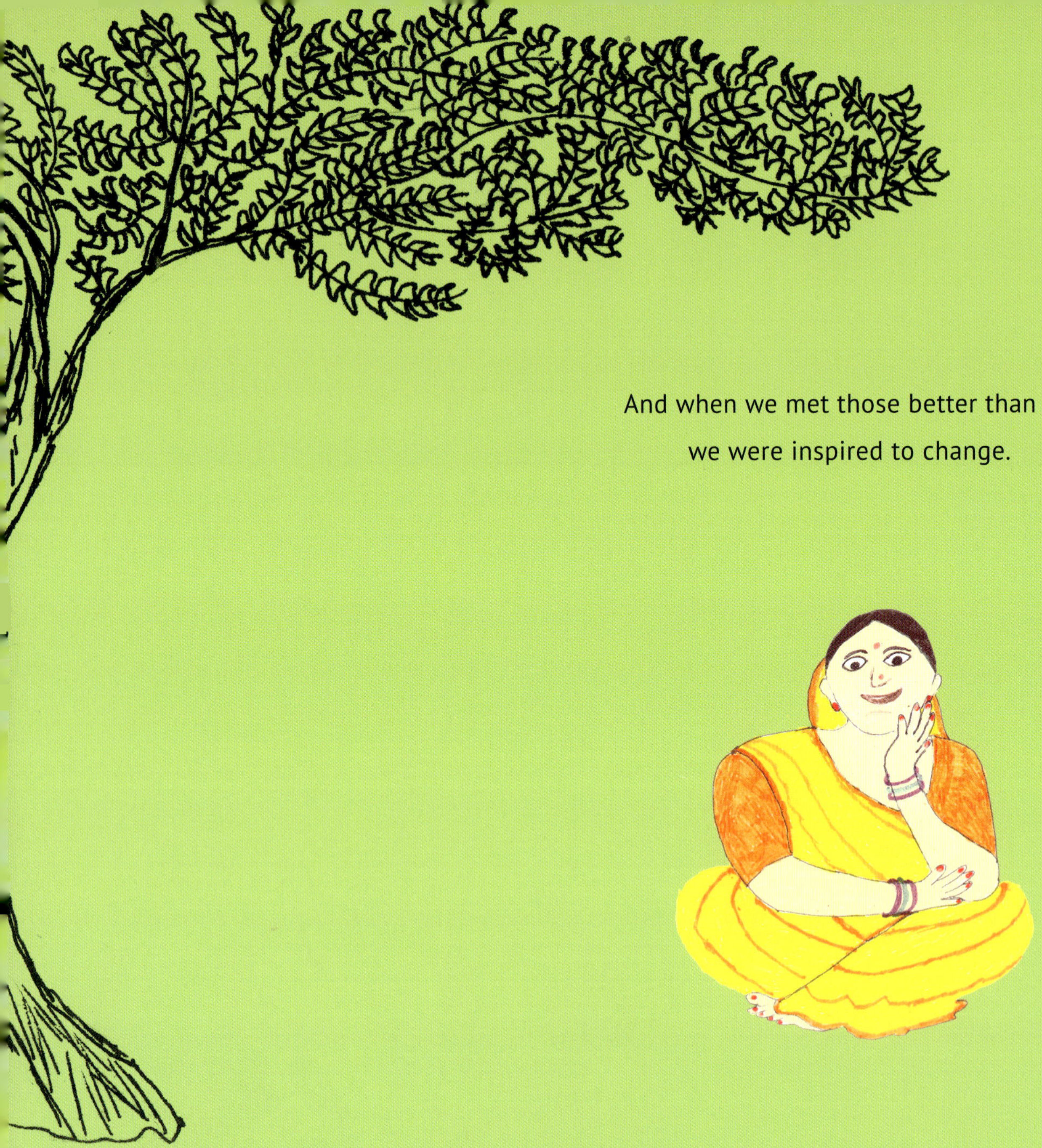

And when we met those better than us,
we were inspired to change.

PROTESTING PATRIARCHY

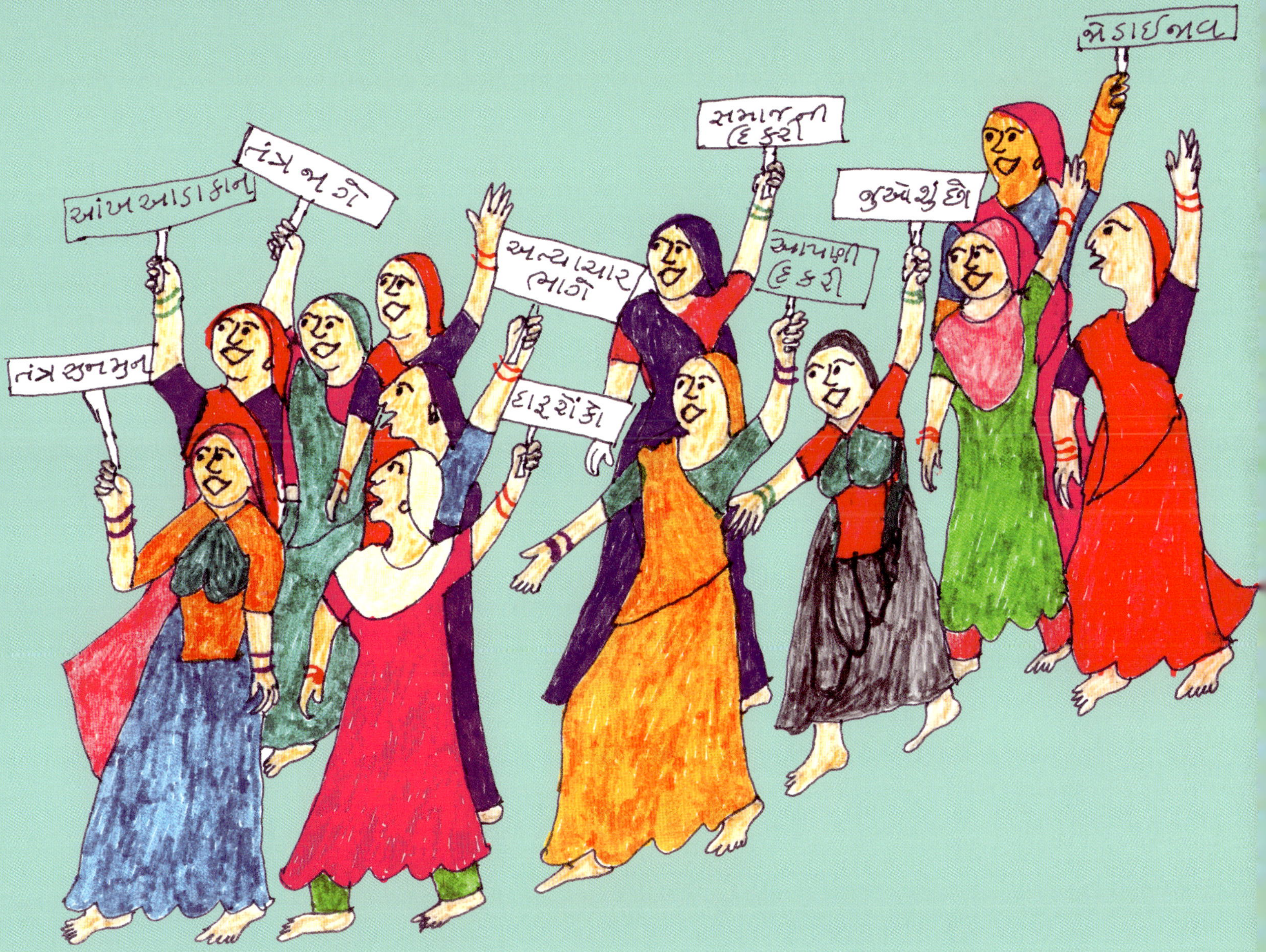

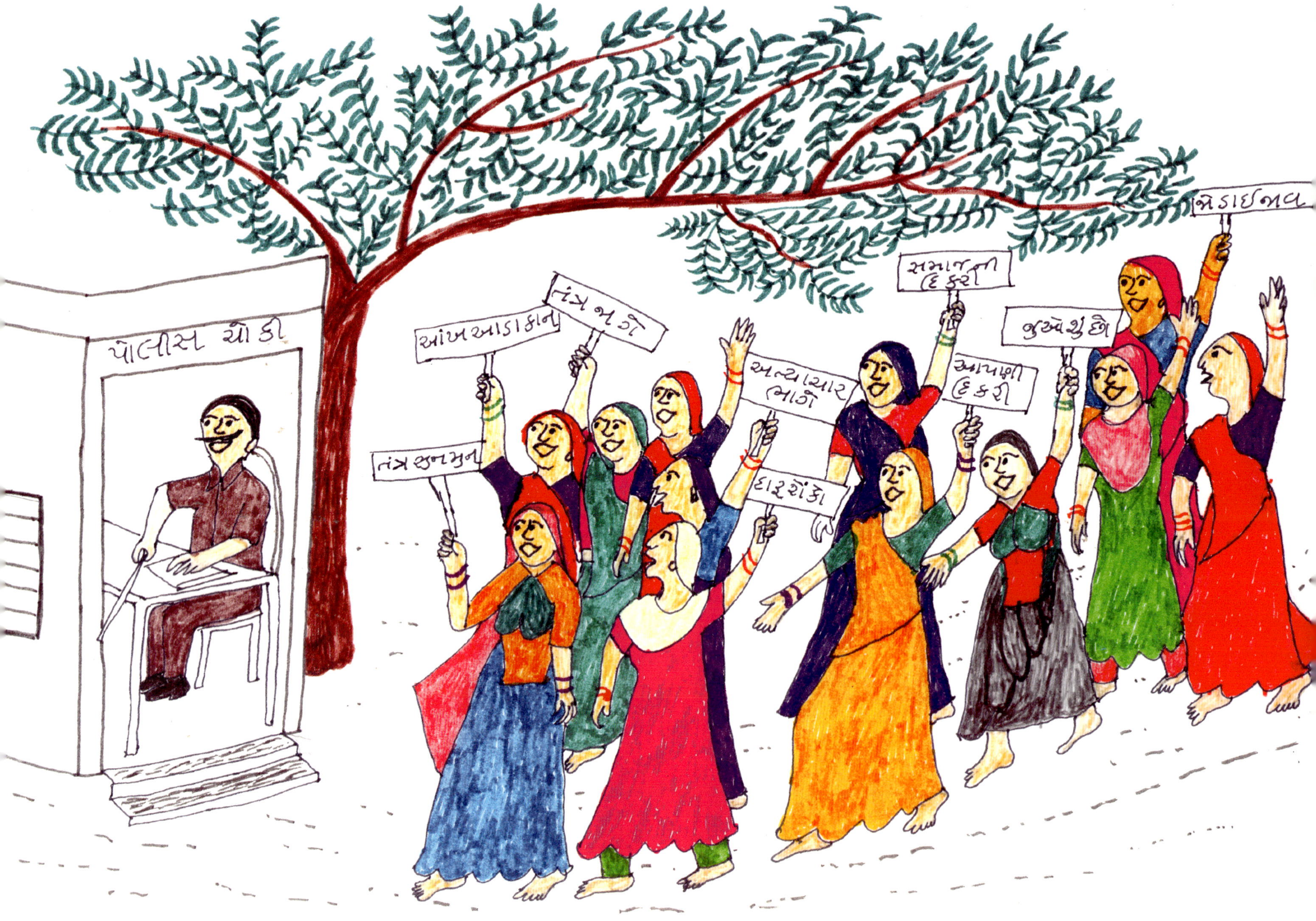
પોલીસ ચોકી
આંખ આડા કાન
તંત્ર જાગે
તંત્ર સુનમુન
અત્યાચાર ભાગે
દારૂ રોકો
સમાજની દીકરી
આપણી દીકરી
જુએ શું છે
જોડાઇ જાવ

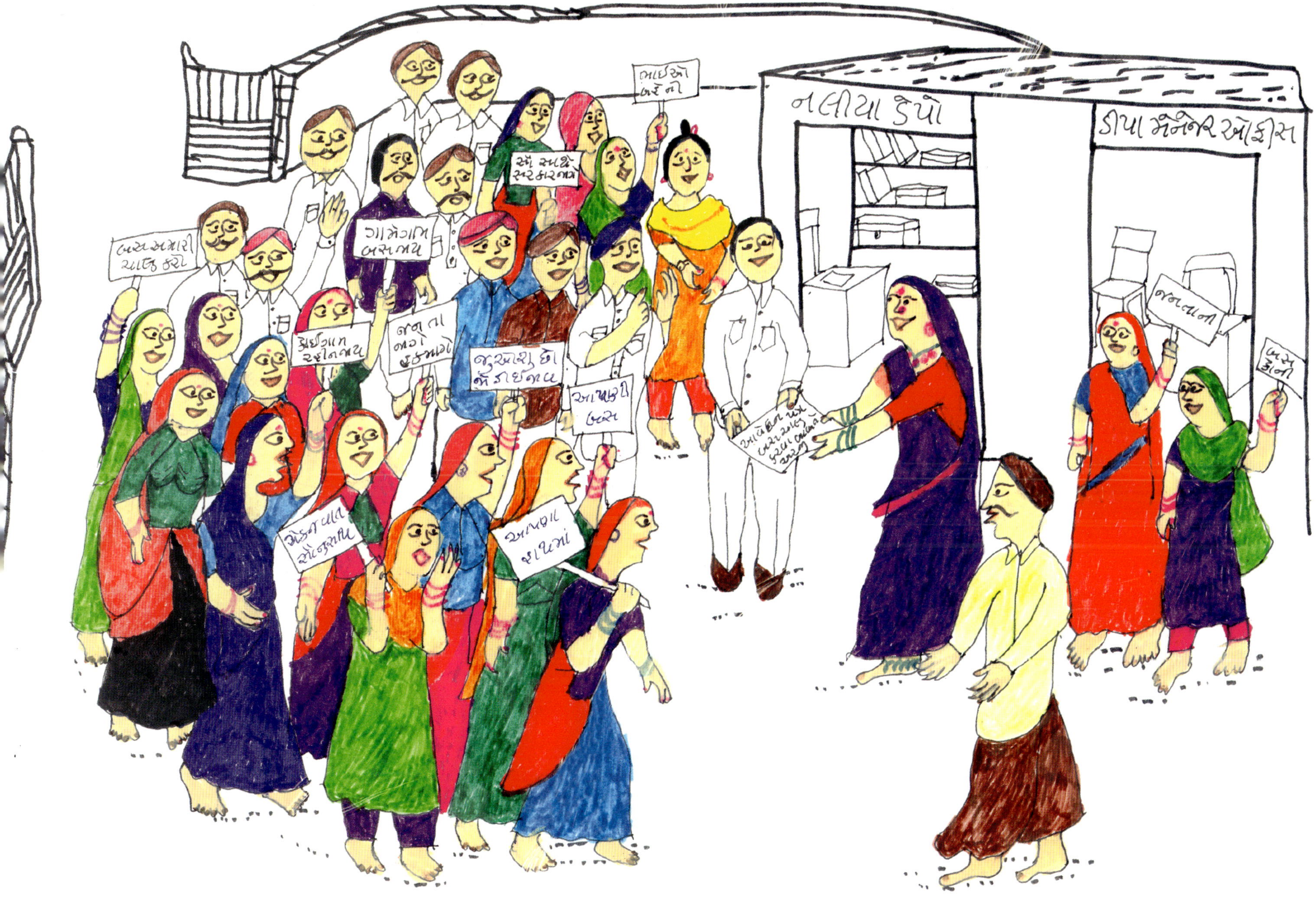
નલીયા ડેપો
ડેપો મેનેજર ઓફિસ

Our mangled uteruses found utterance

when we learnt to listen to our bodies speak.

And they spoke volumes, in spaces that cared to listen.

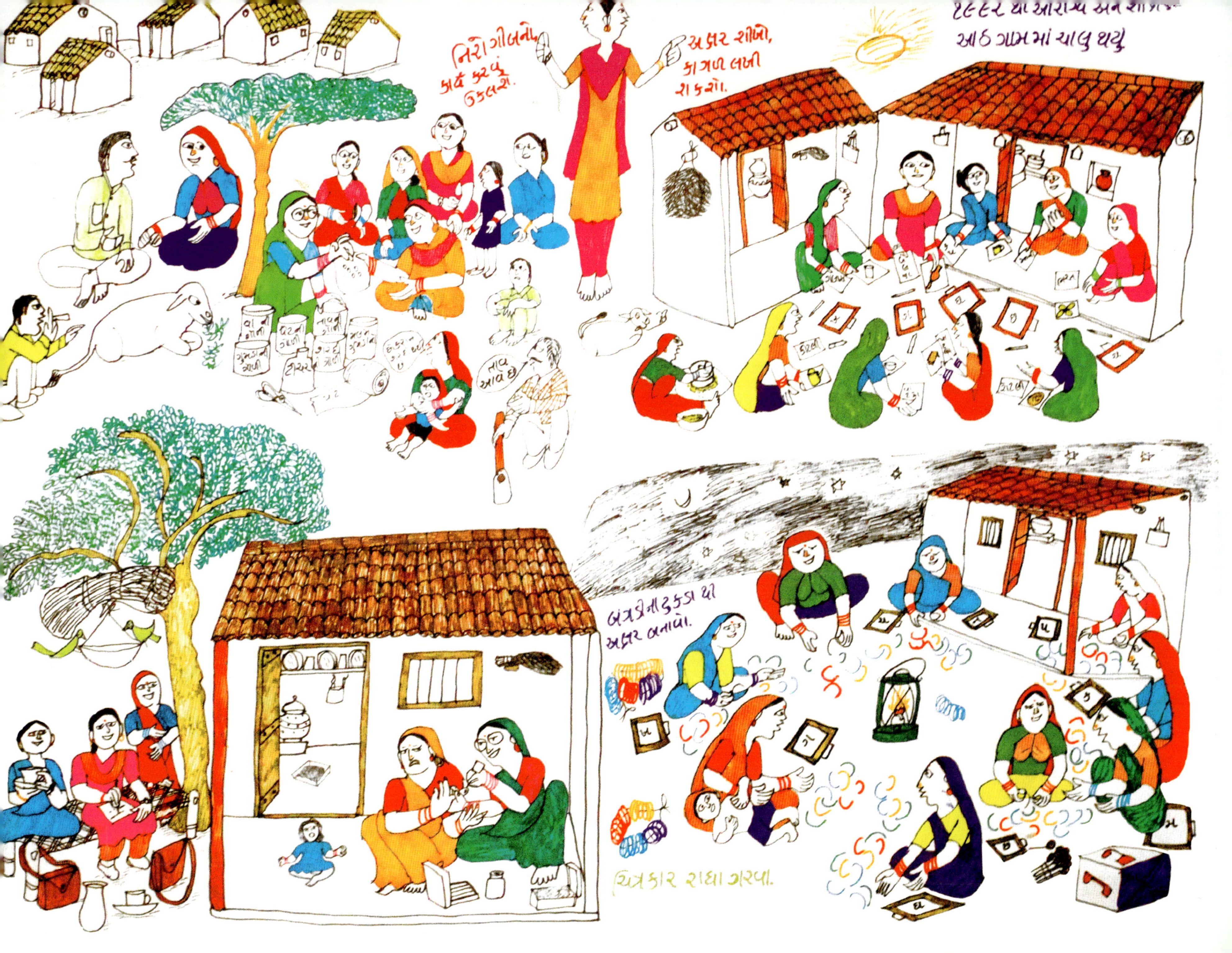
૧૯૯૨ થી આરોગ્ય અને
આઠ ગામ માં ચાલુ થયું
નિરોગી બનો
કાર્ય કરવું
ઉકલશે.
અક્ષર શીખો,
કાગળ લખી
શકશો.
બંગડીના ટુકડા થી
અક્ષર બનાવો.
ચિત્રકાર રાધા ગરવા.

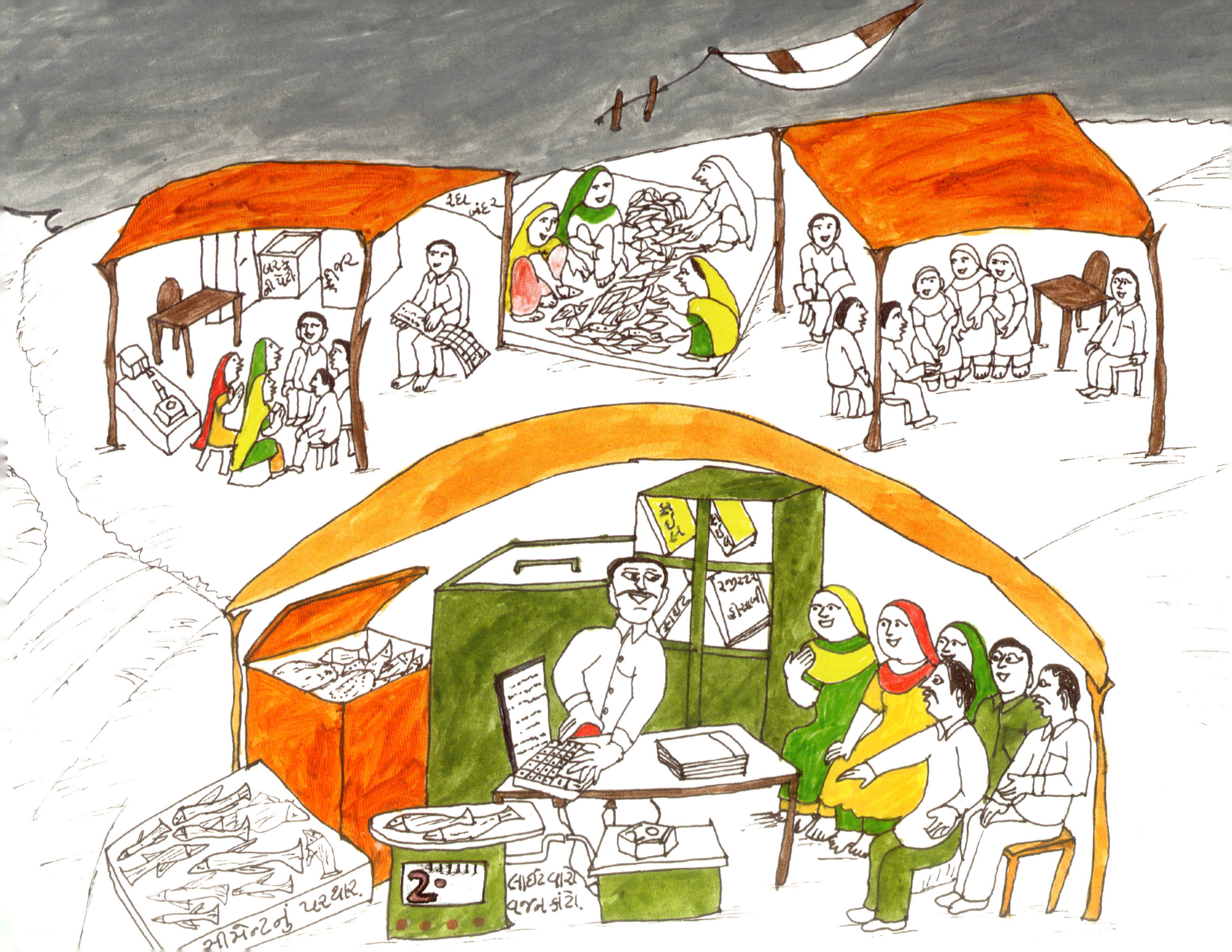
સીમેન્ટનું પરથાર.
લાઈટવારો
વજન કાંટો.

Our ire came in waves – sometimes it was the bus station masters! Sometimes the primary health centres. And often the ration shop. They remained for us the intimate face of the government which fails us where we need it most.

We alternated between waiting for the government to deliver, and initiating our own movement to find solutions. We waited for too long to see big solutions smother our small problems, before we began to demonstrate what we always knew – that small is beautiful.

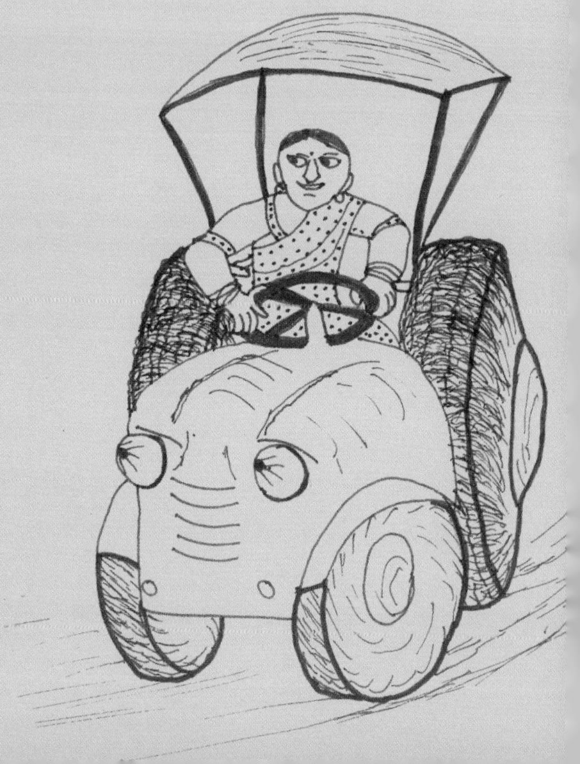

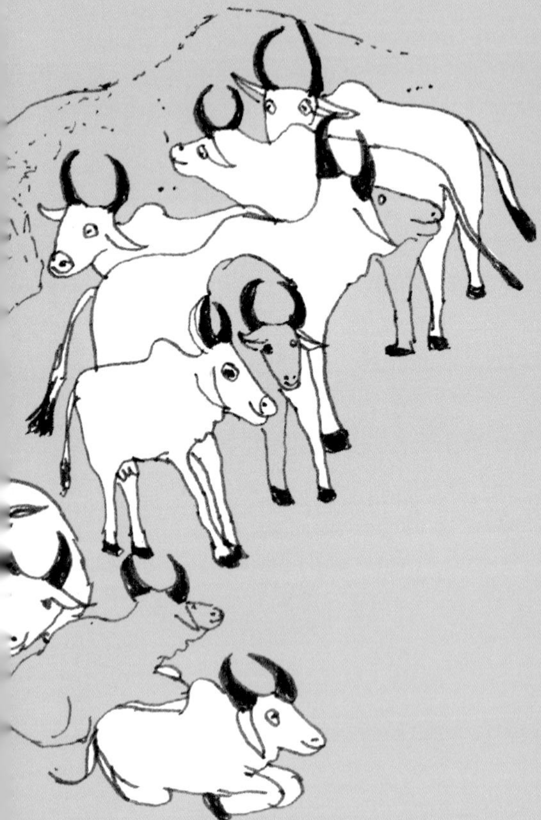

Our demands and dreams for water, fodder, and fuel – something our mothers had in greater abundance – meant that we had to first lead our people away from government doles, impotent water pipelines and free fodder camps.

It meant really that, we had little option but to write the script ourselves, direct it too, and be the main actors!

Empty wells and vacant ponds were revived by our thirst to remind everyone that our rocks, soils, history and wisdom had stories to tell, and could quench our thirst more than remote tubewells and empty pipelines.

And by regenerating our land, ponds, and farms, we were finally reclaiming our villages as our own; earning the respect of our community and our men, and creating faith in the outcomes of a journey which began with us women, but promised to touch everyone.

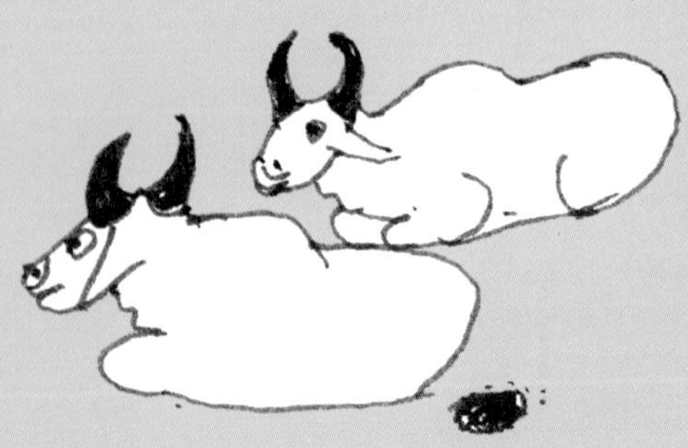

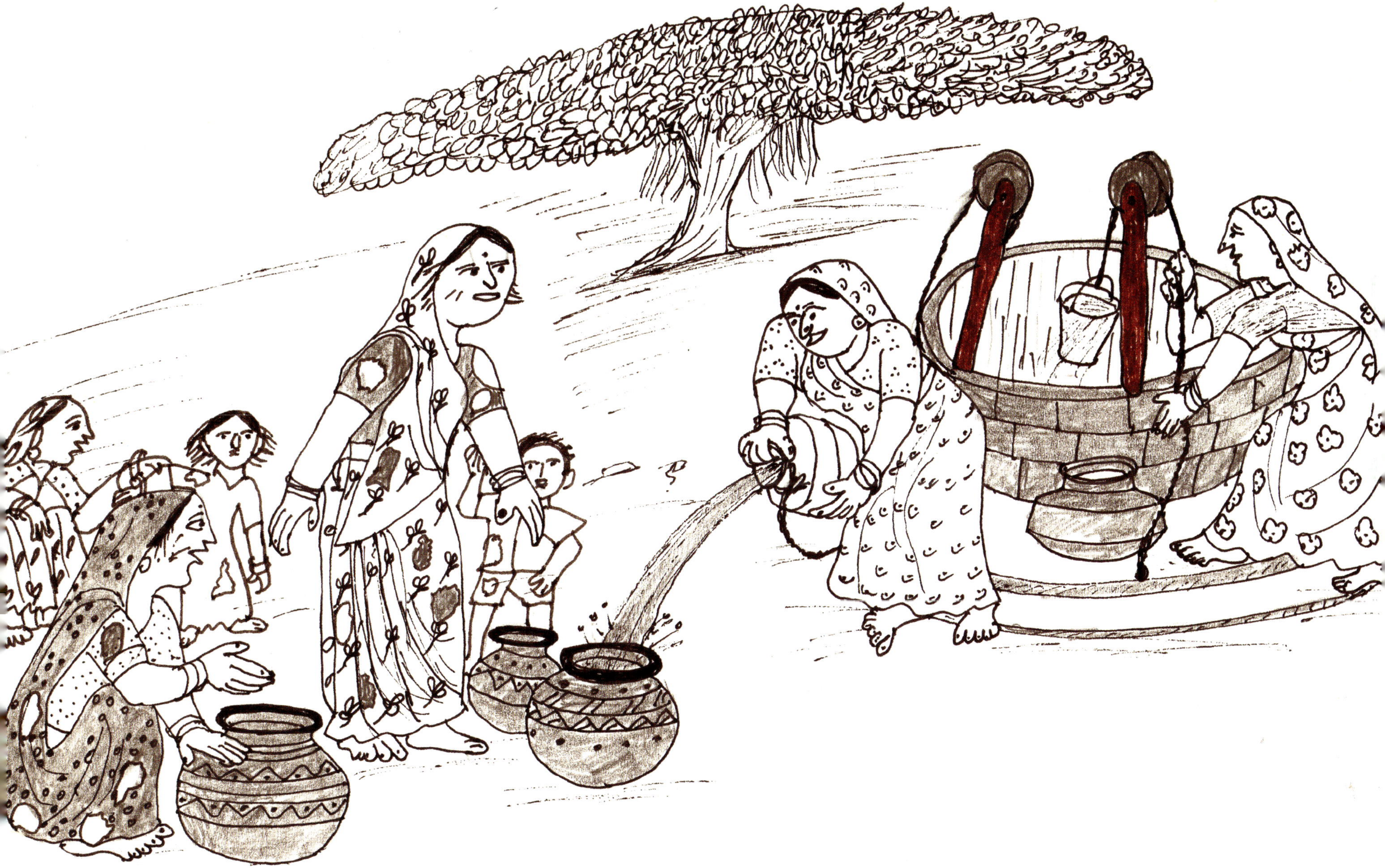

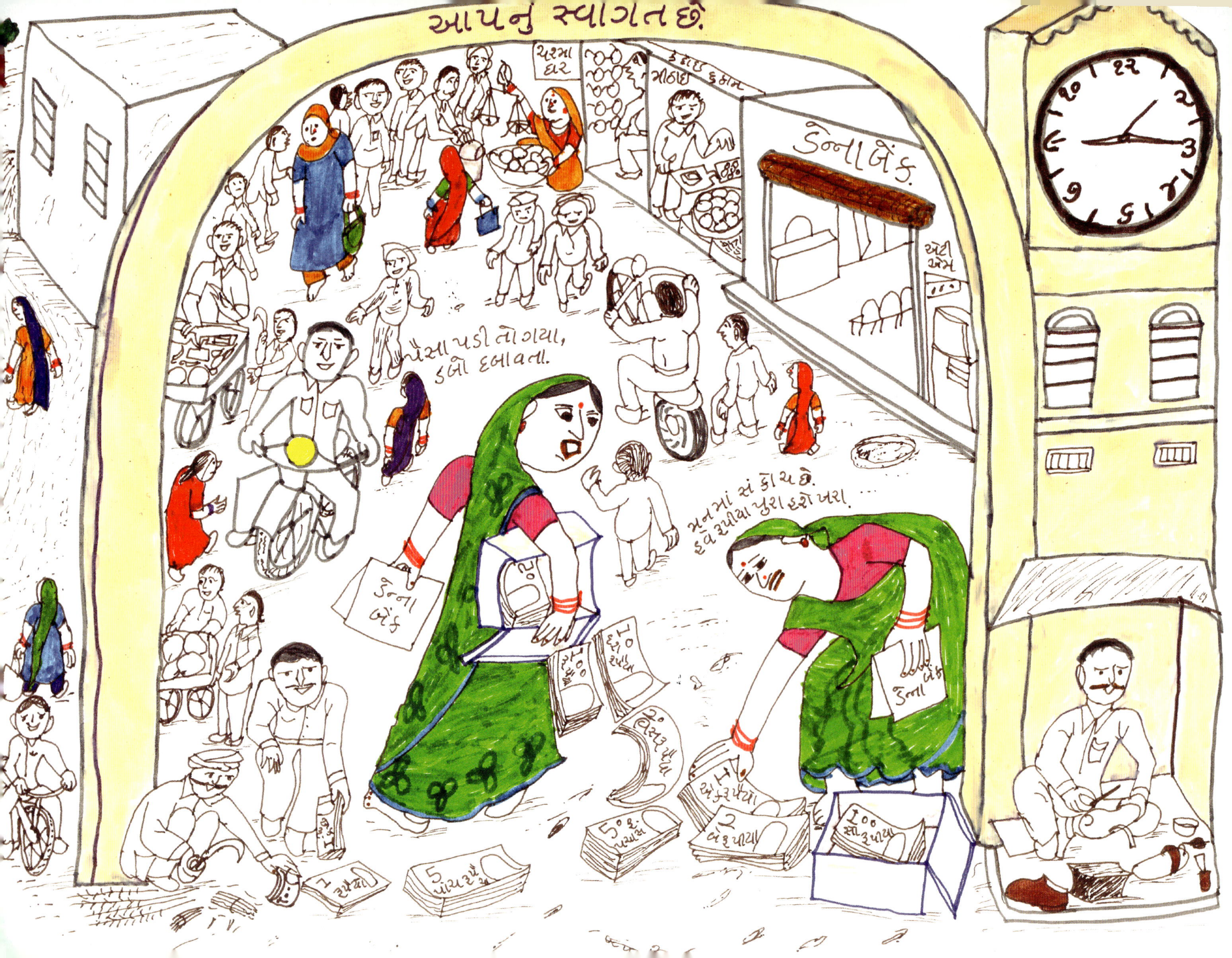

આપનું સ્વાગત છે.
ચશ્મા ઘર
ડેન્નાબેંક.
પૈસા પડી તો ગયા,
ડબો દબાવતા.
મનમાં સંકોચ છે.
હવે રૂપીયા પુરા હશે ખરા....
ડેન્ના બેંક

Our debts were rising and we were too poor for the banks. So we started our own! Our gatherings to save and lend became a pretext really, to let our relationships with each other multiply at greater speed than the money.

In this way, we discovered the anatomy of trust, and the more faith we had in ourselves, the more we trusted the collective.

The amount of Rs 30,000 that Jiva needed as a loan was too large!

How could so many of us, waiting for our smaller loans, be turned back?

But we turned back. And gave her the loan. Jiva was dying of cancer. This loan would not be returned, we knew. This 30,000 would not save her. But it saved our love, and some hope, in our hurry to be good bankers!

Meanwhile, more women were killed in our kitchens than people in road 'accidents' in our state!

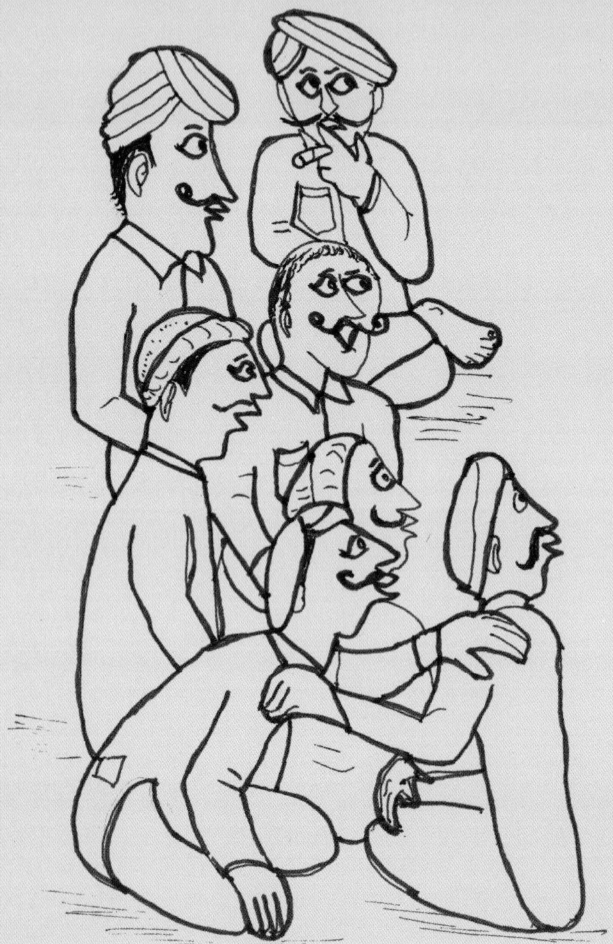

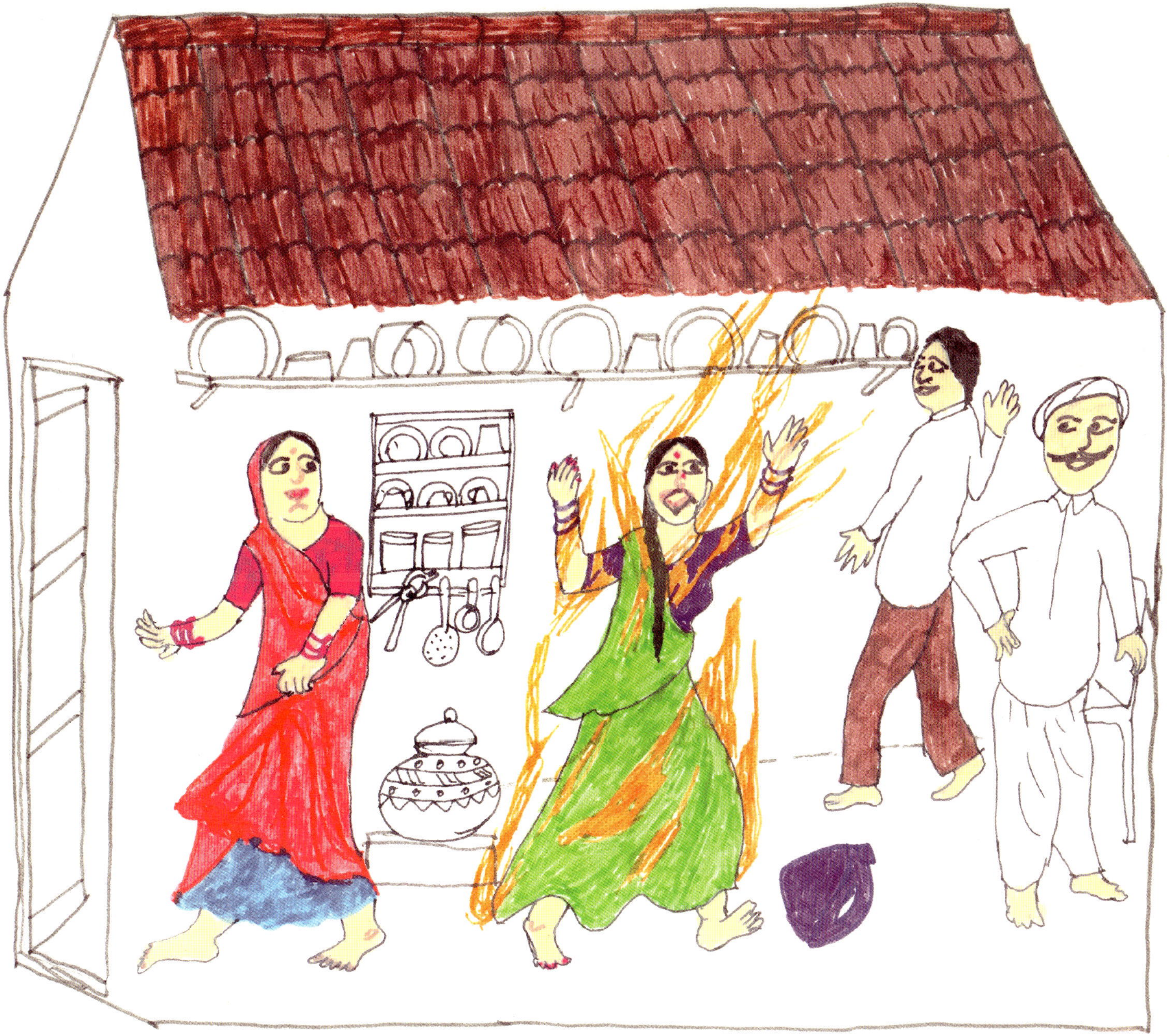

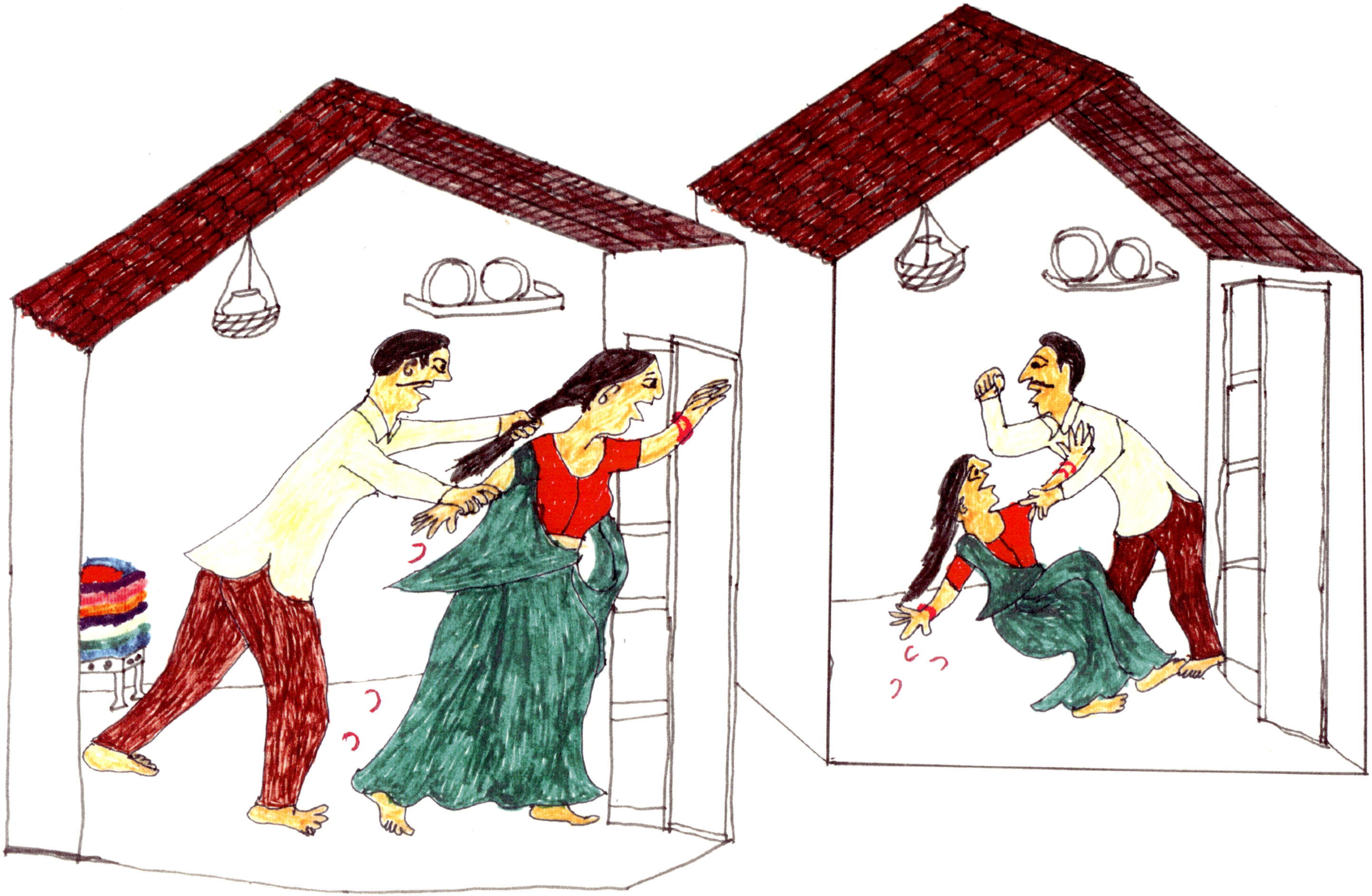

And more dowry was extorted by every community than by bandits in our entire country.

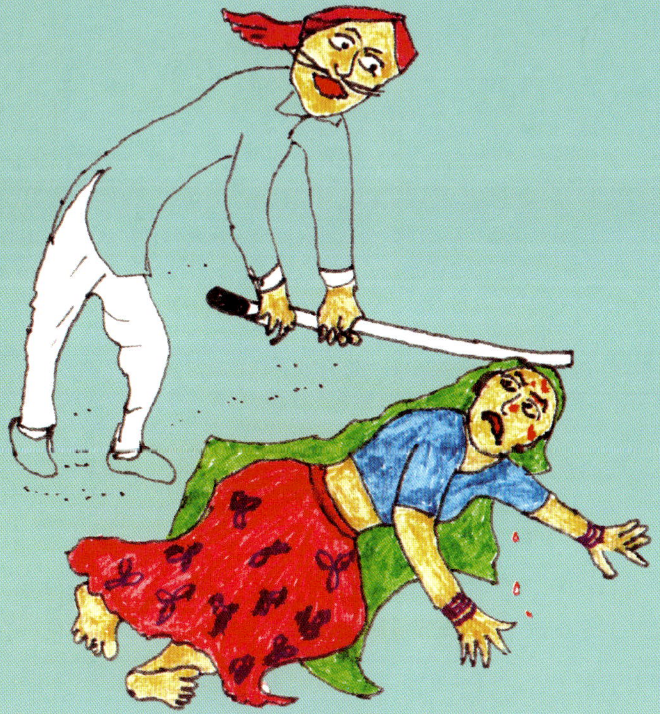

We shamed the families who destroyed a life, but were dismayed by parents who abandoned their child and brokered deals over their dead girl's body. Every day, even today, a daughter is betrayed, more than a daughter-in-law. And we continue to hunt for laws to book them.

With the shattered who survive and cope, we cajole, counsel and take care to care. But that is barely enough. We learn our laws, and pore over those things called FIRs or First Information Reports while we counter the language of chastity, virginity, suspicion and greed.

Alert to the patriarchy of the police, the courts, the lawyers and judges, we also partner with them to build a world which is safe and secure for women.

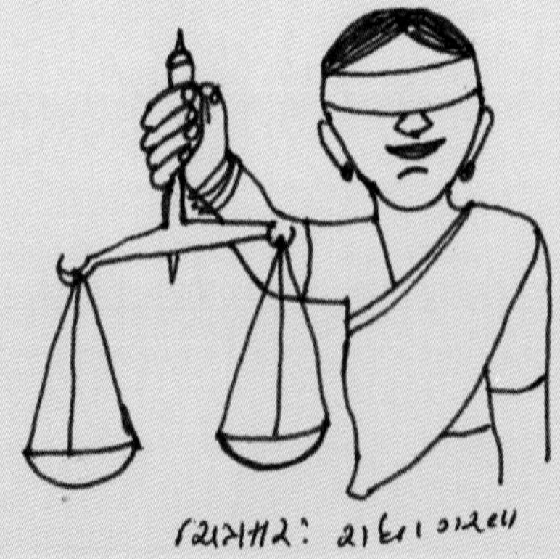

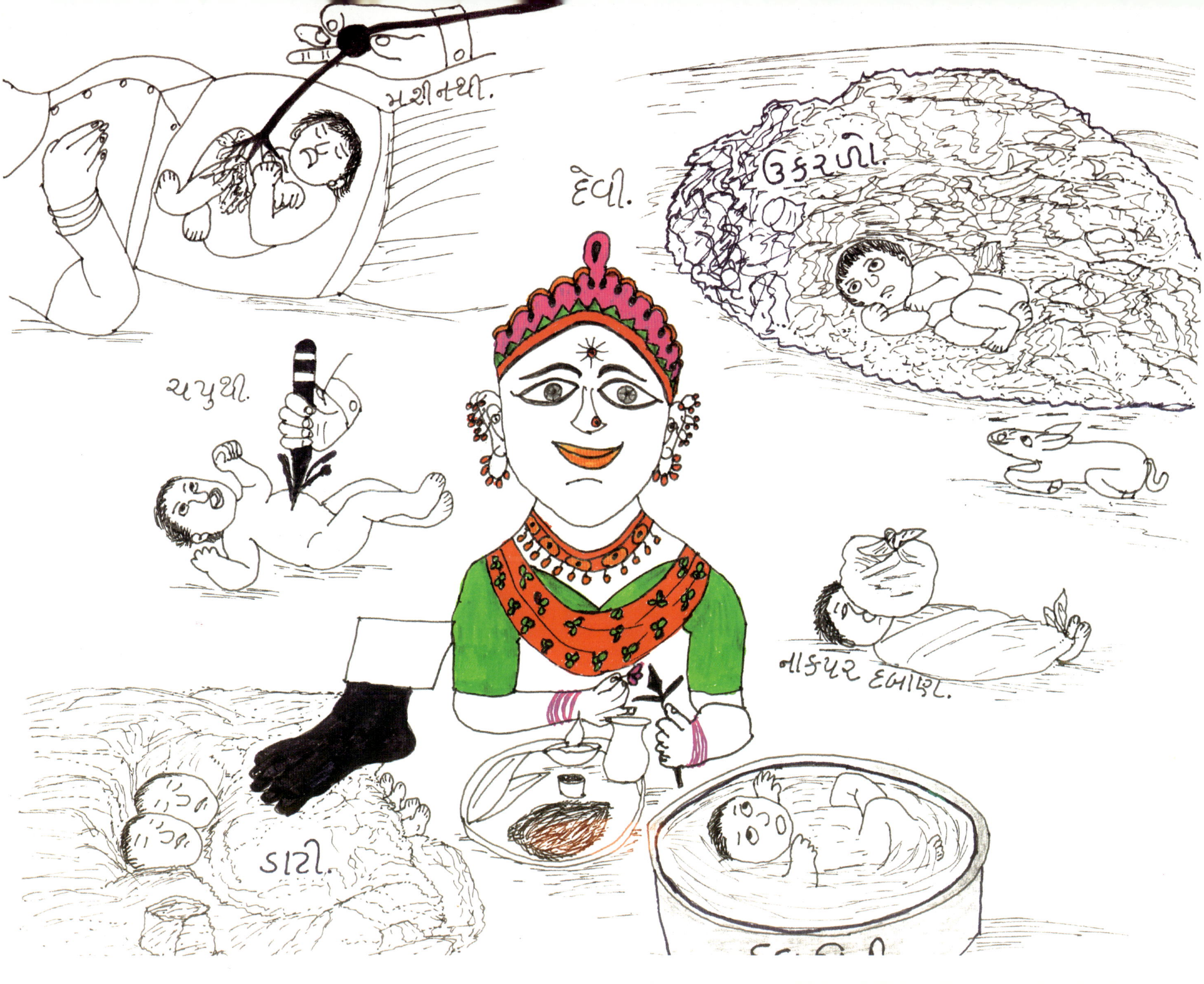
મશીનથી.
ઉકરડો.
દેવી.
ચપુથી.
નાકપર દબાણ.
ડાટી.

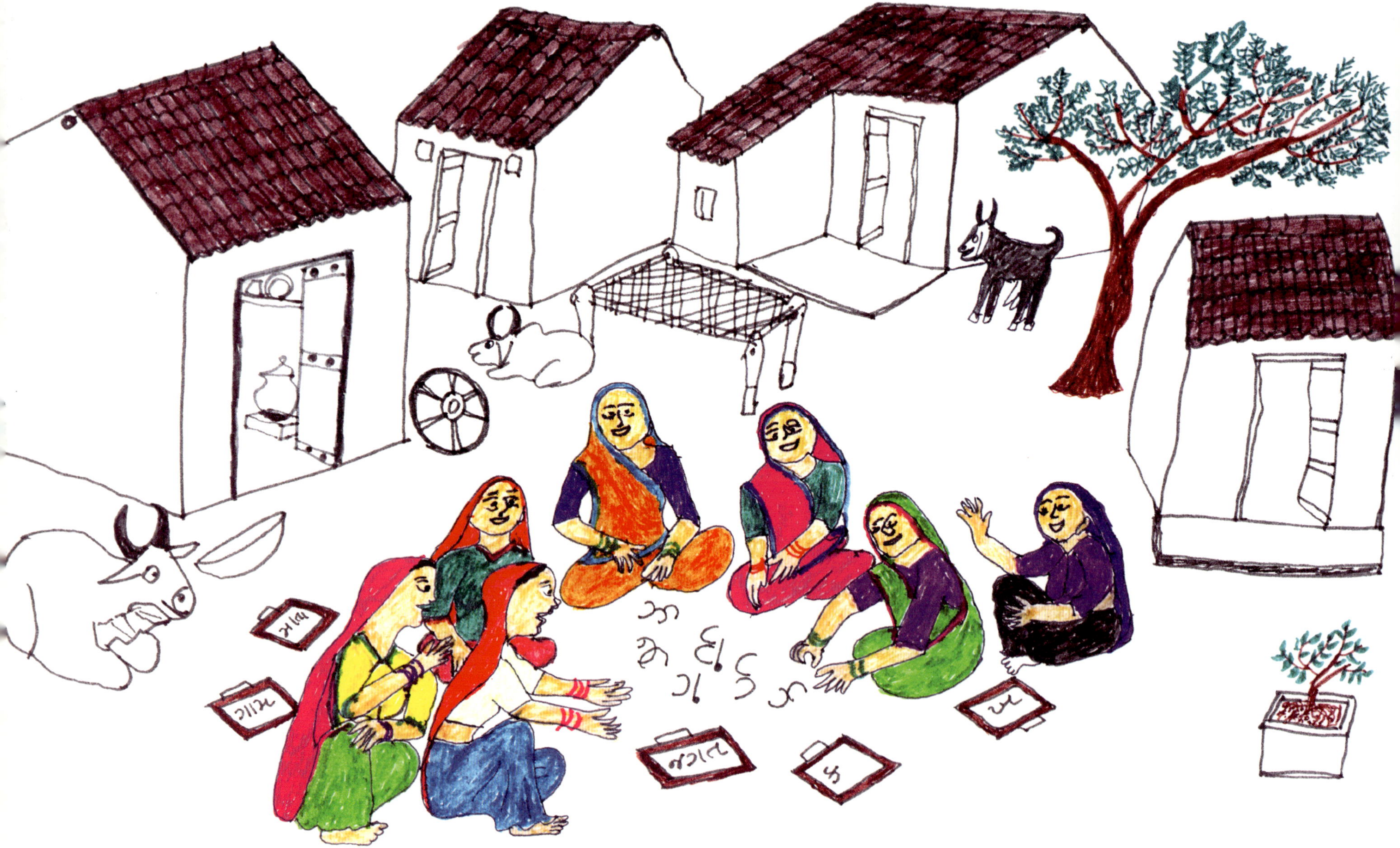

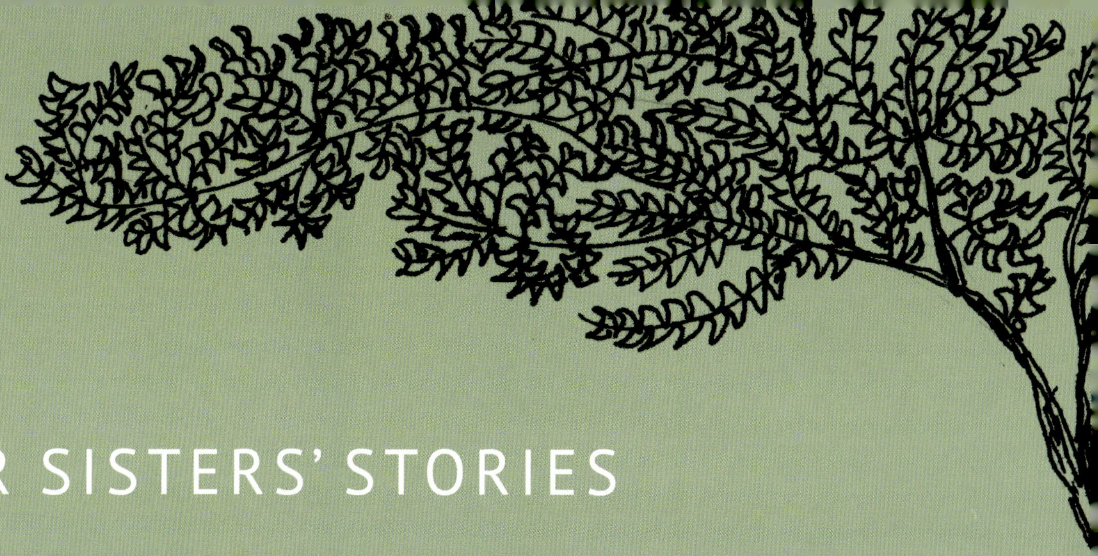

OUR SISTERS' STORIES

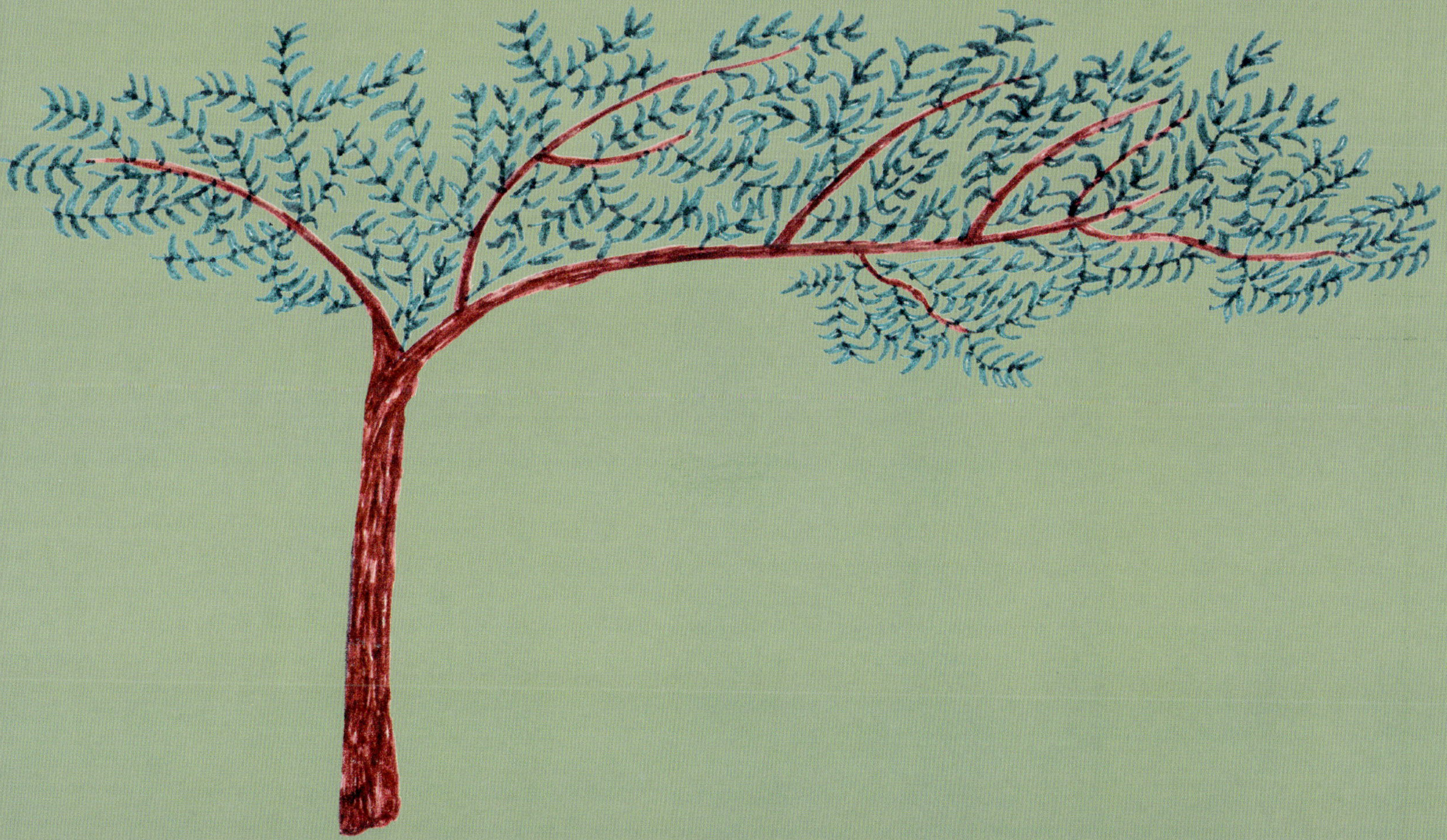

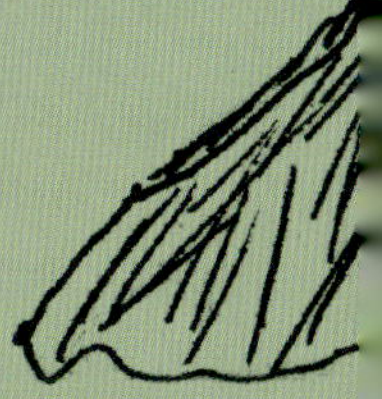

Tales from other lives likes ours, stories of struggle and courage from our sisters in places we had never heard of, would travel across geographies and feed our inspired imagination. Chipko was one such.

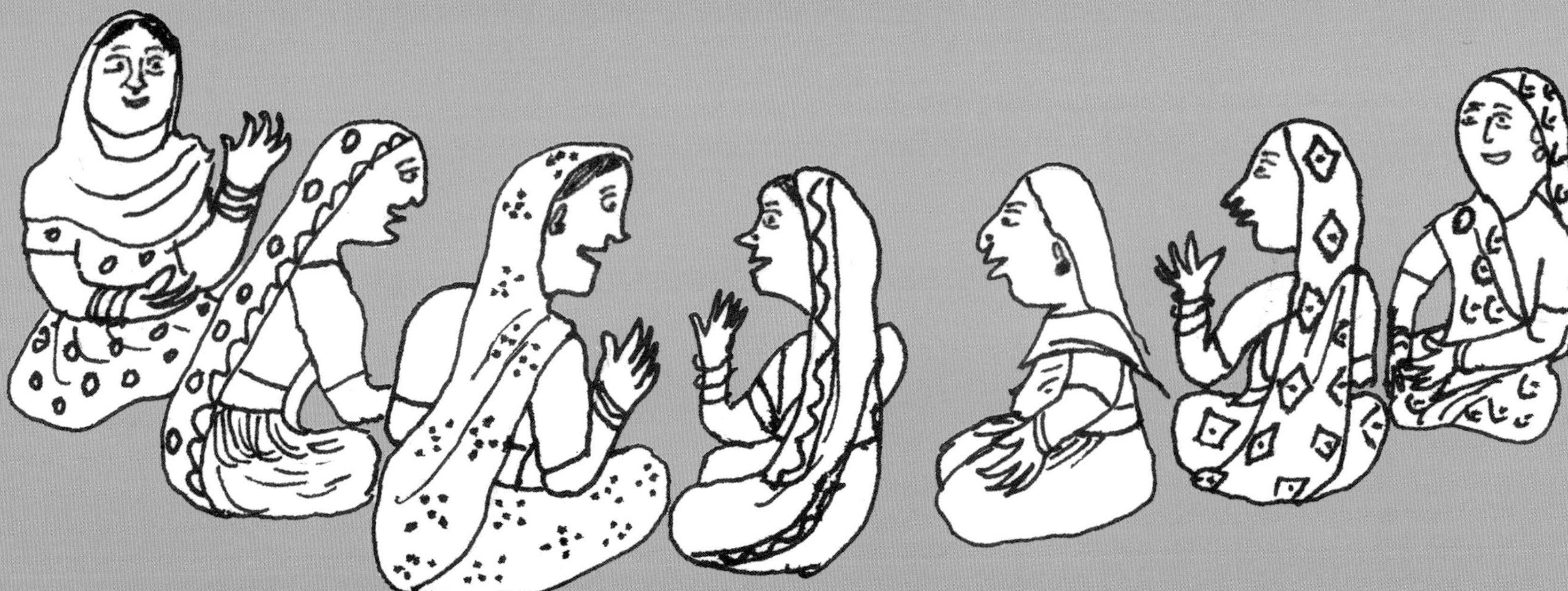

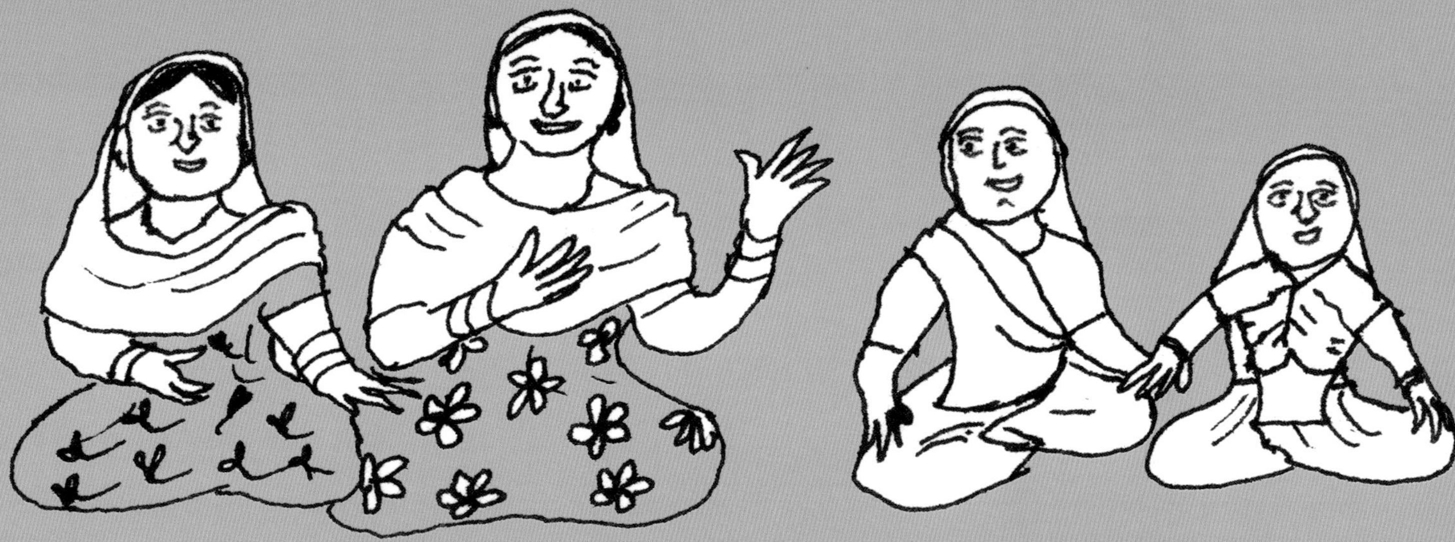

While we were still learning how to embrace each other despite our caste, class and religion, here were women in the Himalayas, who embraced trees, to save their habitat from the gang rape of contractors hungry for wood to shape and sell. They dared the axe to fall on them before it felled the trees. And victory was theirs.

We, of course, had our own battles to win.

And Chipko ignited us in different ways.

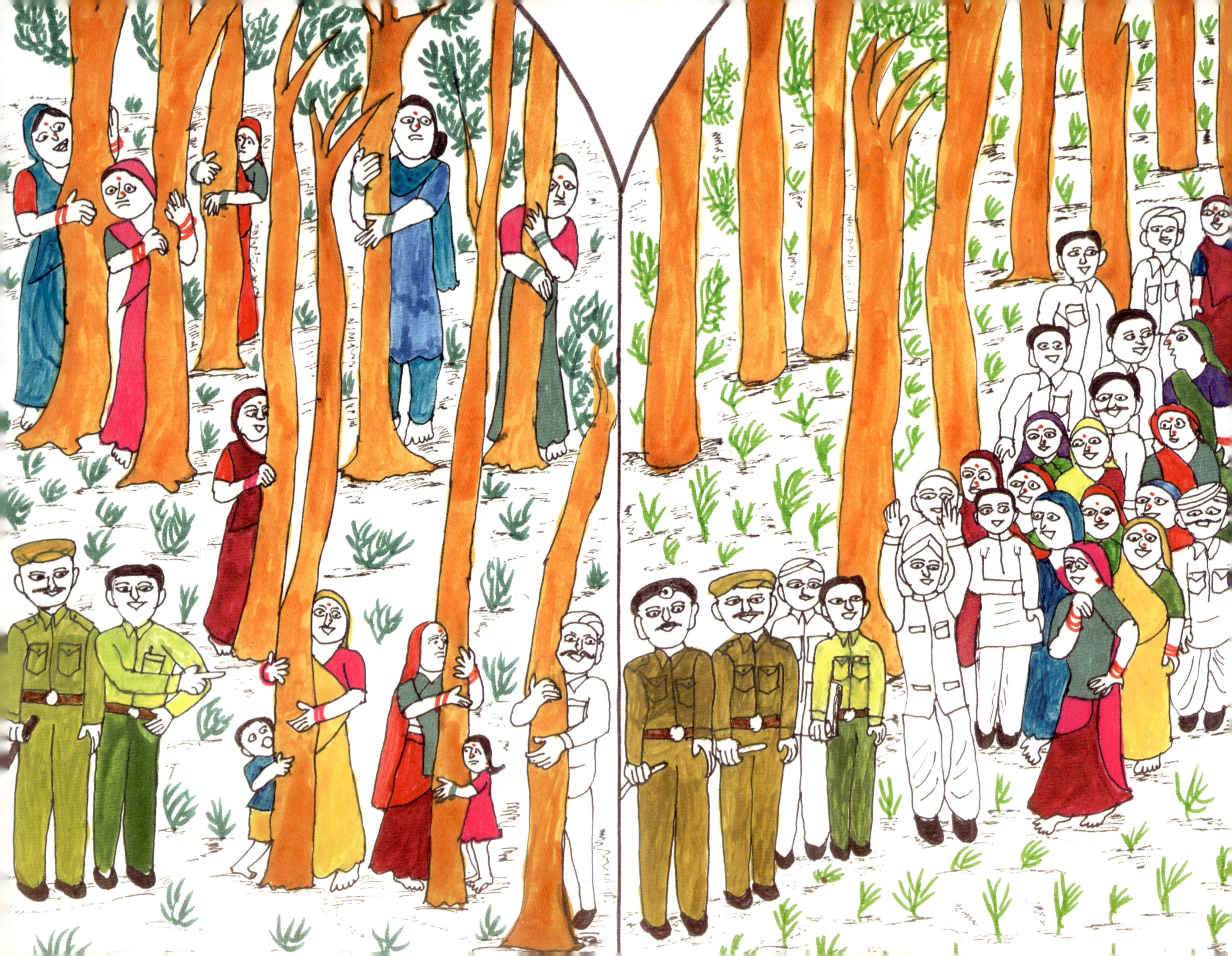

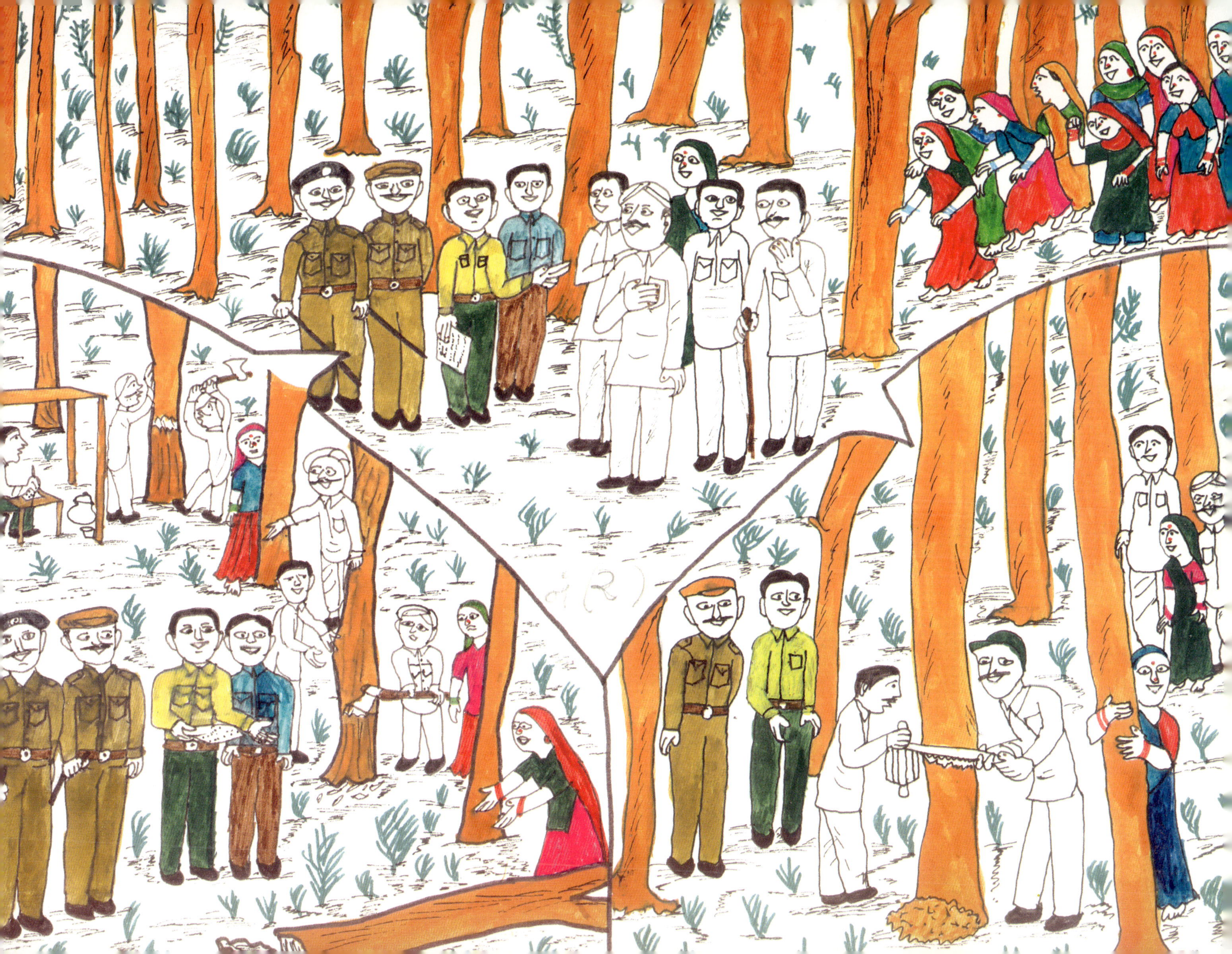

Varjuma, our funny 'kaki' who would have us in splits with her lewd riddles, lost her husband one day. Within a few months, her brother-in-law took over her farm, and she was stripped of her earnings, food and fodder. The fear of courts did not deter him. Nor did our attempts to put pressure on him.

The panchayat looked the other way, as the farm continued to prosper under him.

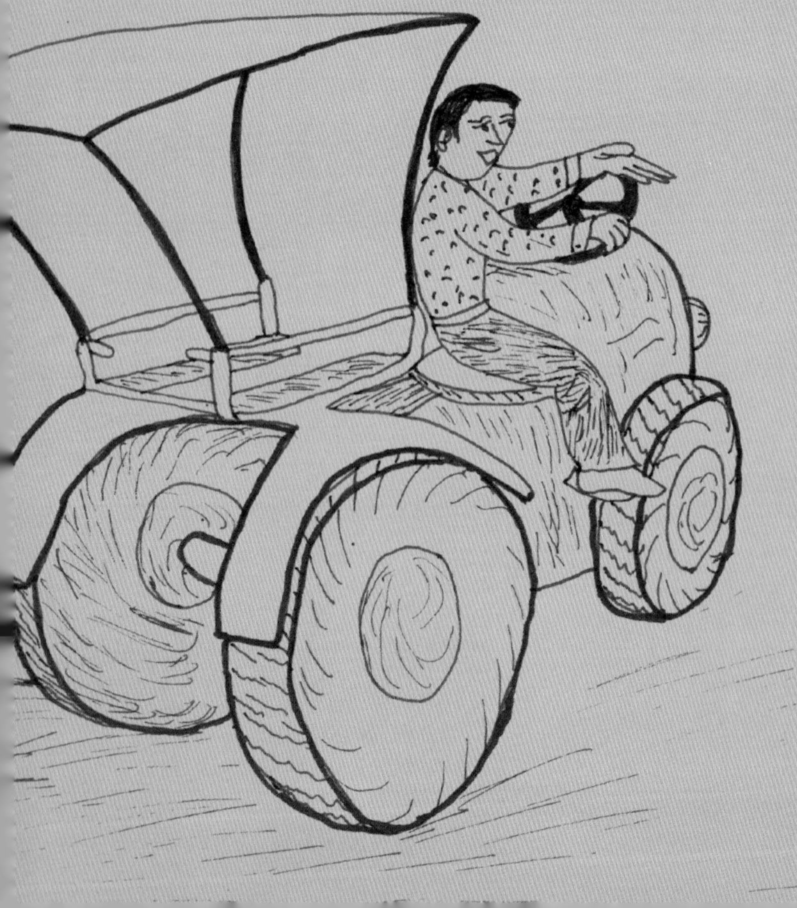

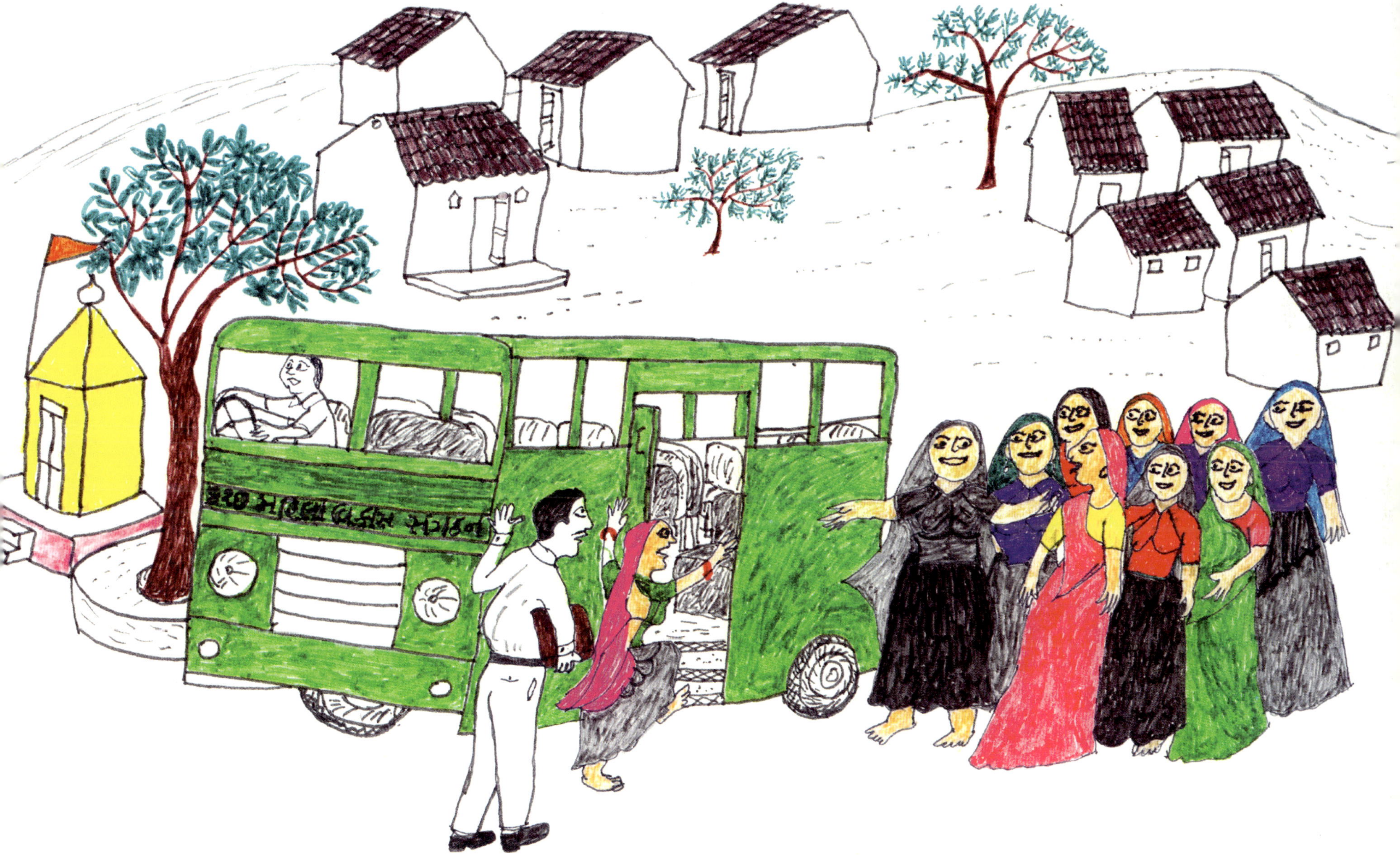

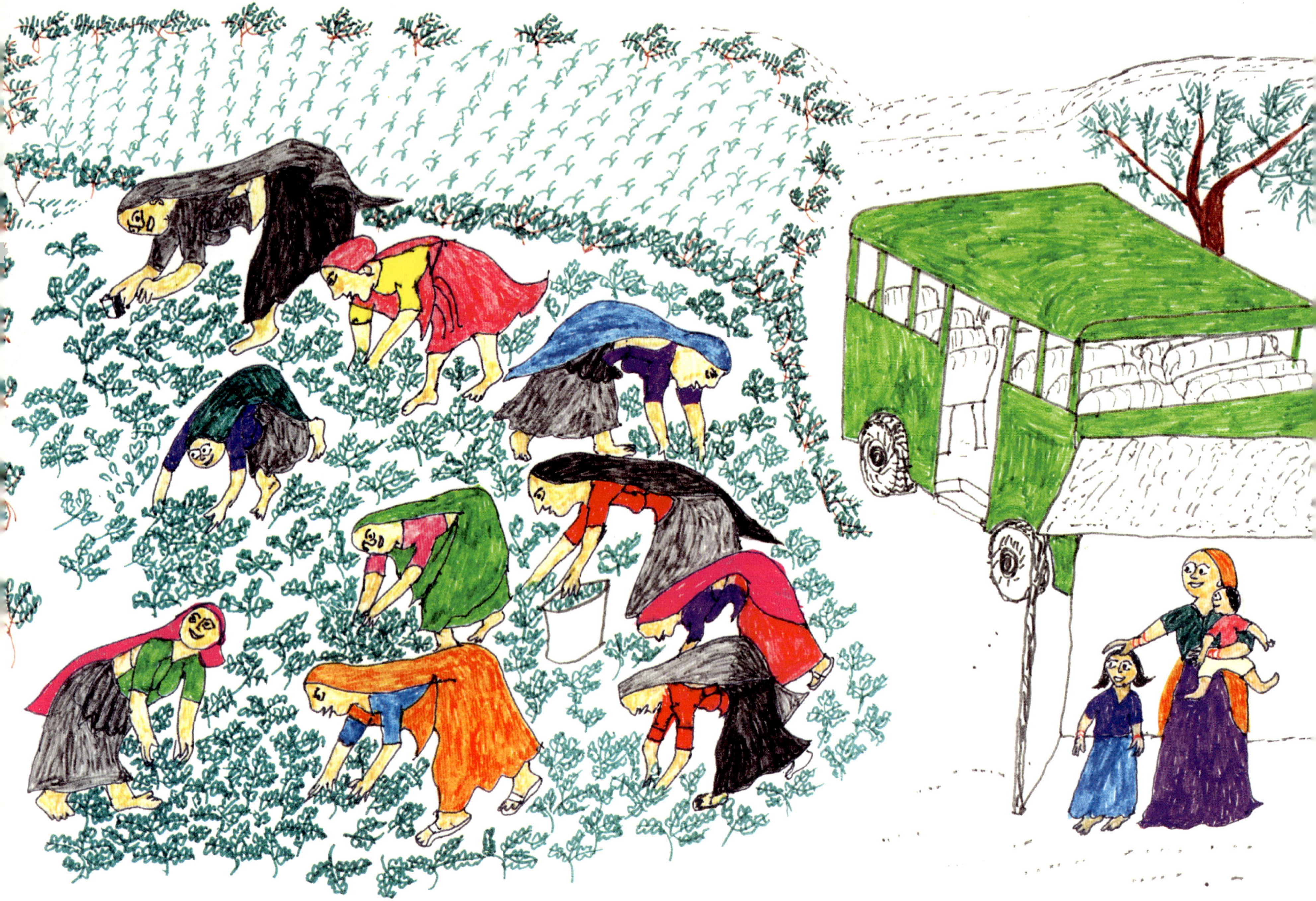

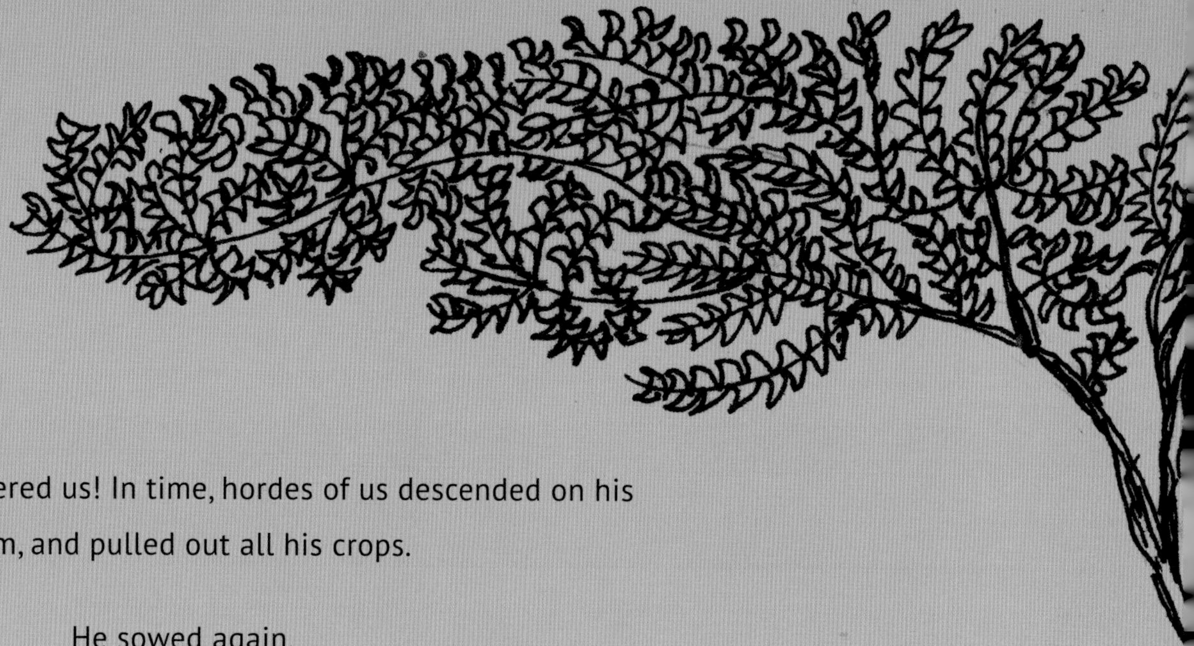

But Chipko had entered us! In time, hordes of us descended on his farm, and pulled out all his crops.

He sowed again.

We removed again.

He sowed. We removed.

Till he returned the land to its rightful owner.

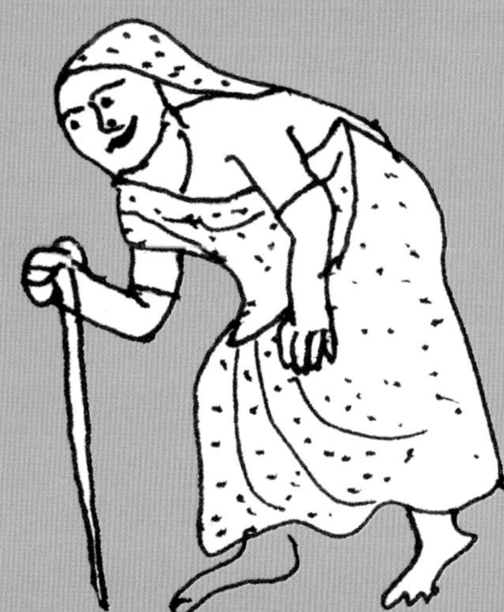

And so we were inundated with requests from many more Varjumas – young and old, all single, struggling to retain their land and dignity in the face of opposition from the patriarchs in their lives.

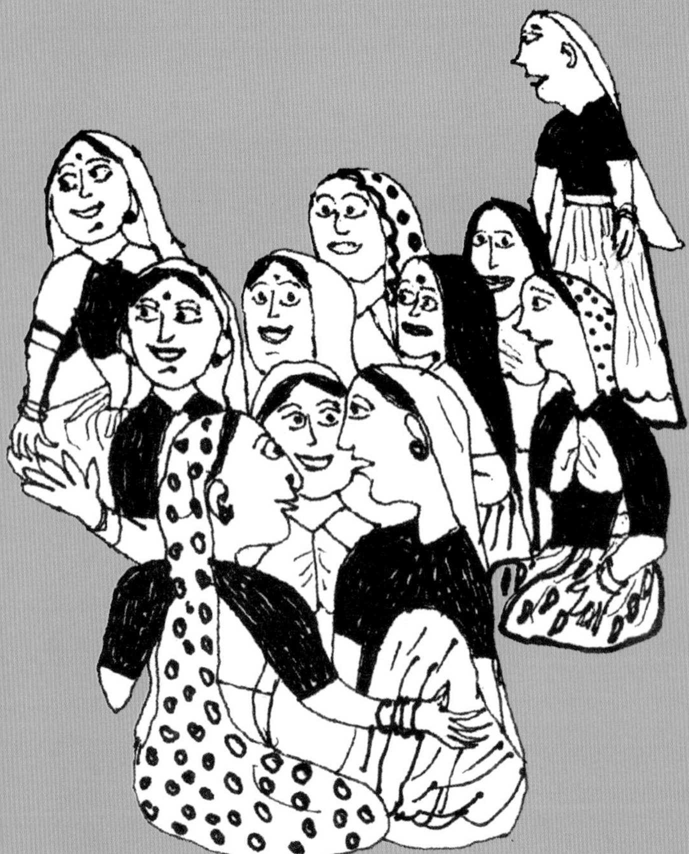

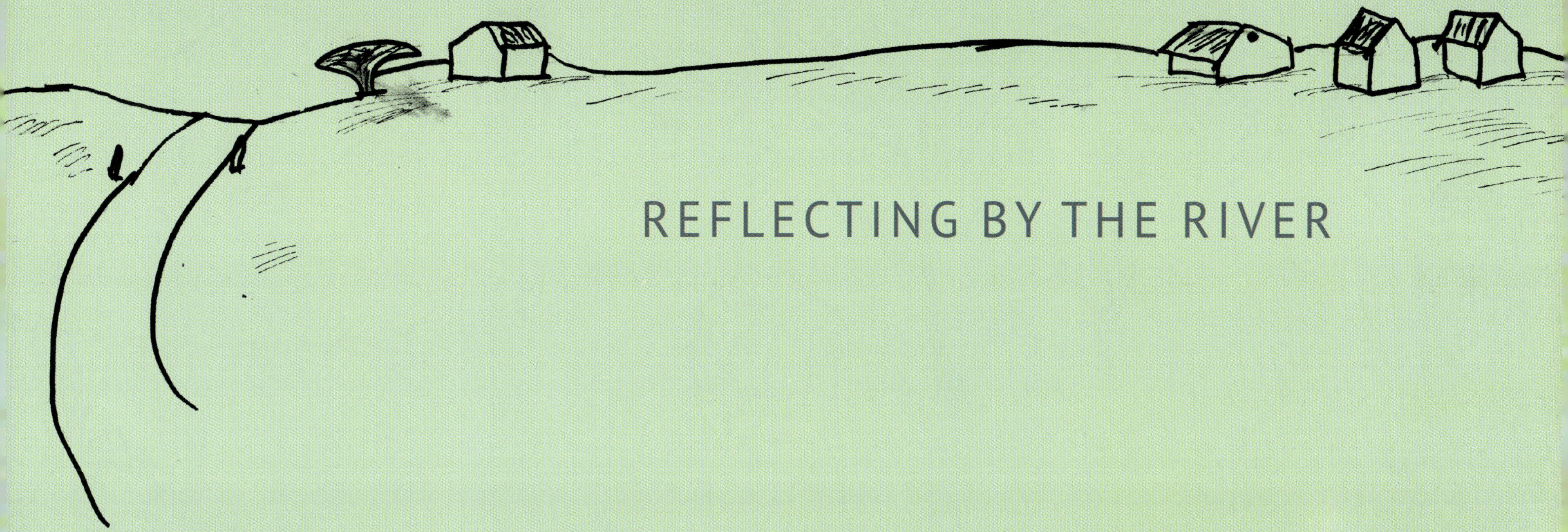

REFLECTING BY THE RIVER

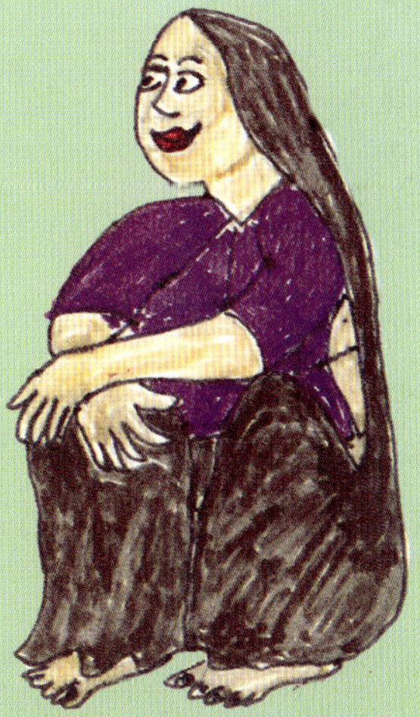

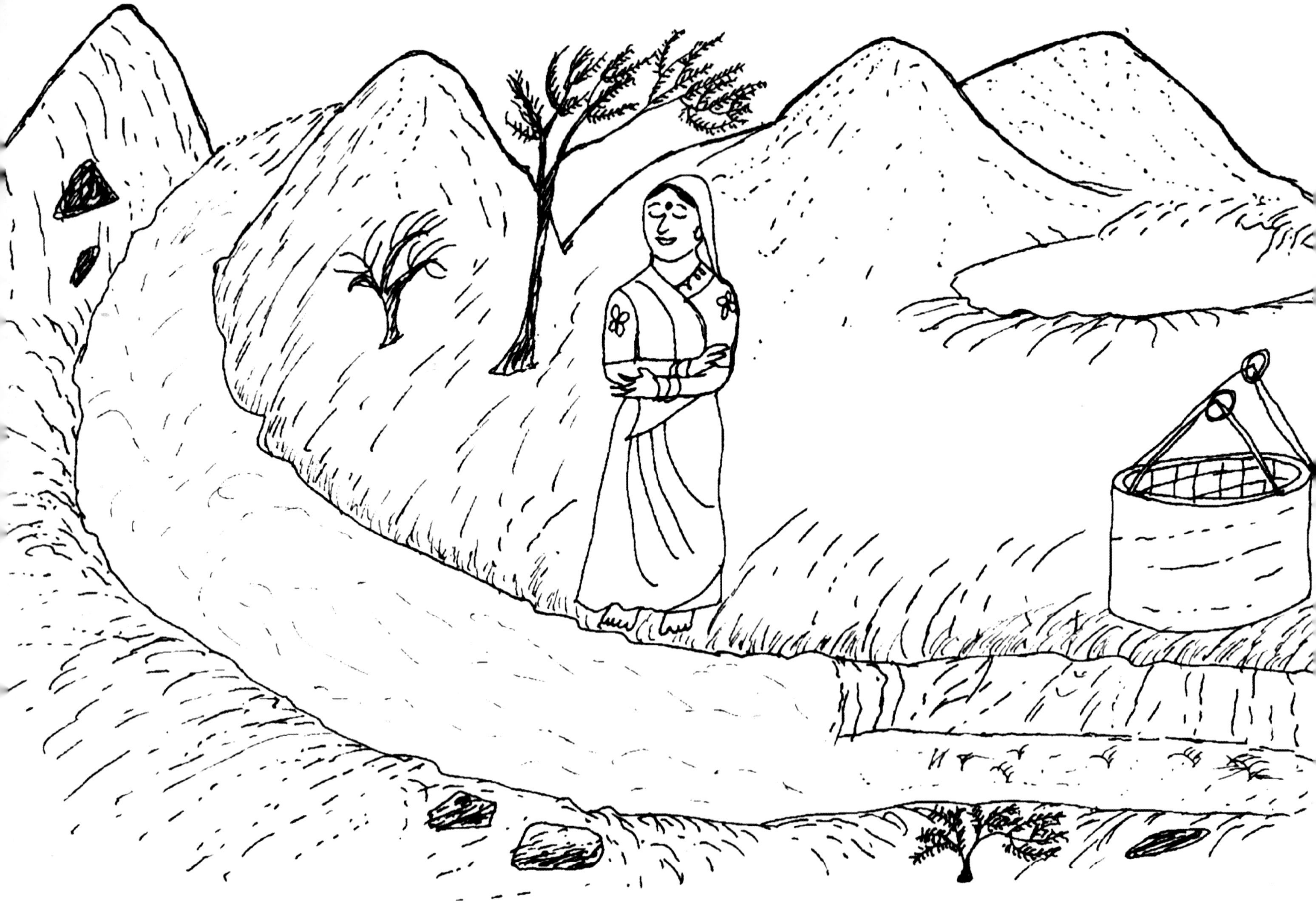

We often pondered . . . do we want to be like the river whose power spreads quietly, invisibly as it meanders through the crevices and corners of the rocks, enters hidden pathways, merges identities, creates new ones, and irrigates the earth with life-giving energy . . .

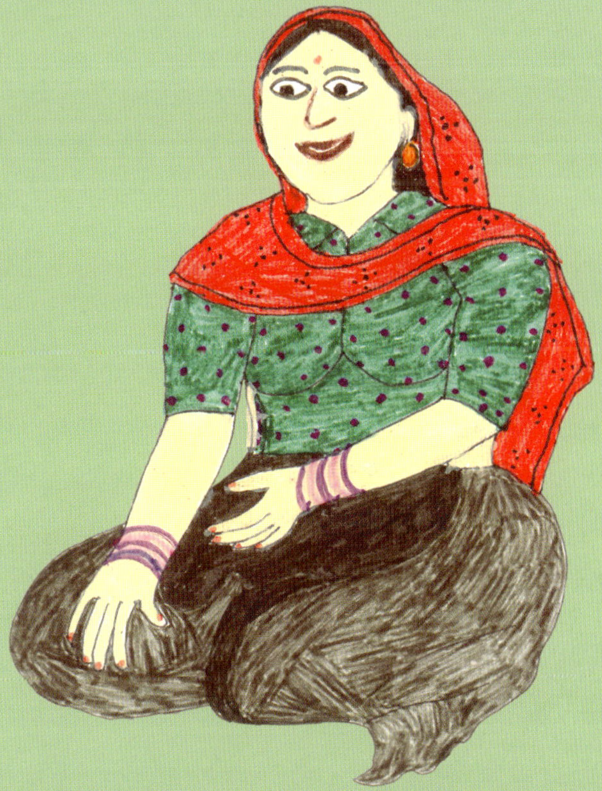

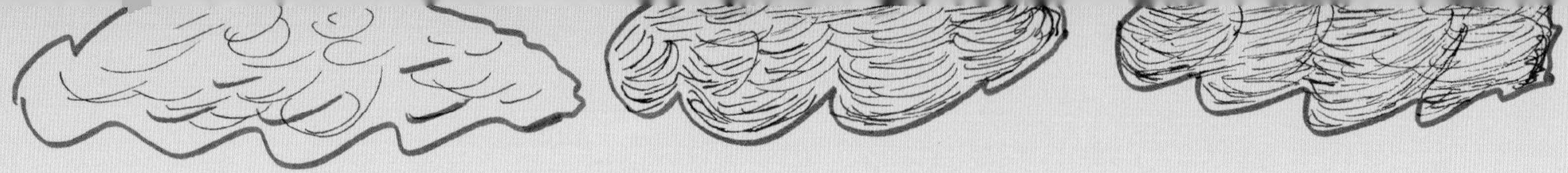

Or would we rather be like the fire, whose power grows as it leaps towards the sky, turns bright and big, consumes and destroys everything that comes in its way, and leaves the earth burnt . . . for its renewal again.

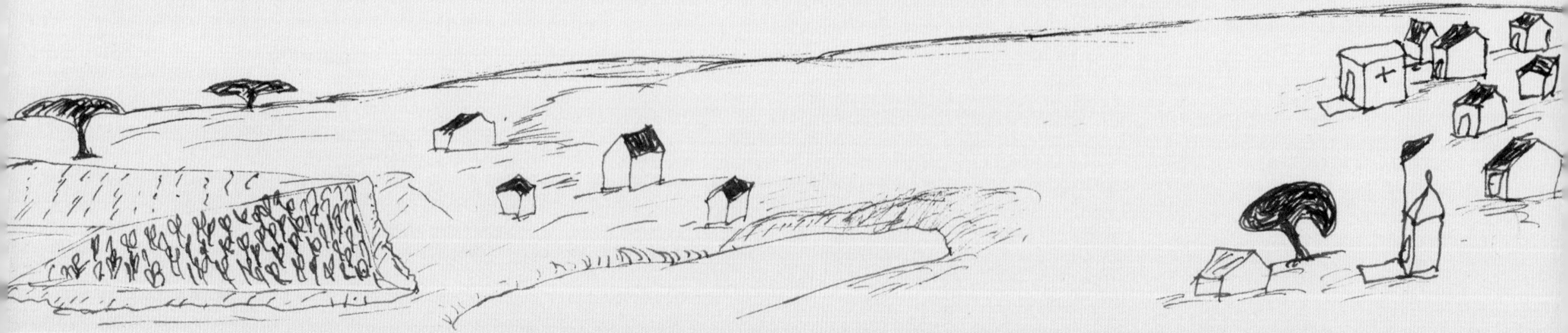

THE DIVIDING LINE

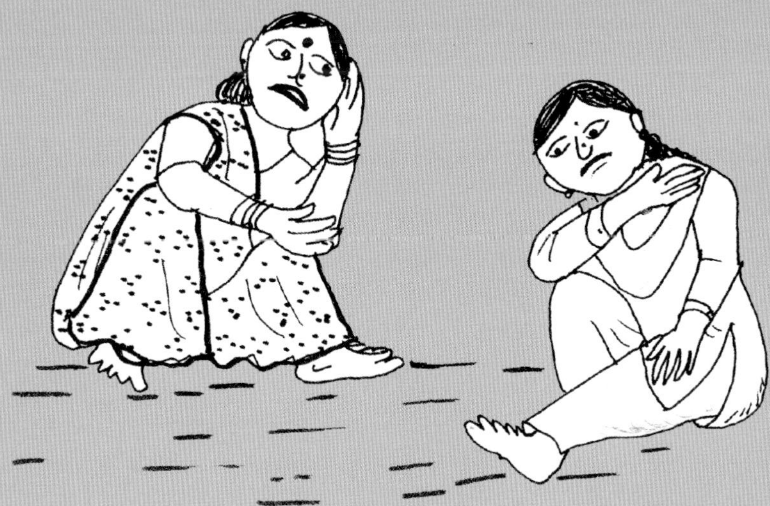

As women we came together, we shifted the boundaries of caste and religion, we pushed them to the very edge of our minds' eye.

Outside of our village, it was easier.

But within our homes, we were not allowed to forget who we were, and what we had been born into.

And we would find ourselves again within the confines of our caste, community and religion.

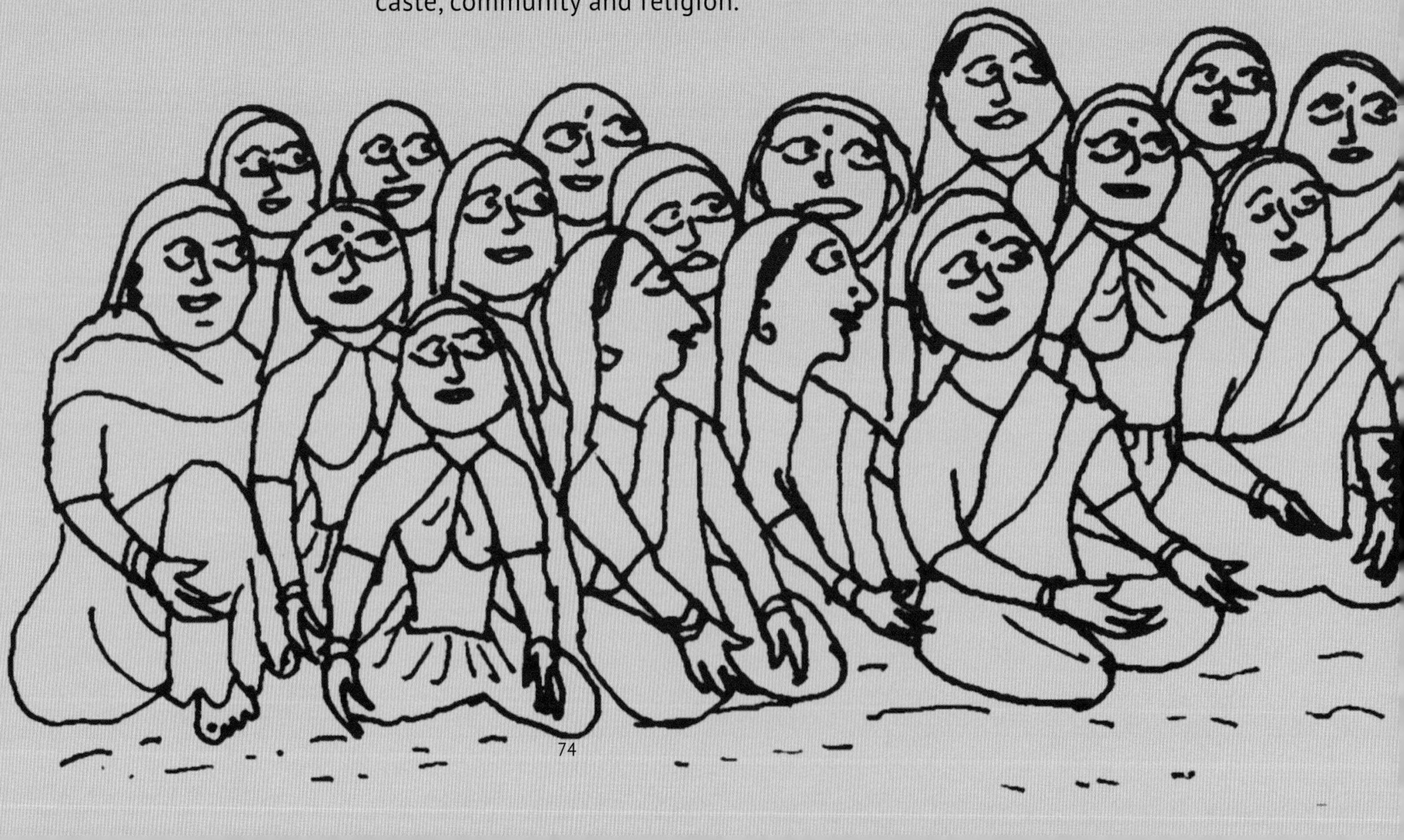

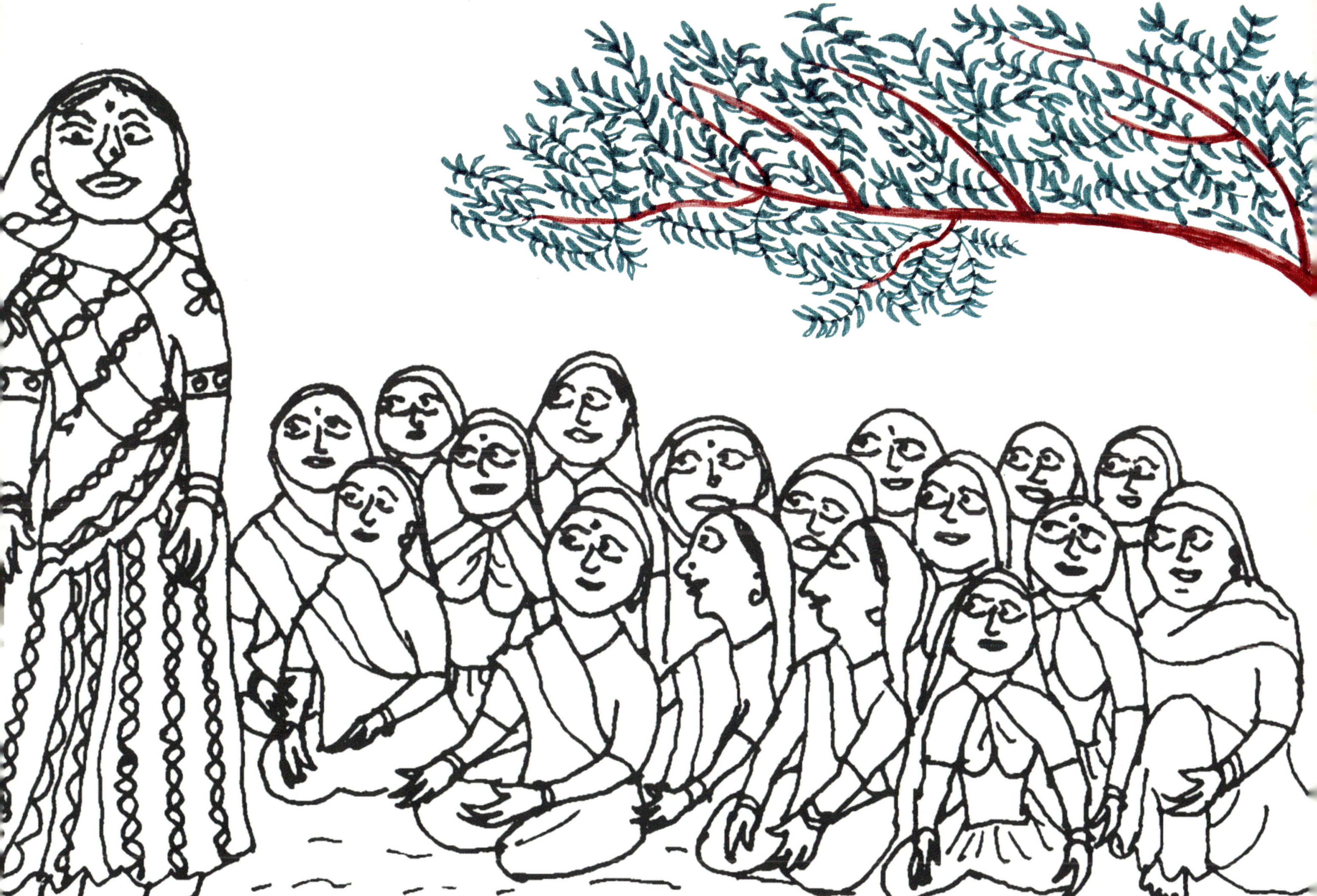

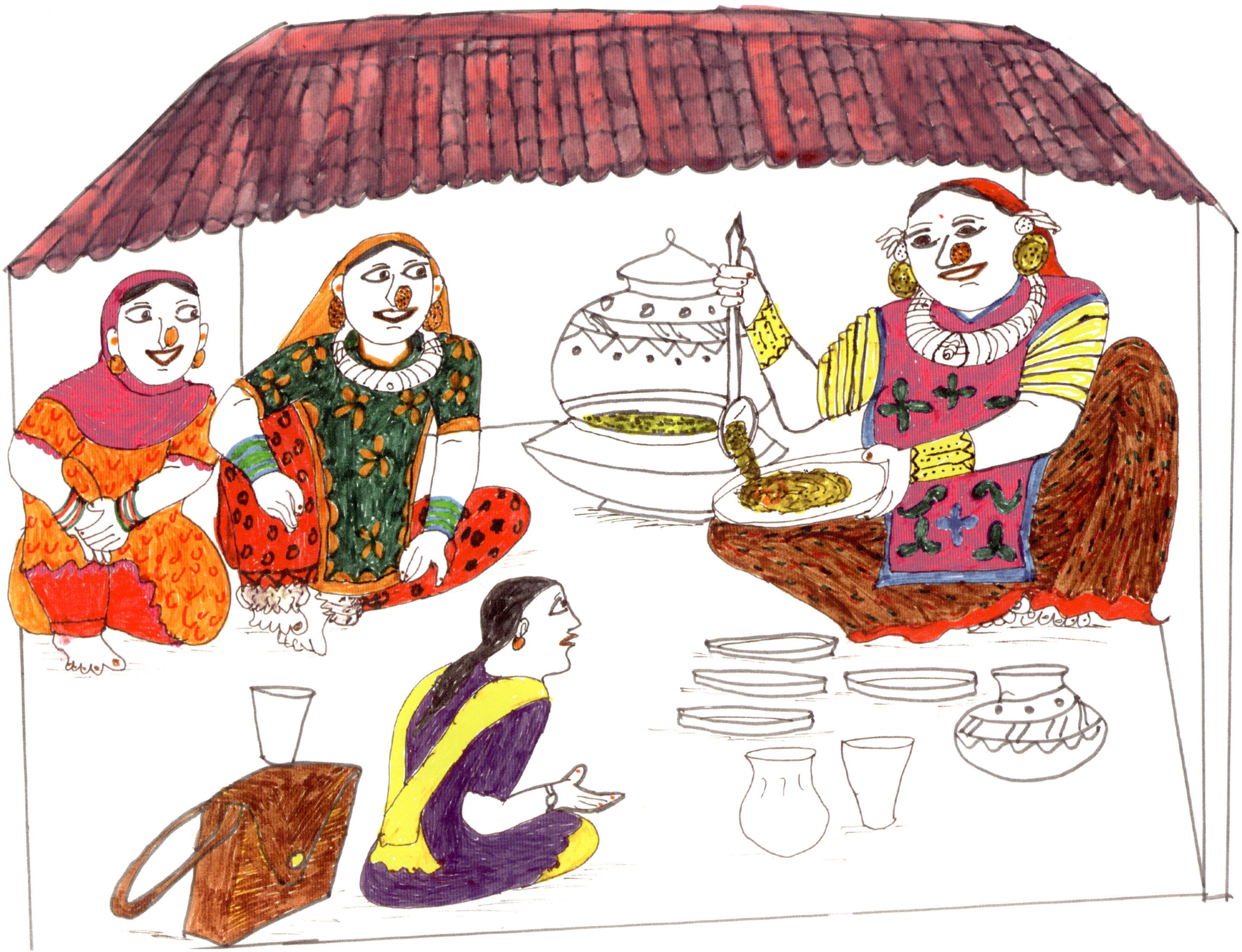

So we would wait: for a husband to travel out before we could slip into each other's kitchens to share some chai and snacks, to gossip a little, to laugh some more, to share our lives.

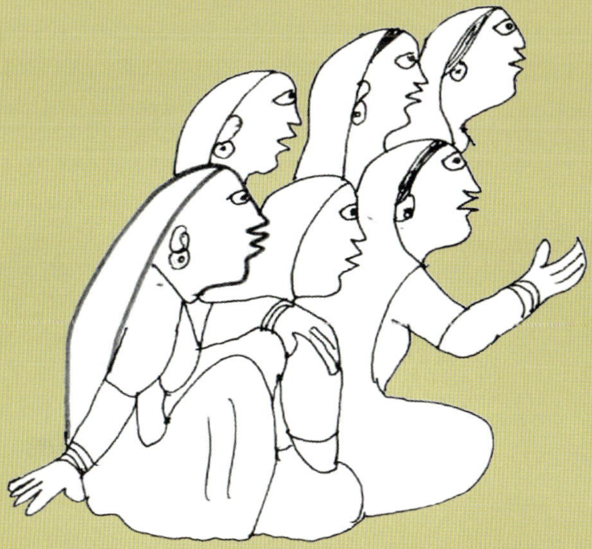

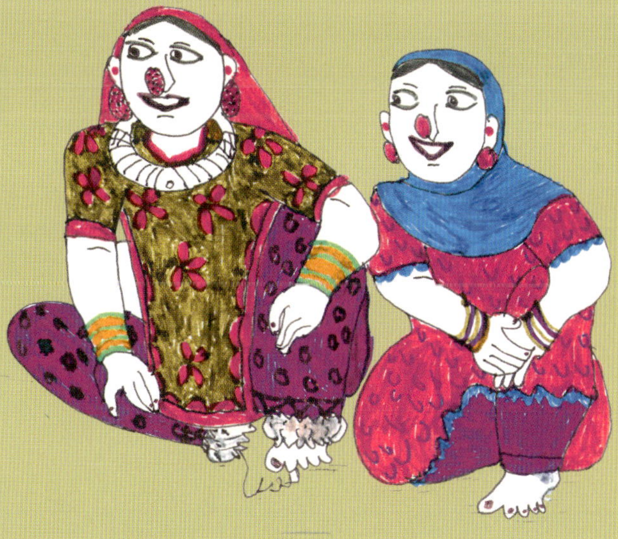

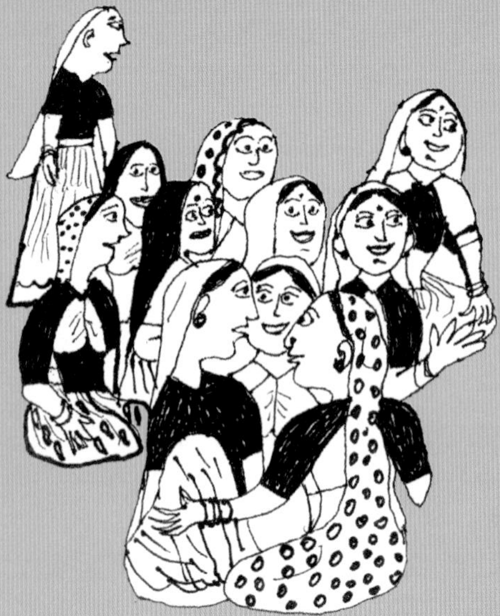

When you are celebrating so much, you do not want to name the fissures within.

When we found ourselves caught in murky conflicts between our communities. We would combat our men in private and resist opposing them in public. And our homes survived.

When we women had tensions which spilled over, we let them spill amongst us, and stayed silent at home.

We were not going to destroy our friendships, our bonds, our future together as women or this collective identity.

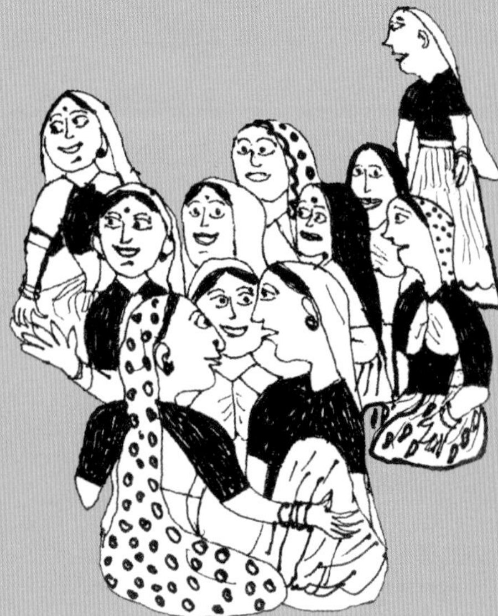

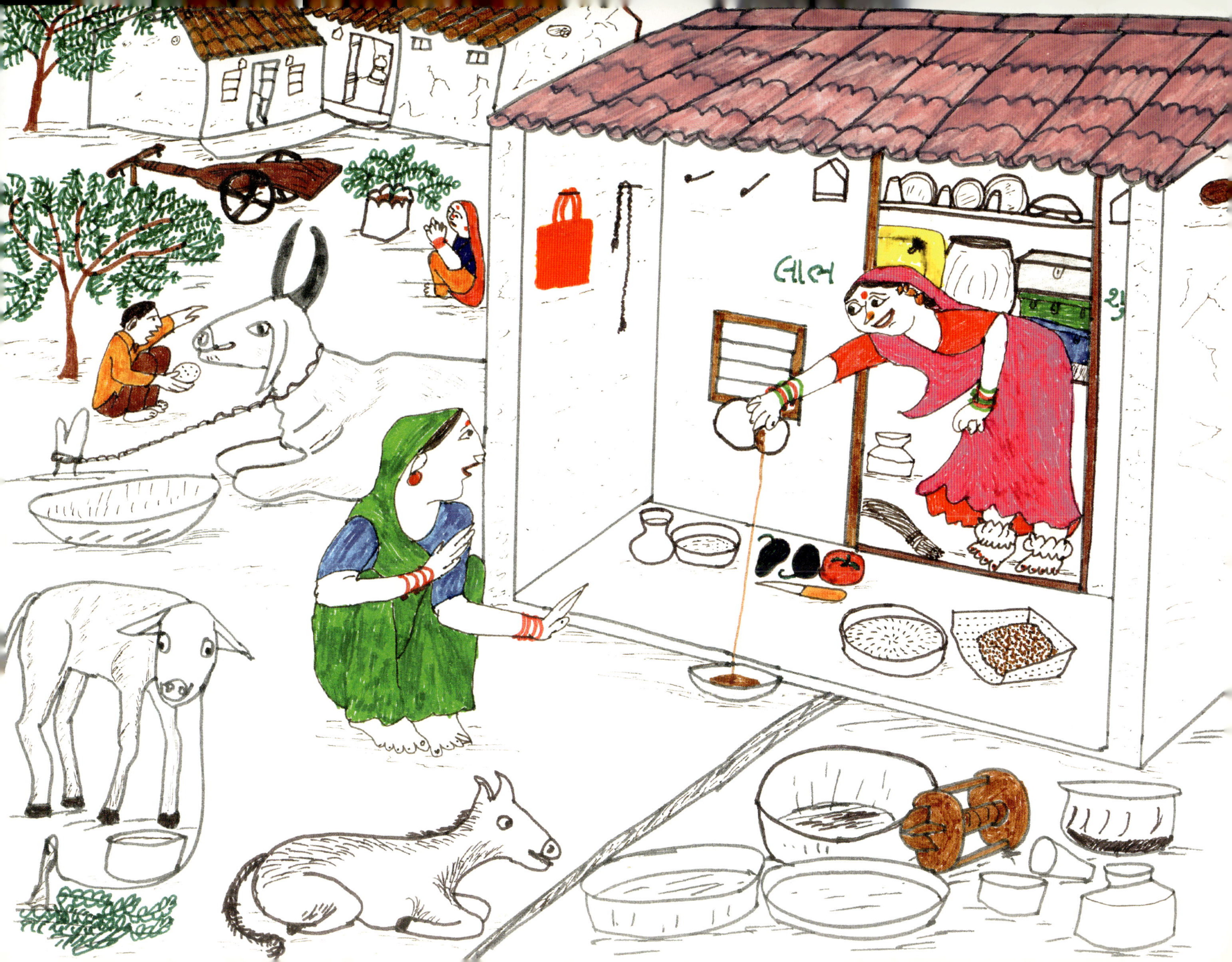
લાલ

This is how we negotiated our complicated lives, by confronting and silencing, opening the wounds, then stitching them, tormented sometimes by our assorted identities.

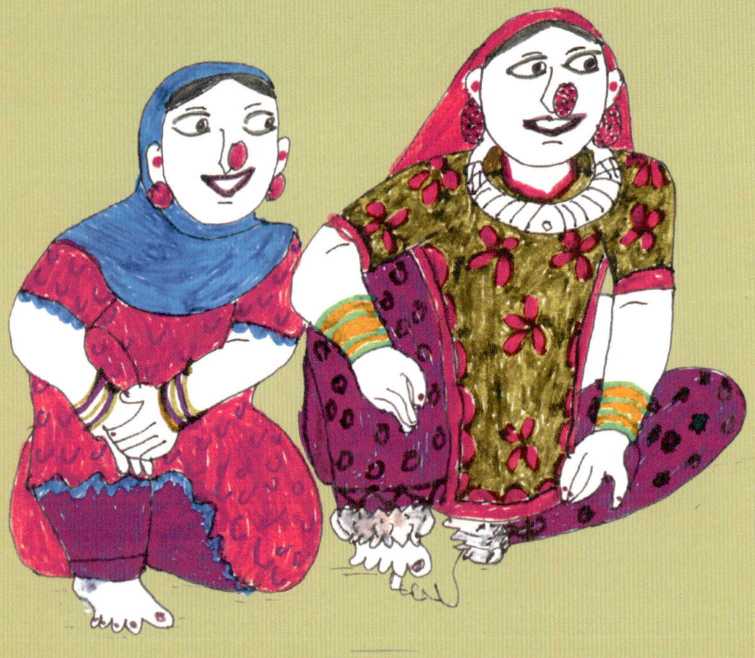

THE POTENT BREW

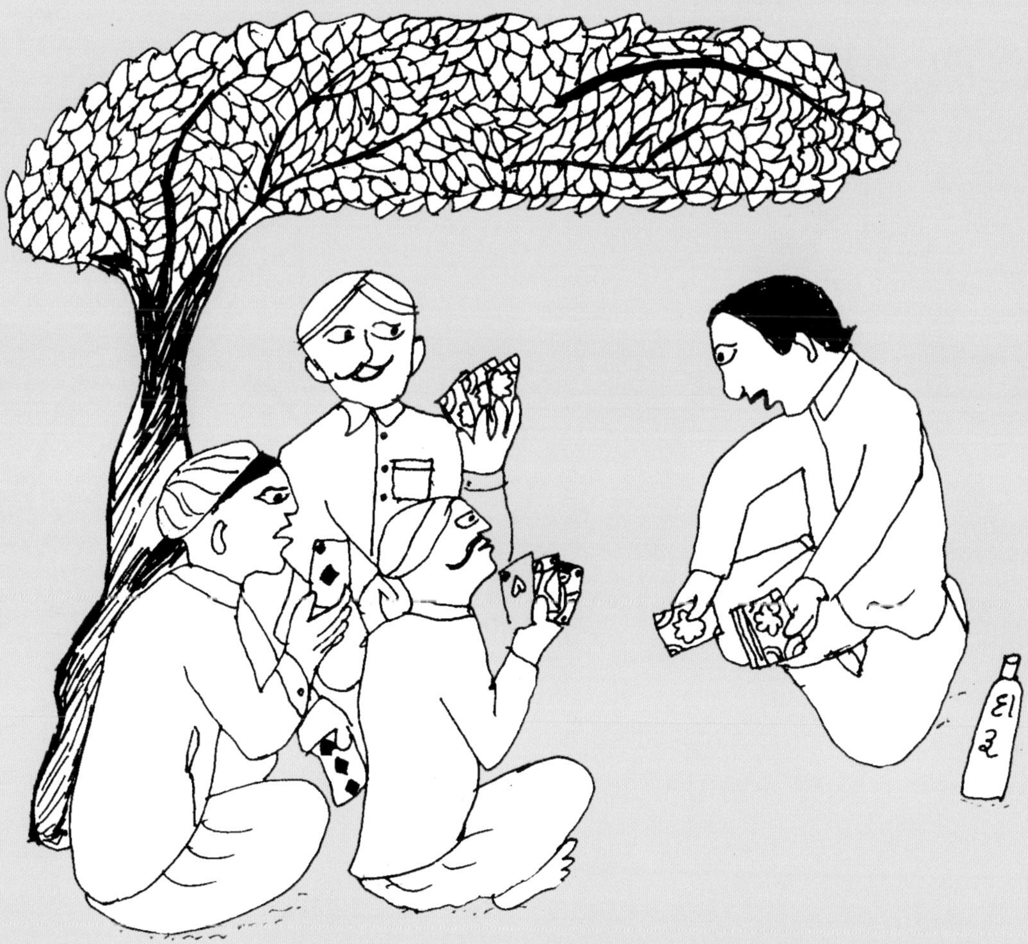

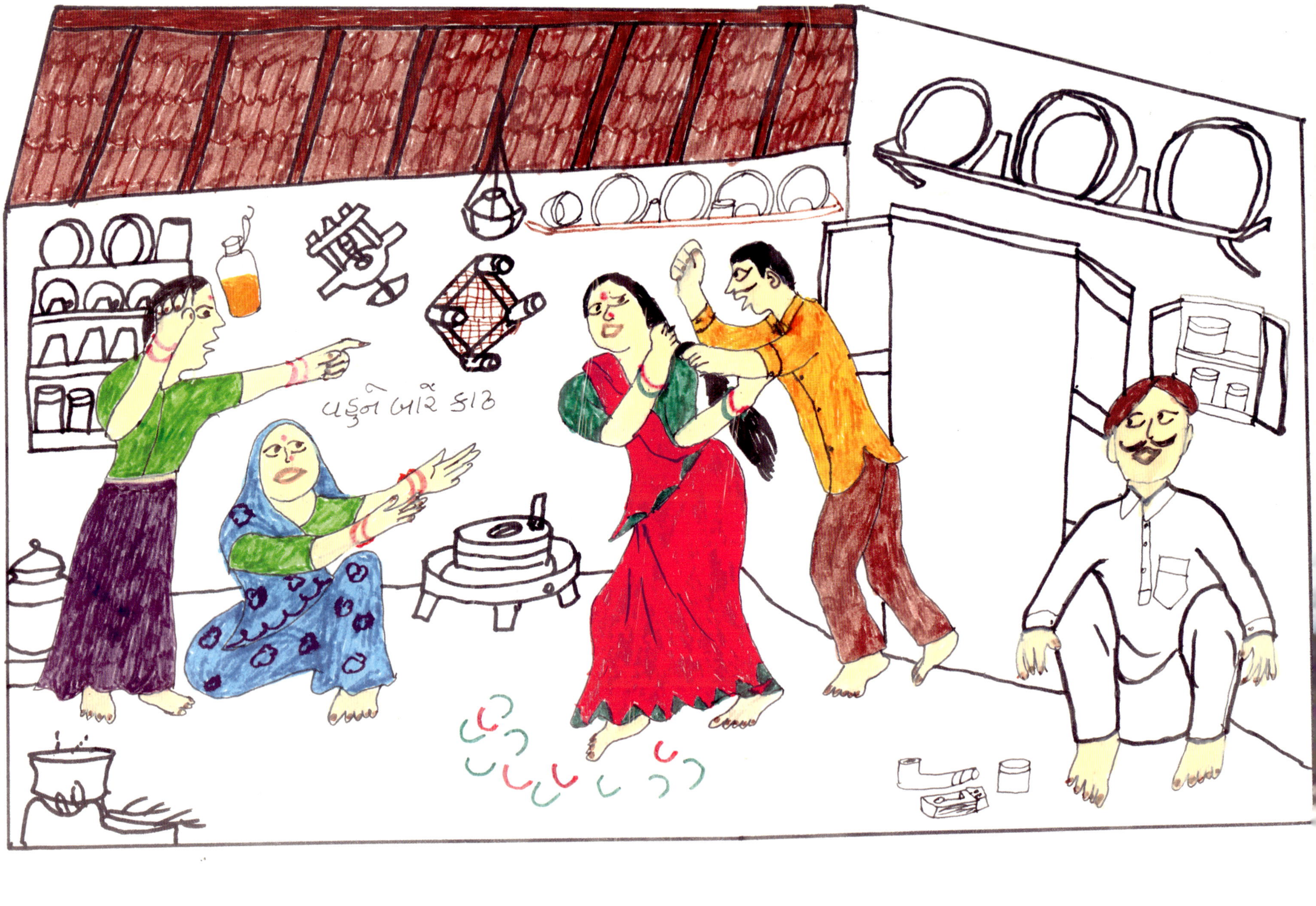
વહુને બારે કાઢ

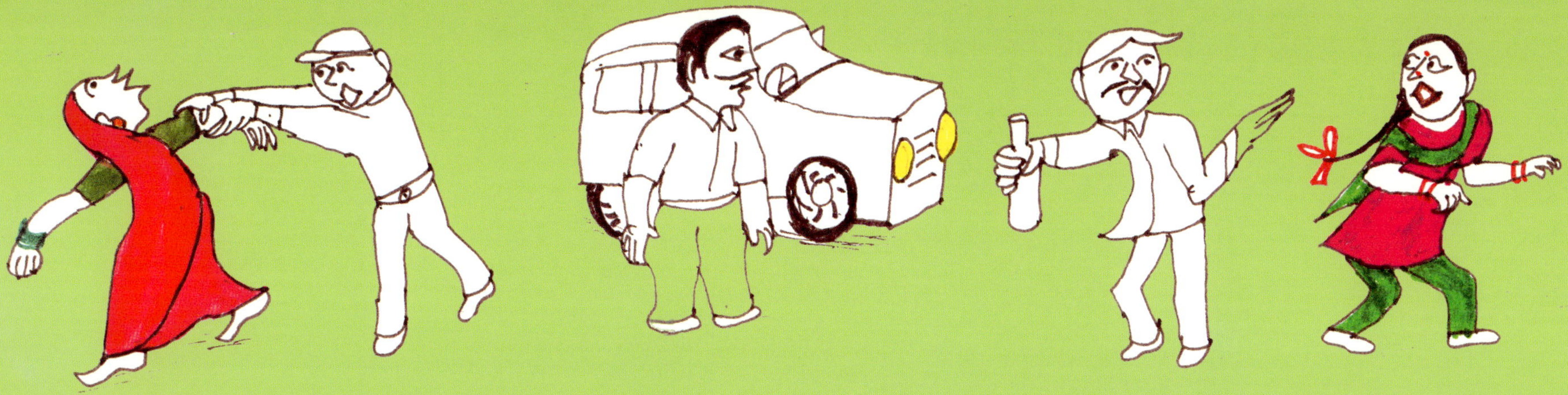

We could not stay intoxicated for too long
on our freshly brewed liberation.

Even as we heard of other women, in other regions battle the bottle, we found ourselves in a fight on many fronts – the police, our own men, the bootleggers of our villages, silken-tongued politicians, widowed Rajput women happy to be employed for brewing alcohol, hapless sangathan women whose addicted husbands needed medical care, and the spiralling violence against us women.

The women of Nellore, we heard, had pulled down a government which sold alcohol to fill its coffers! But what do you do with a government whose 'morality' does not allow it to sell alcohol but which colludes with its poor citizens to get them drunk on fermented batteries and jaggery?

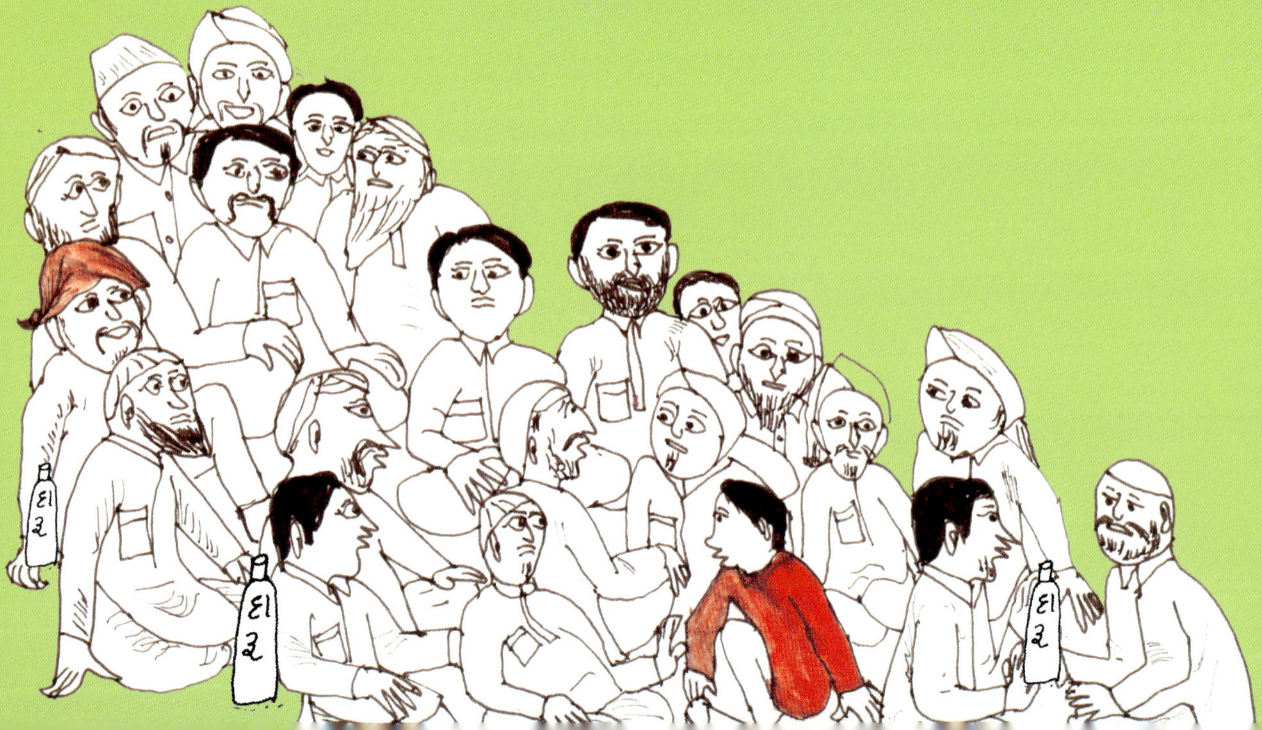

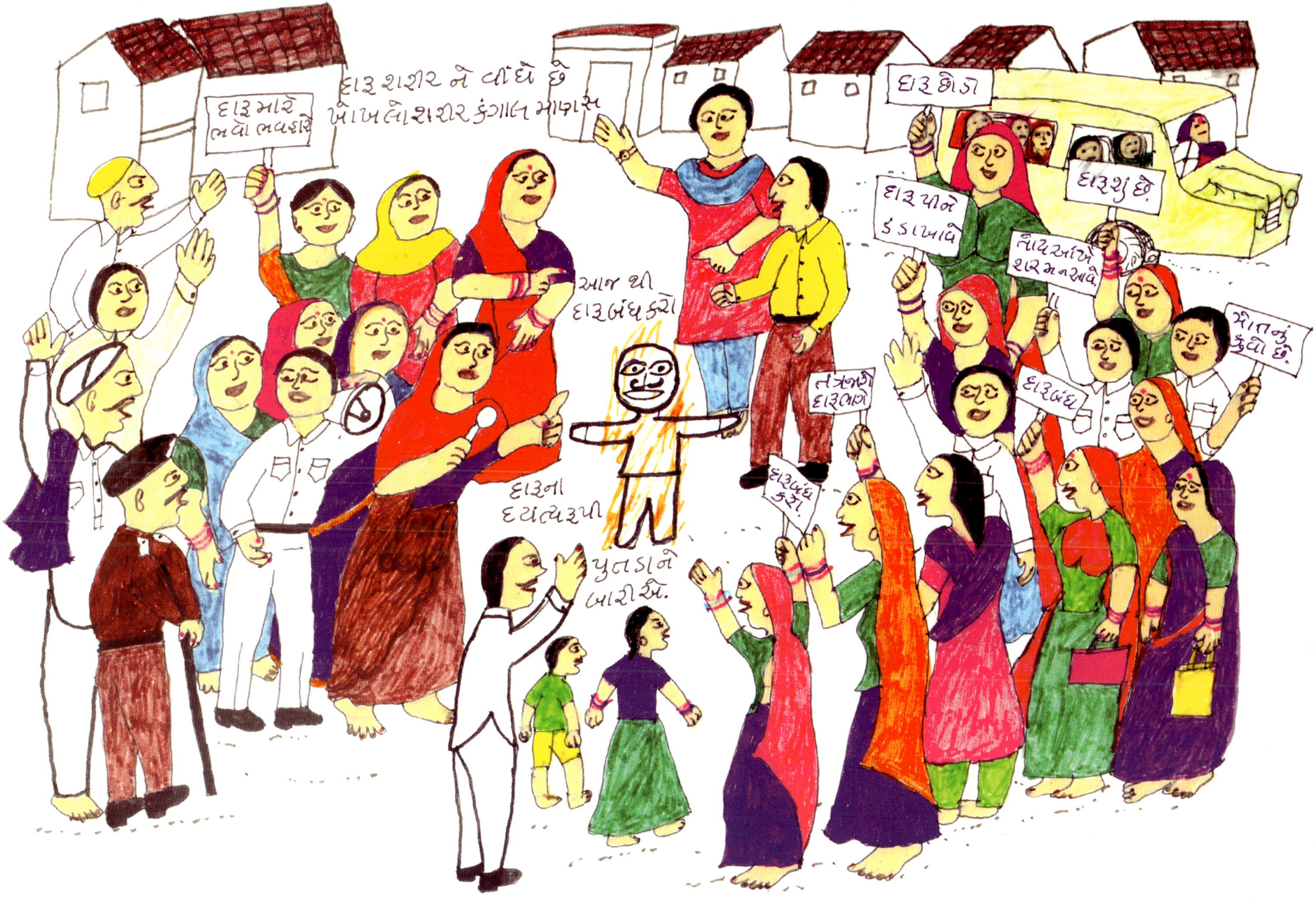
દારૂ મારે
દારૂ શરીર ને વીંધે છે
દારૂ છોડો
દારૂ શું છે.
આજ થી દારૂ બંધ કરો
દારૂના દયંત્યરૂપી
પુતડાને બારીએ.
દારૂ બંધ
દારૂ બંધ કરો.
મોતનું કૂવો છે.

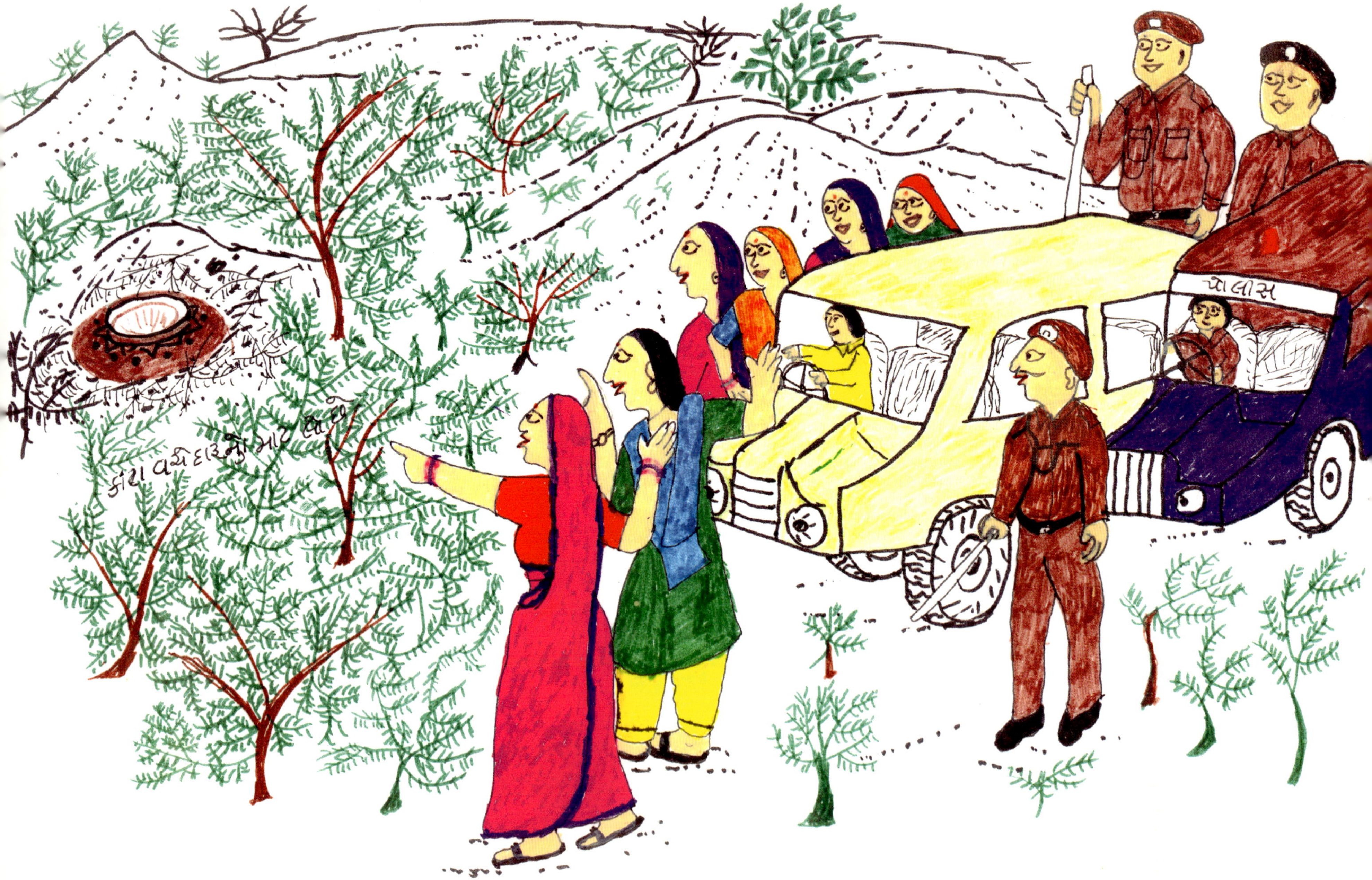

We too were soon spying in the dark through friendly door-cracks, swooping in on liquor dens with surprise and speed, shattering liquor pots in the village square, and spilling onto the streets till they – this drunken world – took us seriously.

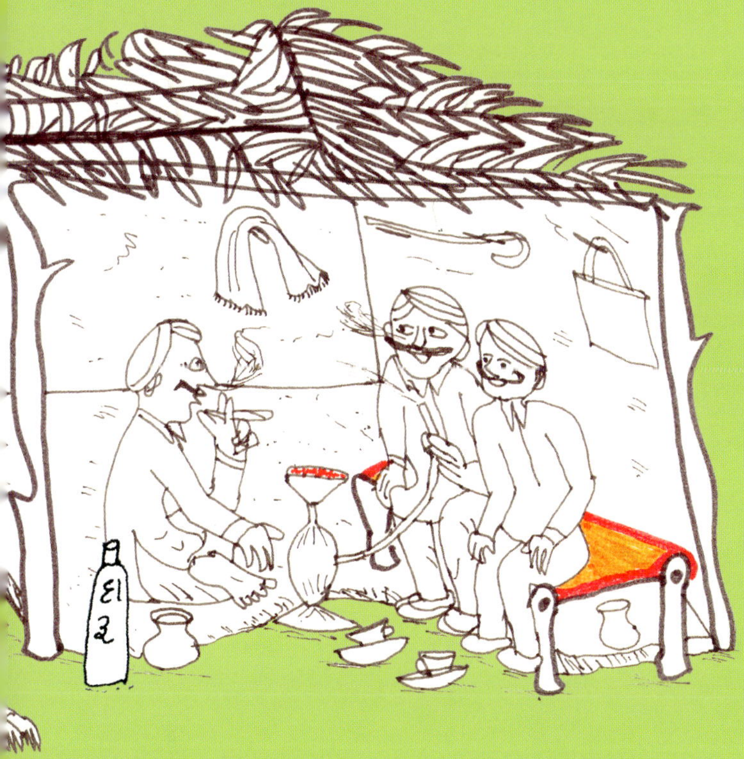

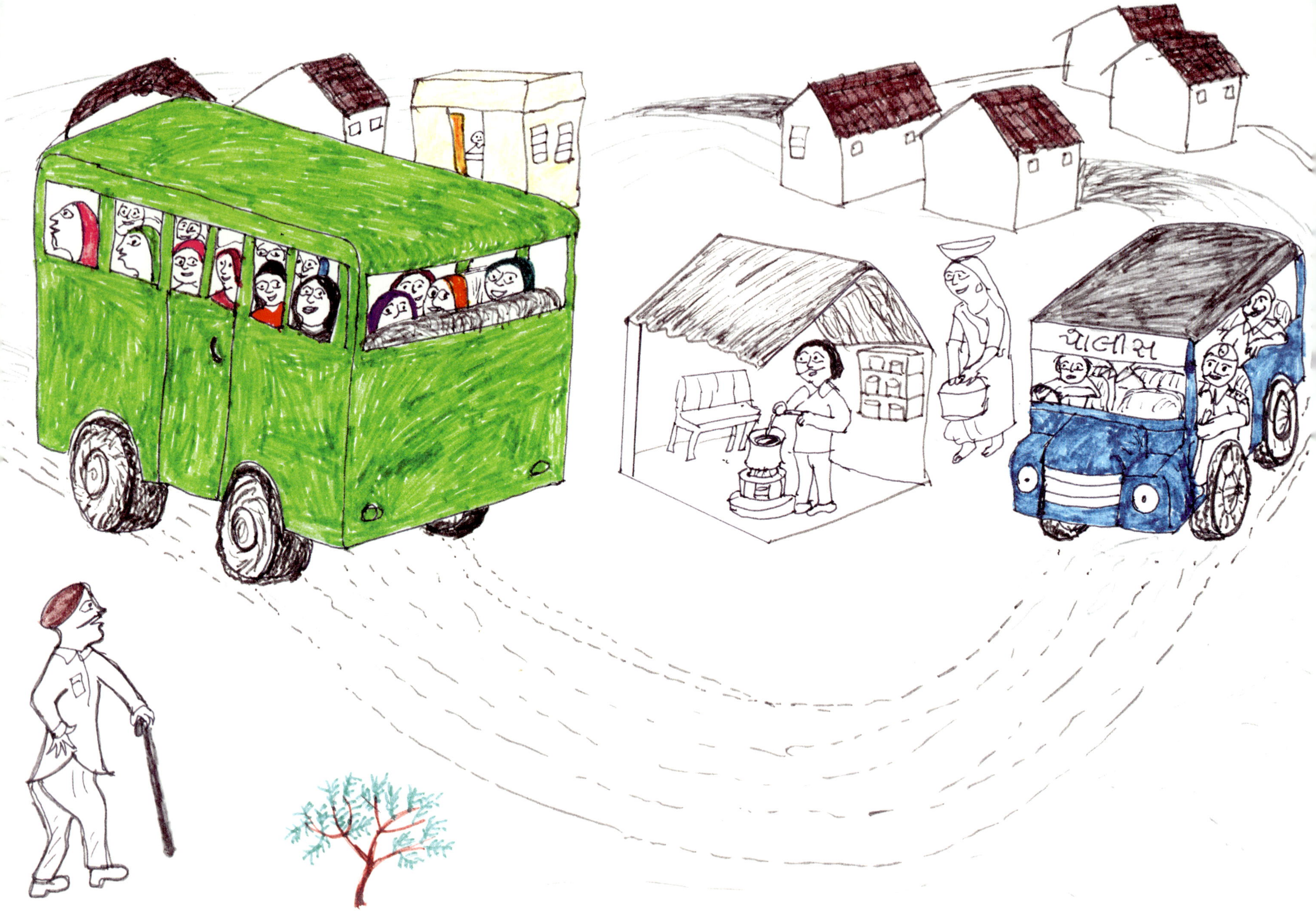
પોલીસ

SCRIPTING CHANGE

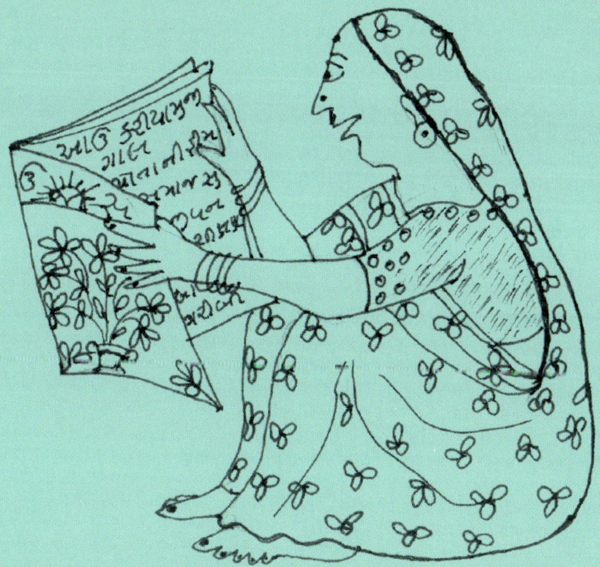

Where we chose to remain silent, or when we could not speak, we wrote. And we learnt the difference between the spoken and the written word. Our newsletter *Ujjas*, which sprang out of a literacy camp, unlocked within us a new stream of consciousness.

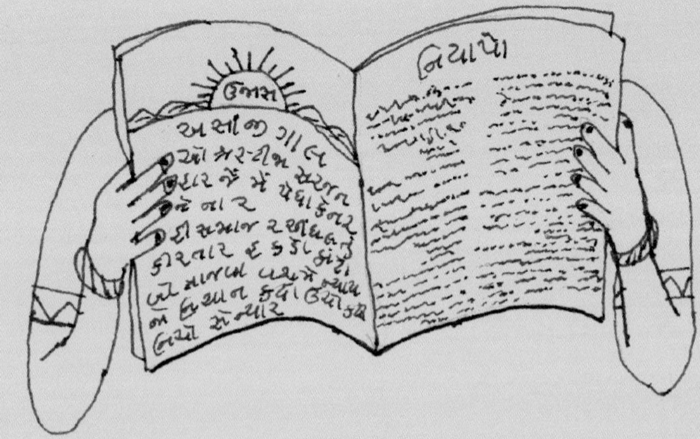

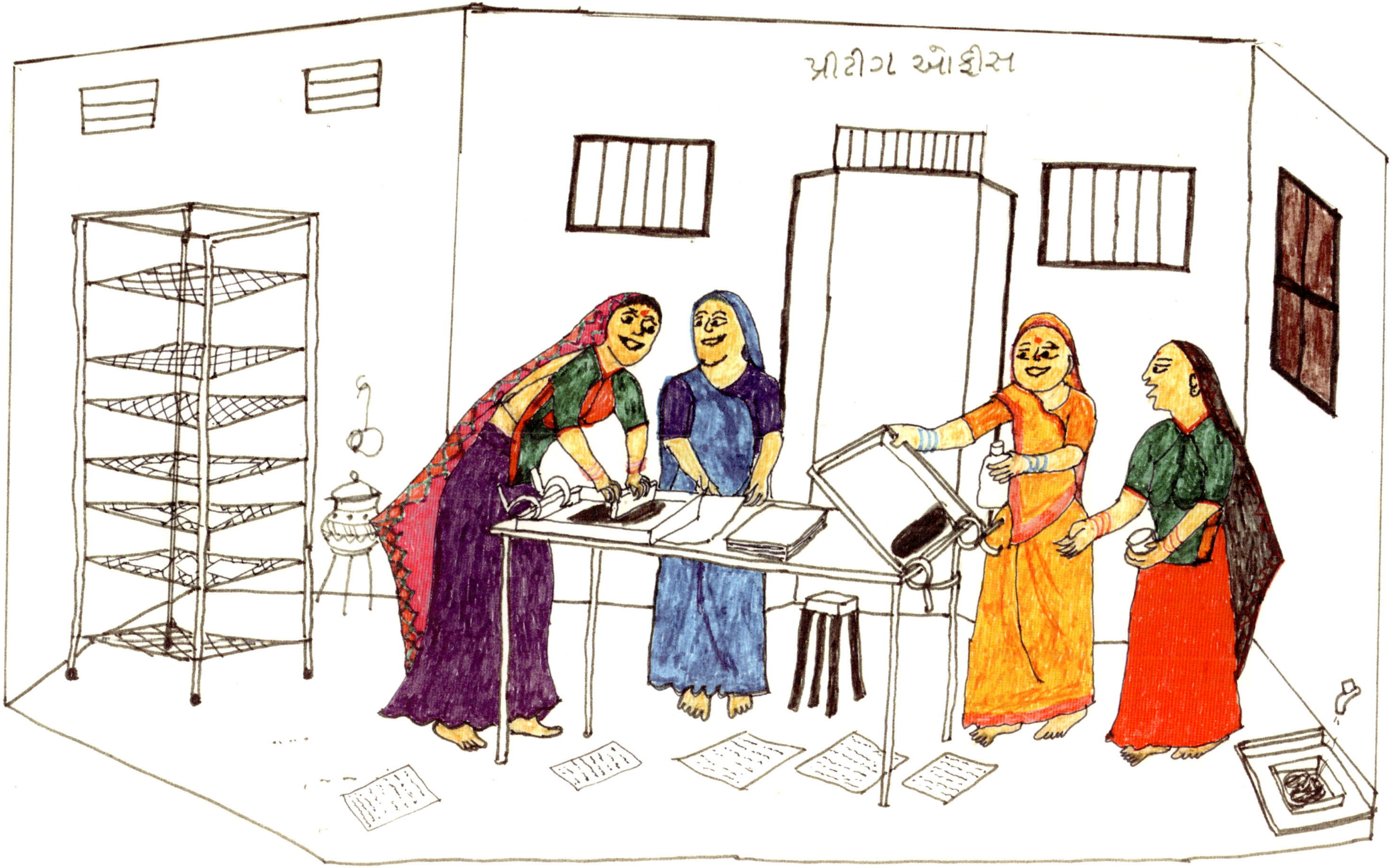
પ્રીટીગ ઑફીસ

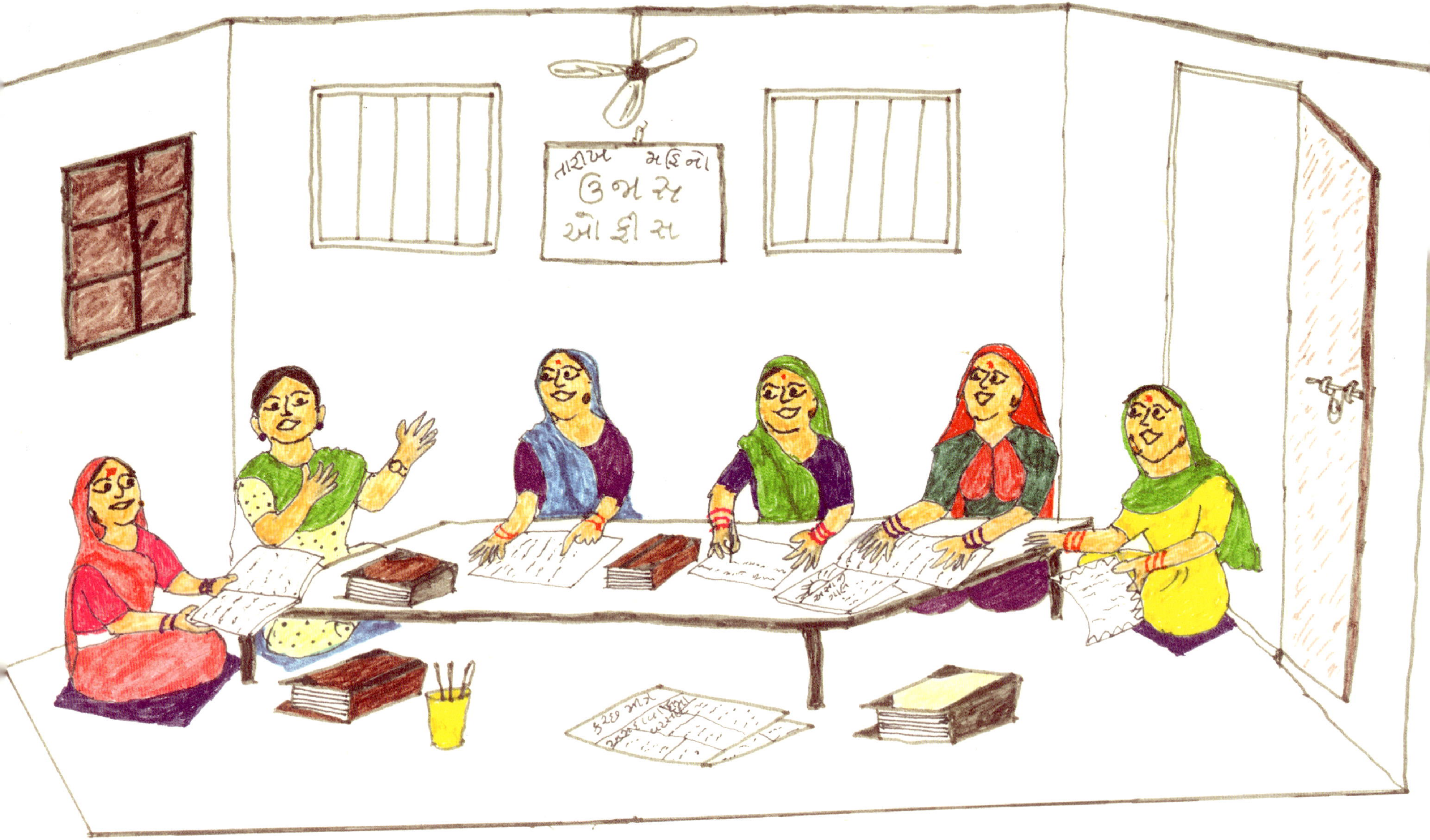

તારીખ
મહિનો
ઉમસ
ઓફીસ

When we wrote the truth, we strangely experienced its power more than when we spoke it! It was almost as if our spoken word got certified by our inner selves. Perhaps, when we spoke, we revelled in our strength, our power; but when we wrote, we celebrated the power of those for whom we wrote.

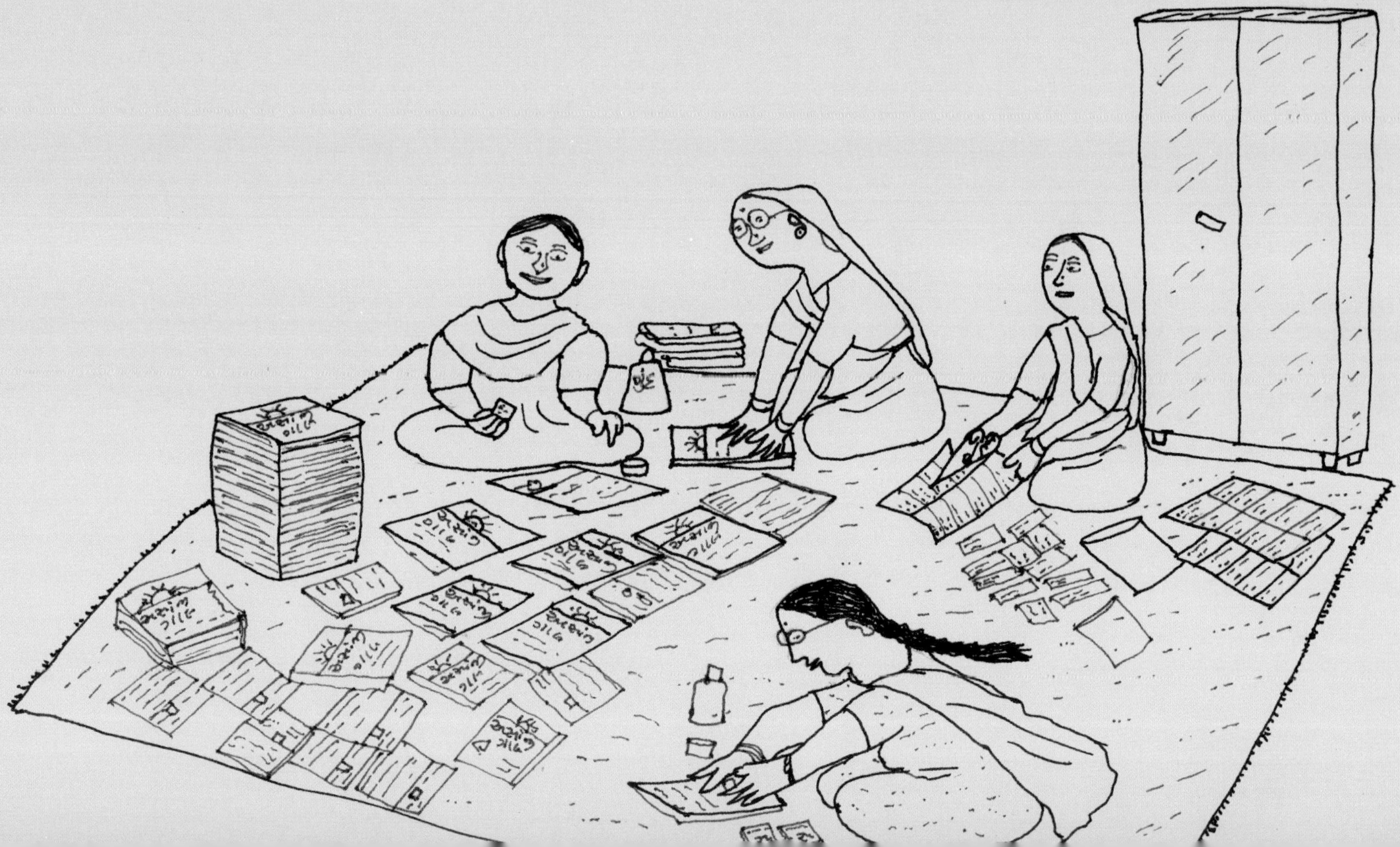

We stirred up our environment with our newsletter as we peeled away the layers of untruth that so effectively covered the rampant adulteration, corruption, land grabs, violence and patriarchy. Its presence was all around us, in every blade of grass, in every village from where news would come pouring in as women had begun to believe that justice could be ours if we laid bare the truth.

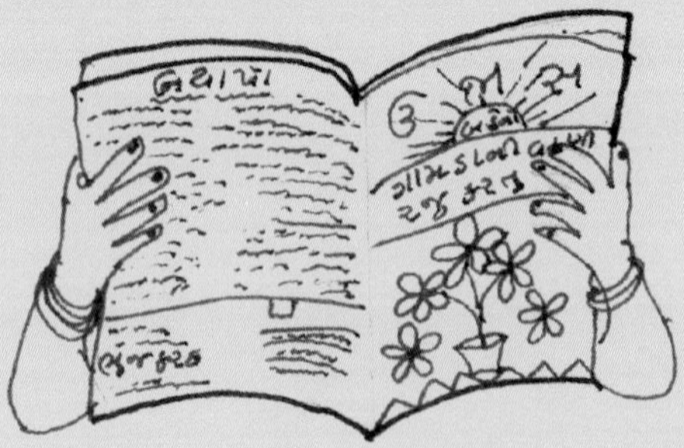

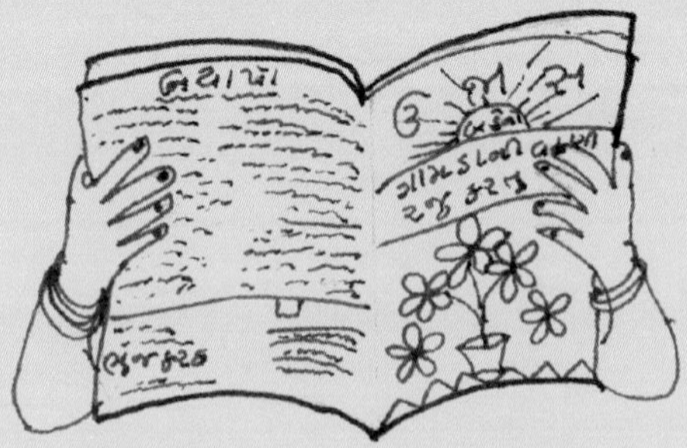

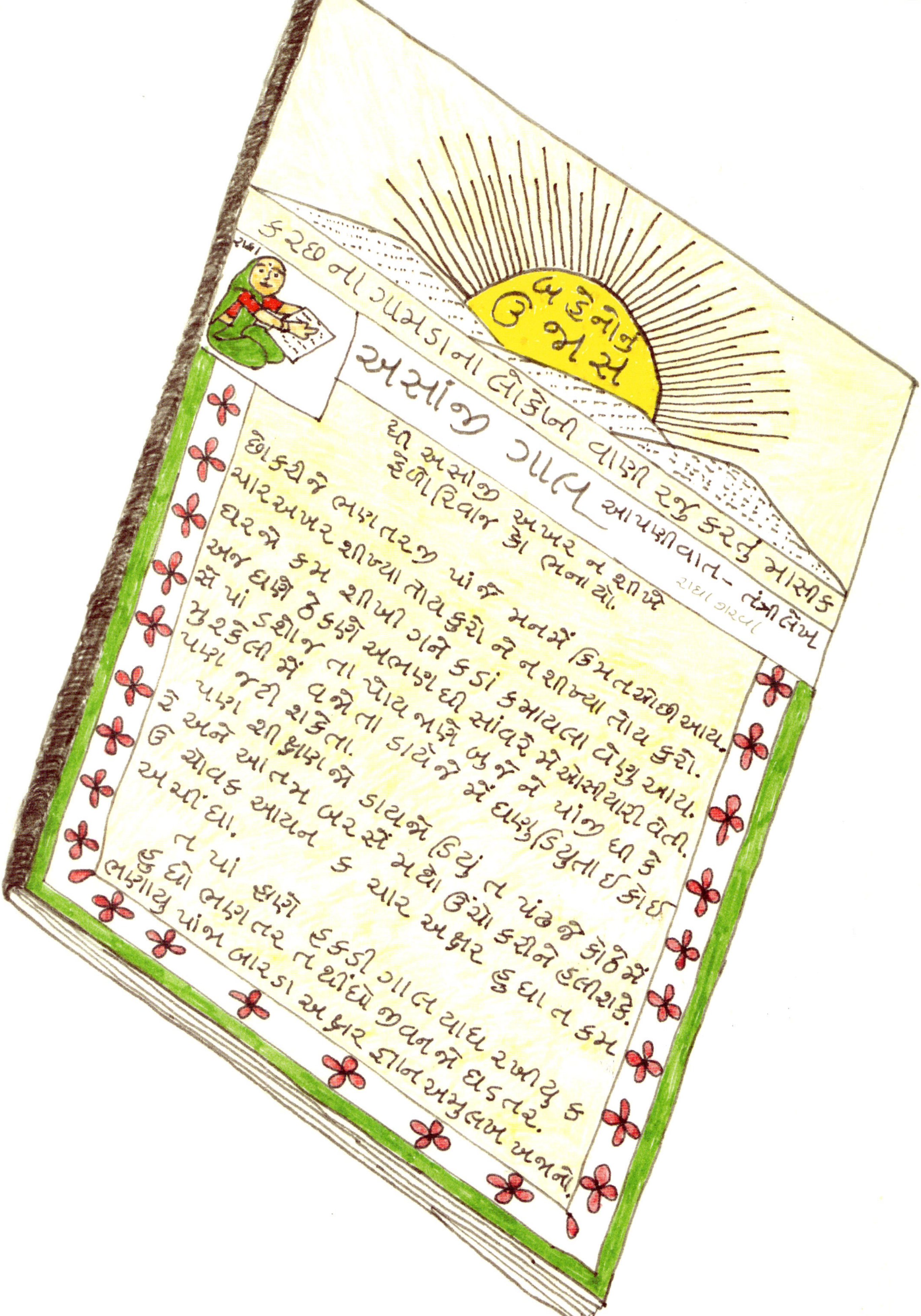
કચ્છ ના ગામડાના લોકોની વાણી રજૂ કરતું માસિક
અસાંજી ગાલ
આપણીવાત - તંત્રીલેખ
રાધા ગારવા
હી અસાંજી અખર ન શાખે
હેલો રિવાજ કો ભેના ચો.
છોકરીજે ભણતરજી પાંજે મનમેં કિમતઓછી આય.
ચારઅખર શીખ્યા તોય કુરો ને ન શીખ્યા તોય કુરો.
ઘરમે કમ શીખી ગને કડાં કમાયલા વેણું આય.
અજ ઘણે ઠેકાણે ભણધી સાંવરે મે ઓસીયારી વેતી.
સે પાં કશીંગ ના પોય જાણે બુ મેં ને પાંજી ધી કે
ગુડકેલી મેં વજે તા ડાયેજે મેં ઘણુંકિયુતાઈ કોઈ
પપા જટી શકેતા.
રે અને શીખ્યાજે કાયજે હિયું ત પંઢજે કોઠેમેં
ઉ ચોવક આતમ બરસેં મથો ઉંચો કરીને હલીશકે.
અસાંધા.
ત પાં કણે ઉકડી ગાલ યાદ રખાયું ક
હુંધો ભણતર ત થીંધો જીવનજો ઘડતર.
ભણાયું પાંજ બારડા અખ્રાર જ્ઞાન અમુલખ અજનો.

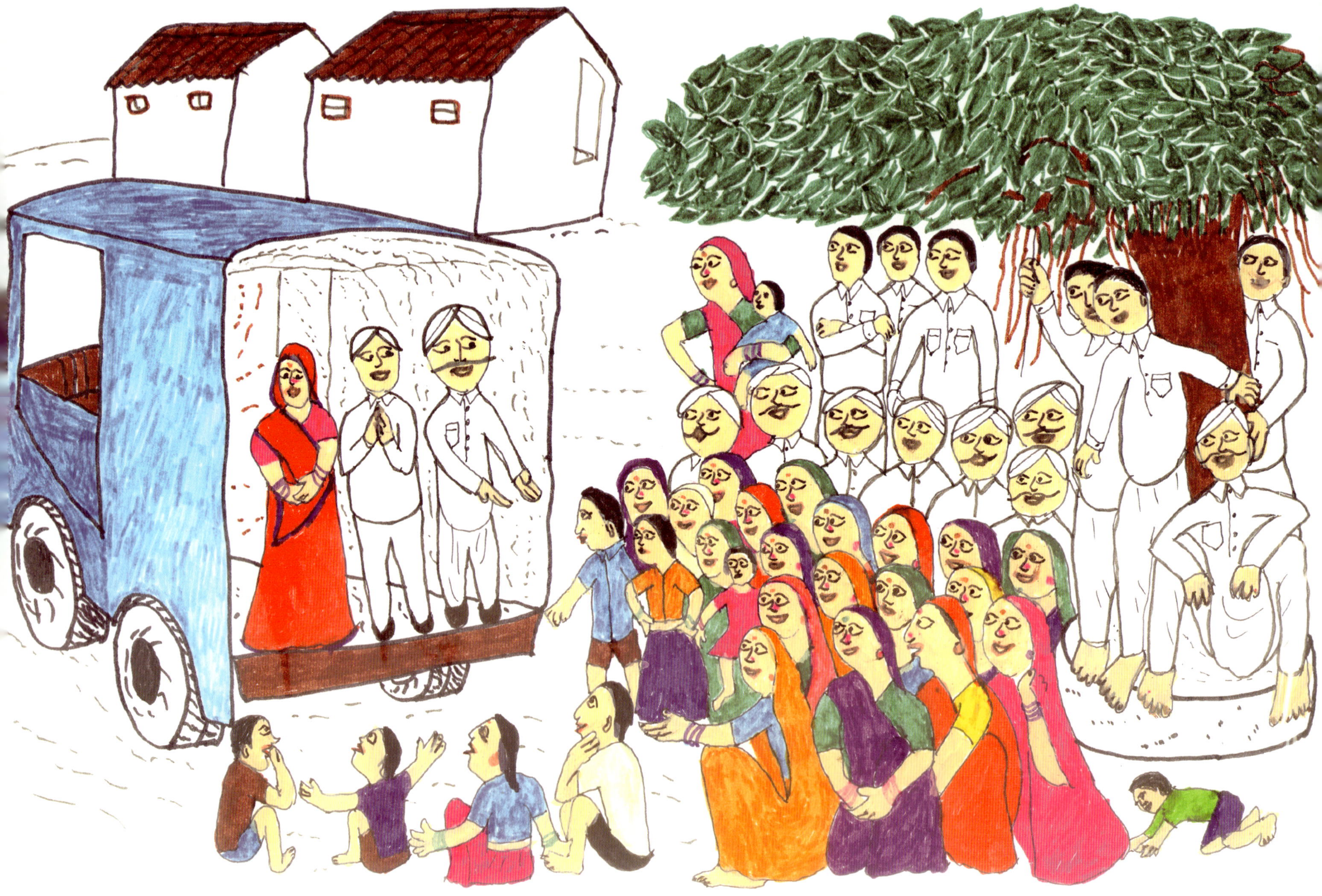

When we exposed the kerosene theft by our PDS shops and their nexus with the gambling dens and the sellers of illicit liquor, and named the key leaders, we also earned our first defamation case by the local leader! Later, he withdrew it and apologized in public.

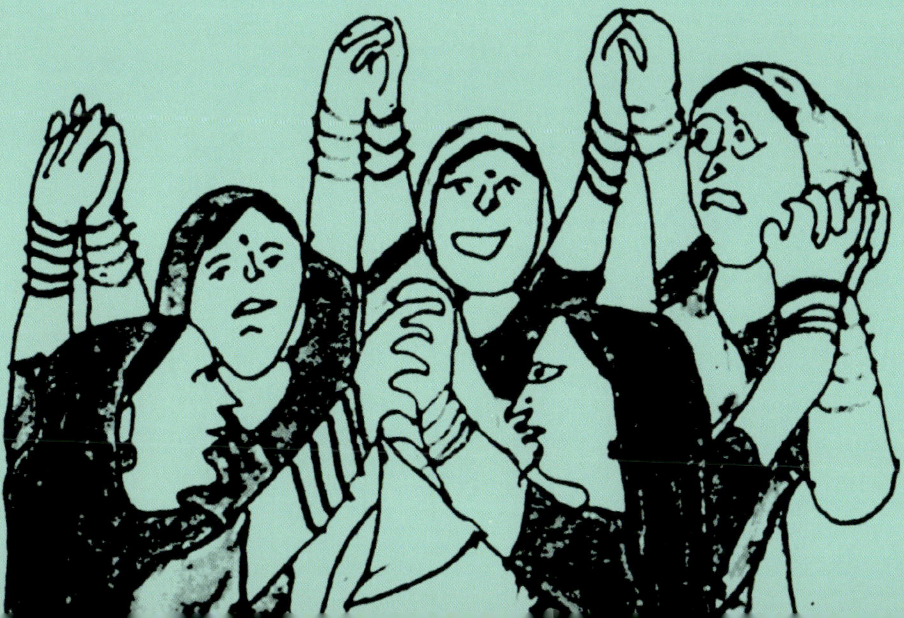

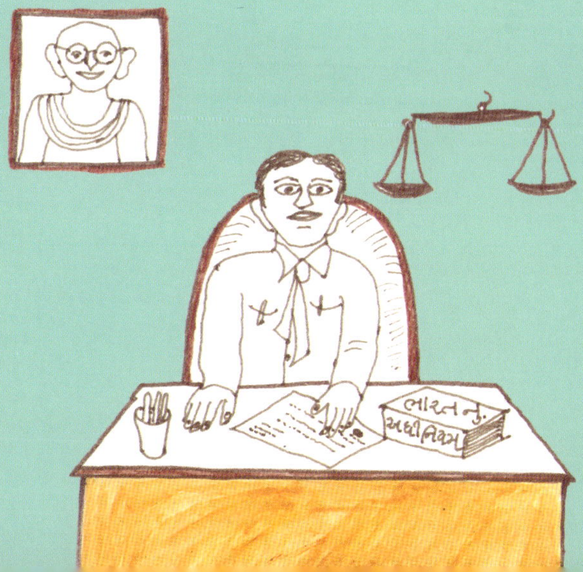

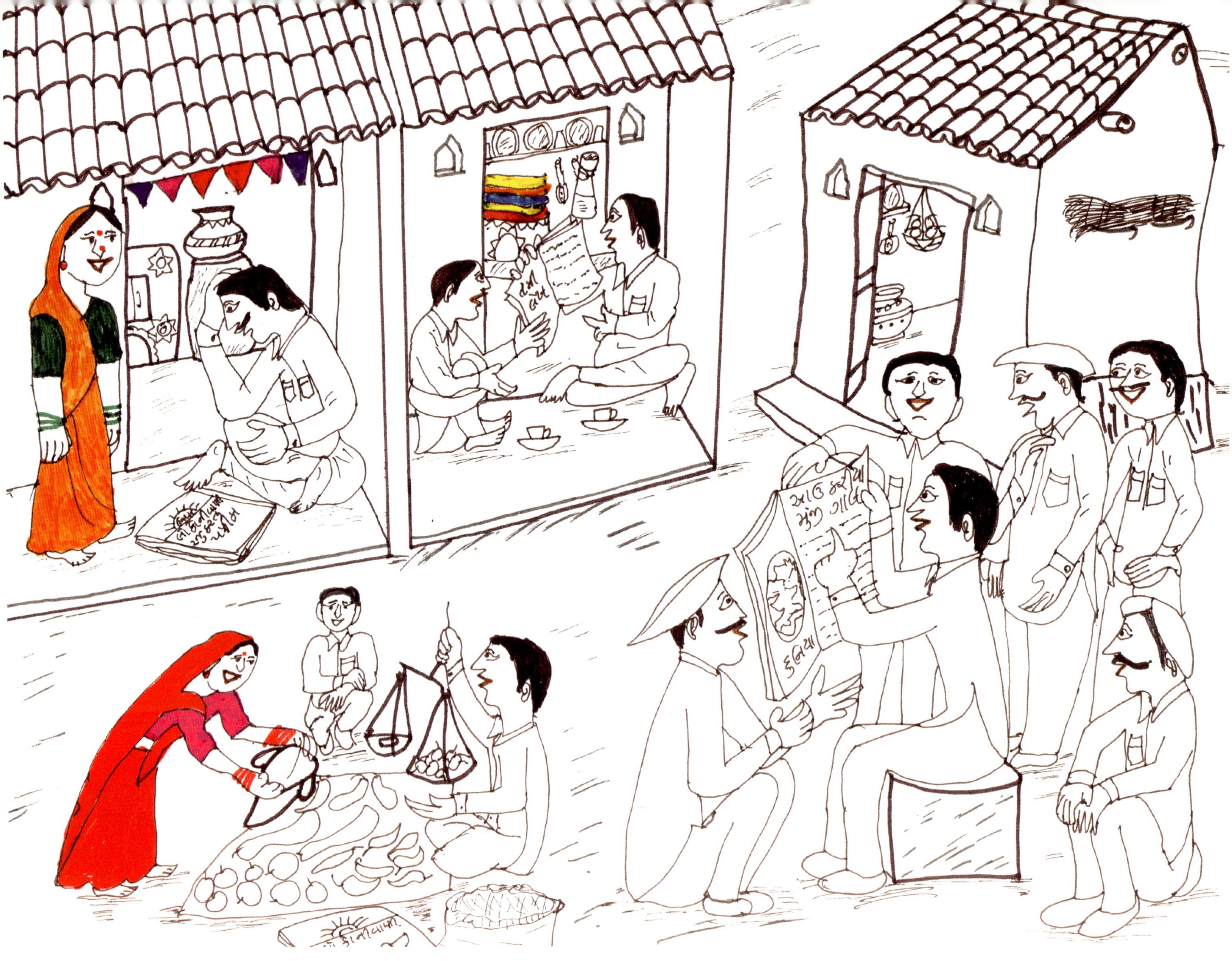

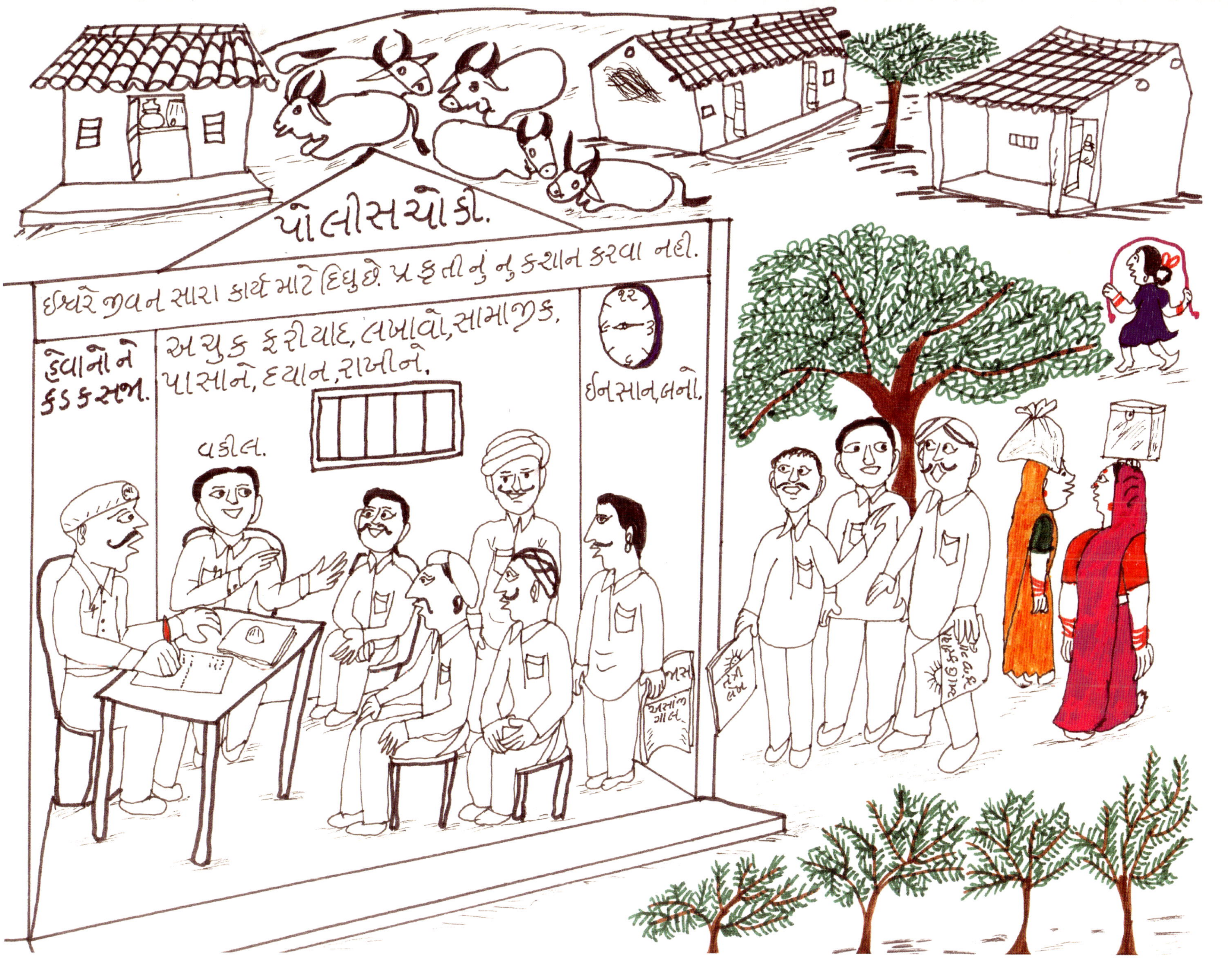
પોલીસચોકી.
ઈશ્વરે જીવન સારા કાર્ય માટે દિધુ છે. પ્રકૃતી નું નુકશાન કરવા નહી.
હેવાનોને કડક સજા.
અચુક ફરીયાદ, લખાવો, સામાજીક, પાસાને, દયાન, રાખીને,
ઈનસાન, બનો.
વકીલ.

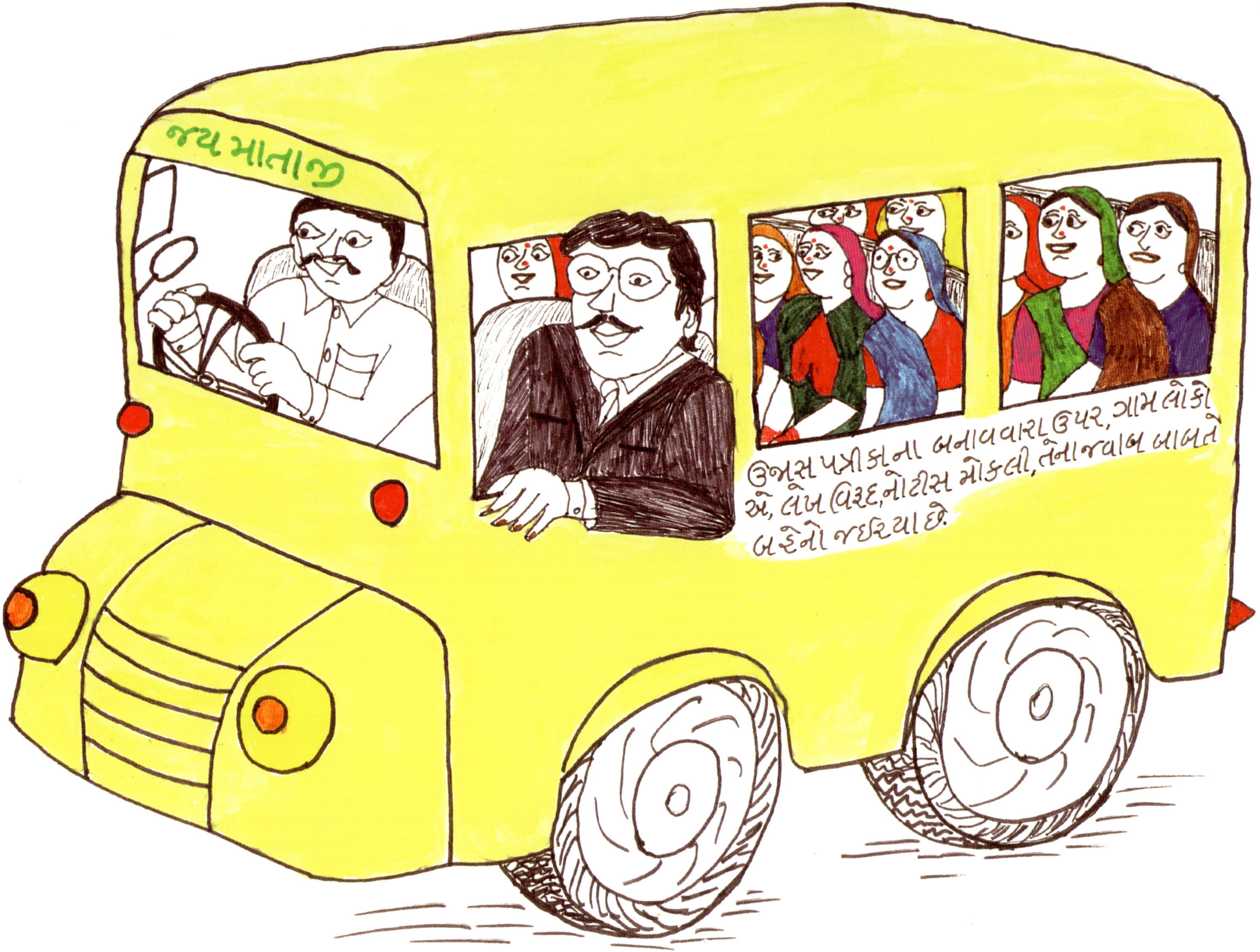

જય માતાજી
ઉજાસ પત્રીકાના બનાવવારૂ ઉપર, ગામ લોકો
એ, લેખ વિરૂદ્ધ, નોટીસ મોકલી, તેના જવાબ બાબતે
બહેનો જઈરયા છે.

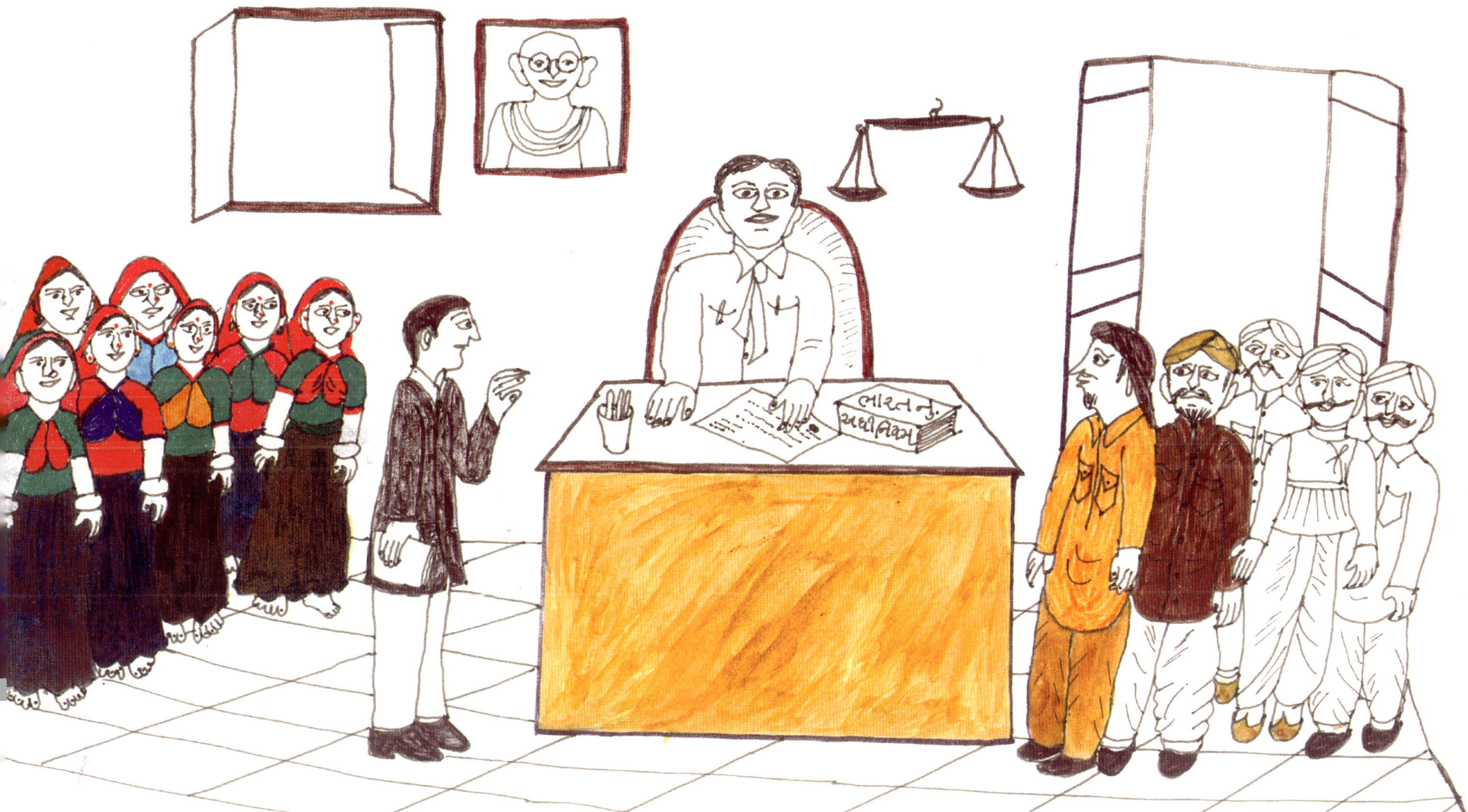
ભારત નું
અધીનિયમ

While we learnt to name and shame, write what we saw, and never walk the edge between truth and half-truth, we also learnt to gather our evidence before we unfurled the truth.

And yes! we also began to learn the laws of defamation.

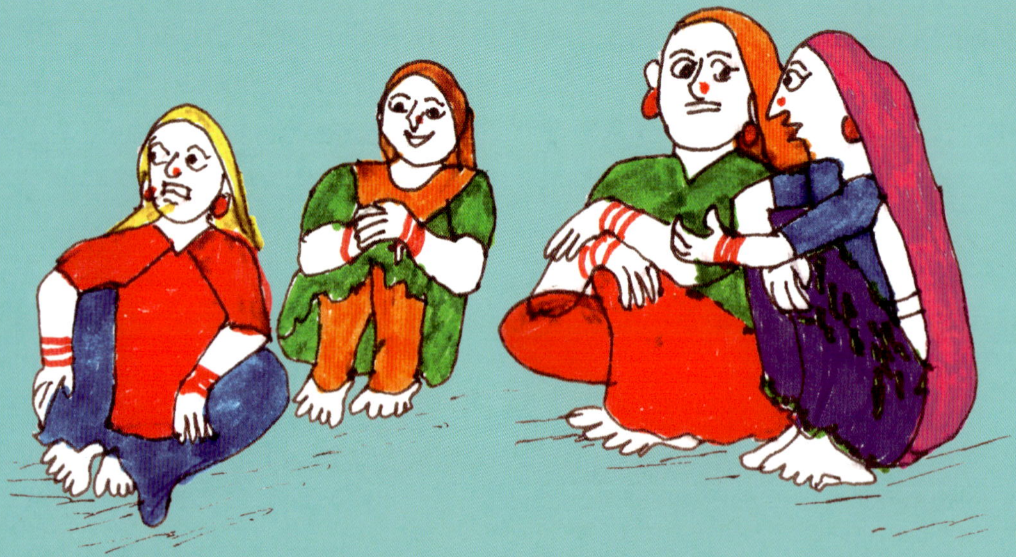

THE SEARCH FOR ALLIES

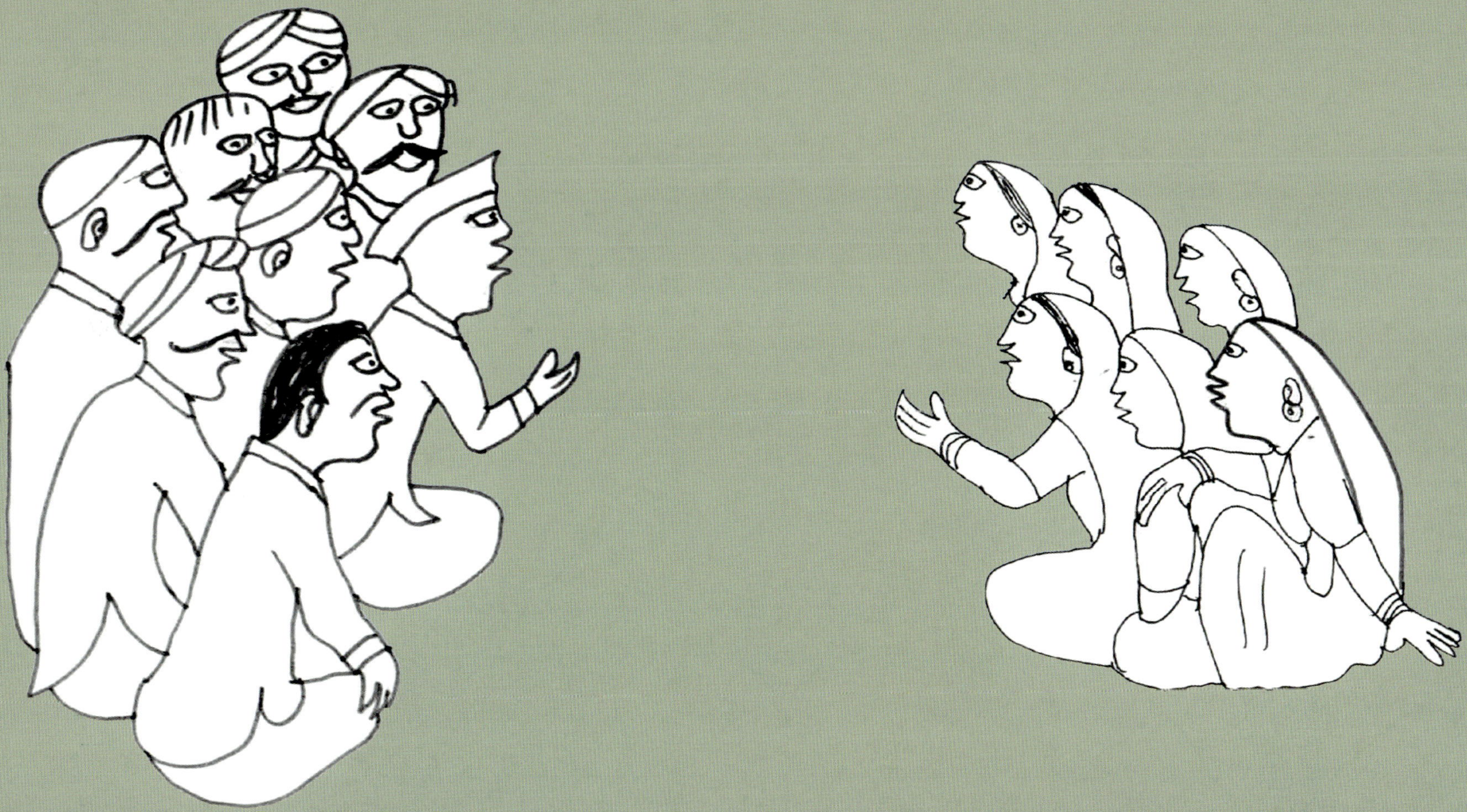

When we began, we learnt to 'see' and 'name' some of the worst acts of violence within the confines of our own 'peaceful' homes. Each time we resisted or prevented this, we brimmed with a sense of power.

But even more empowering was the sheer joy of being able to dialogue with our men, to sensitize them, to help in their transformation – and ours – and to make them allies in a gentler, more caring world.

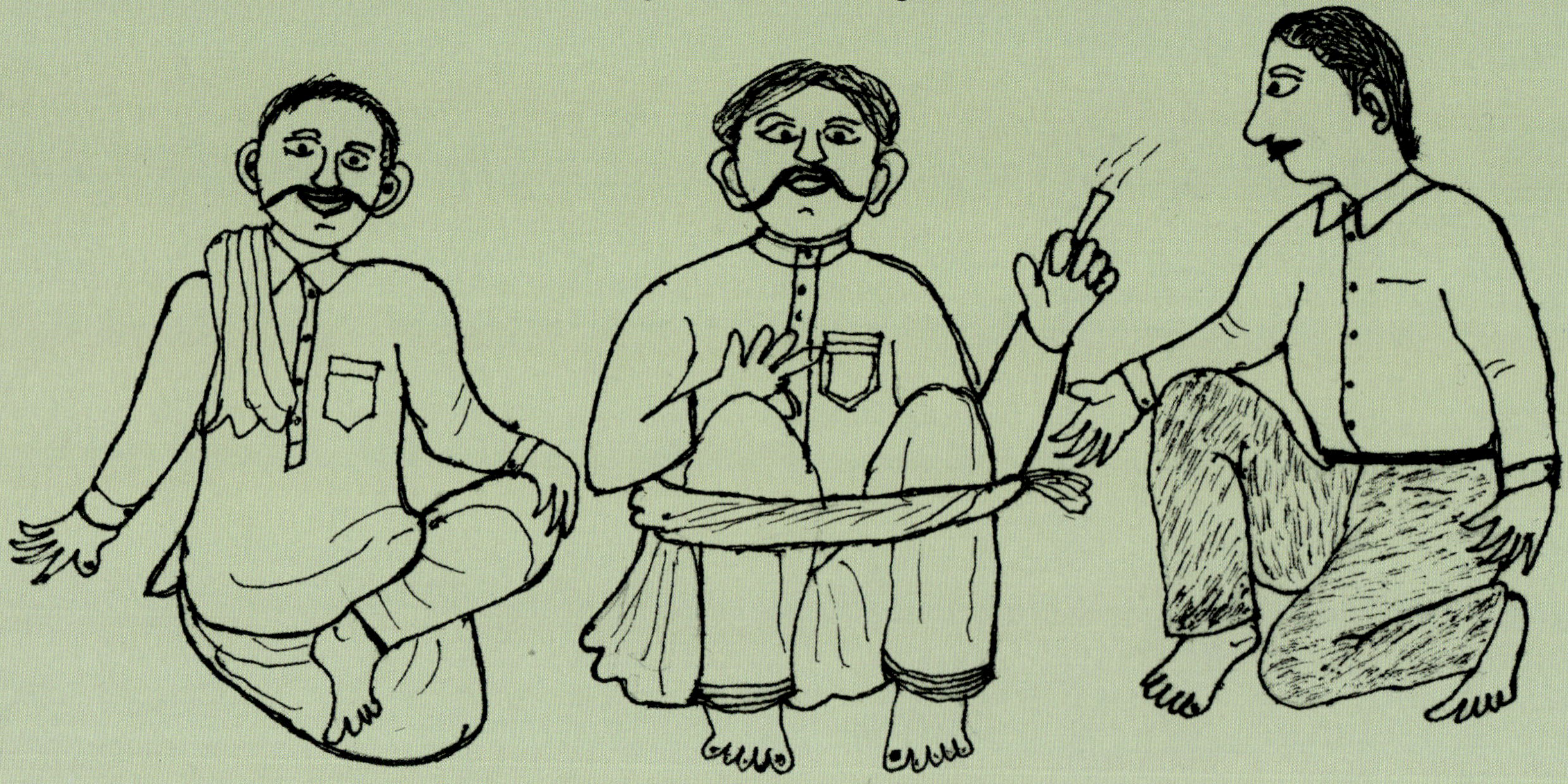

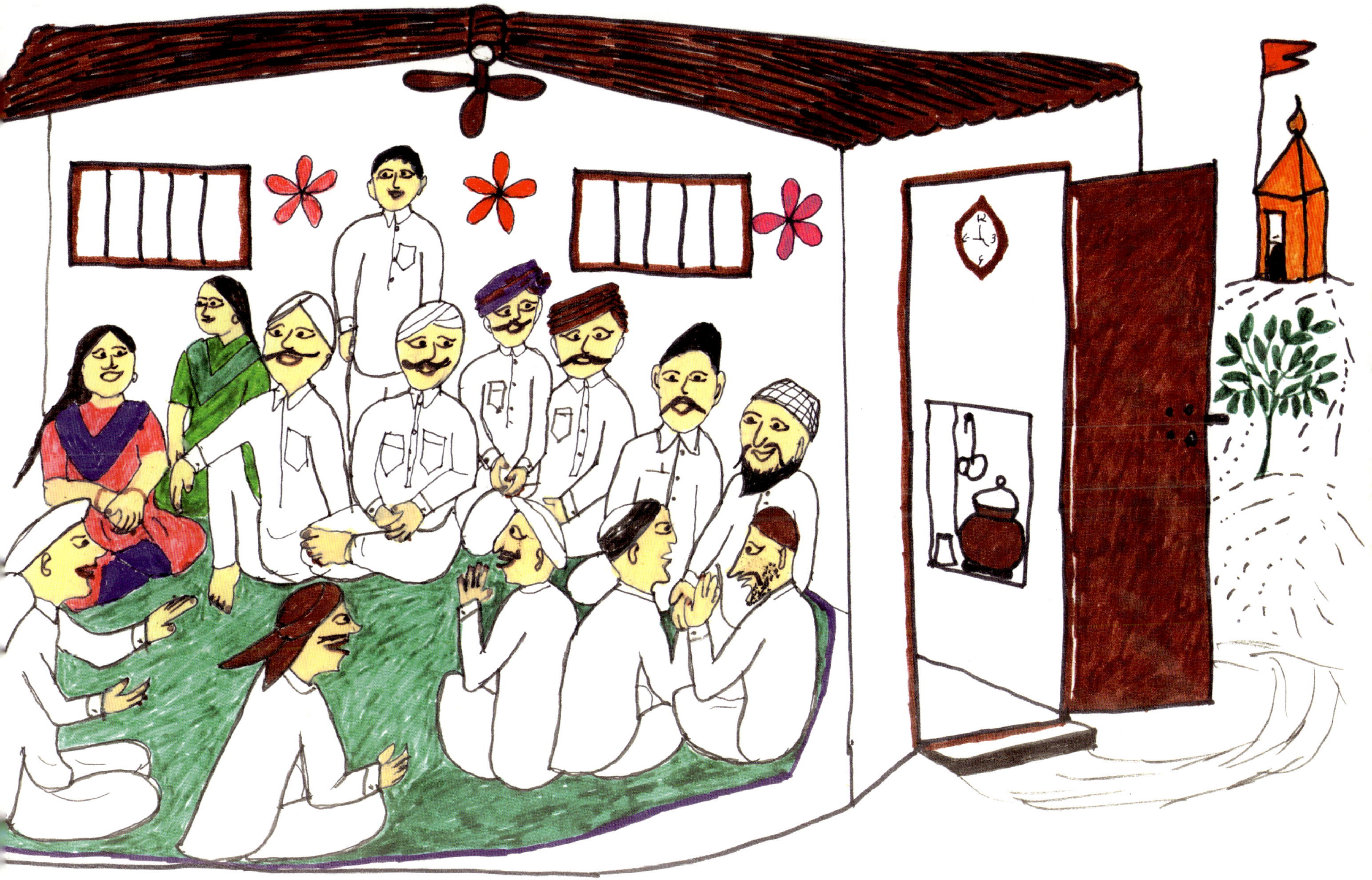

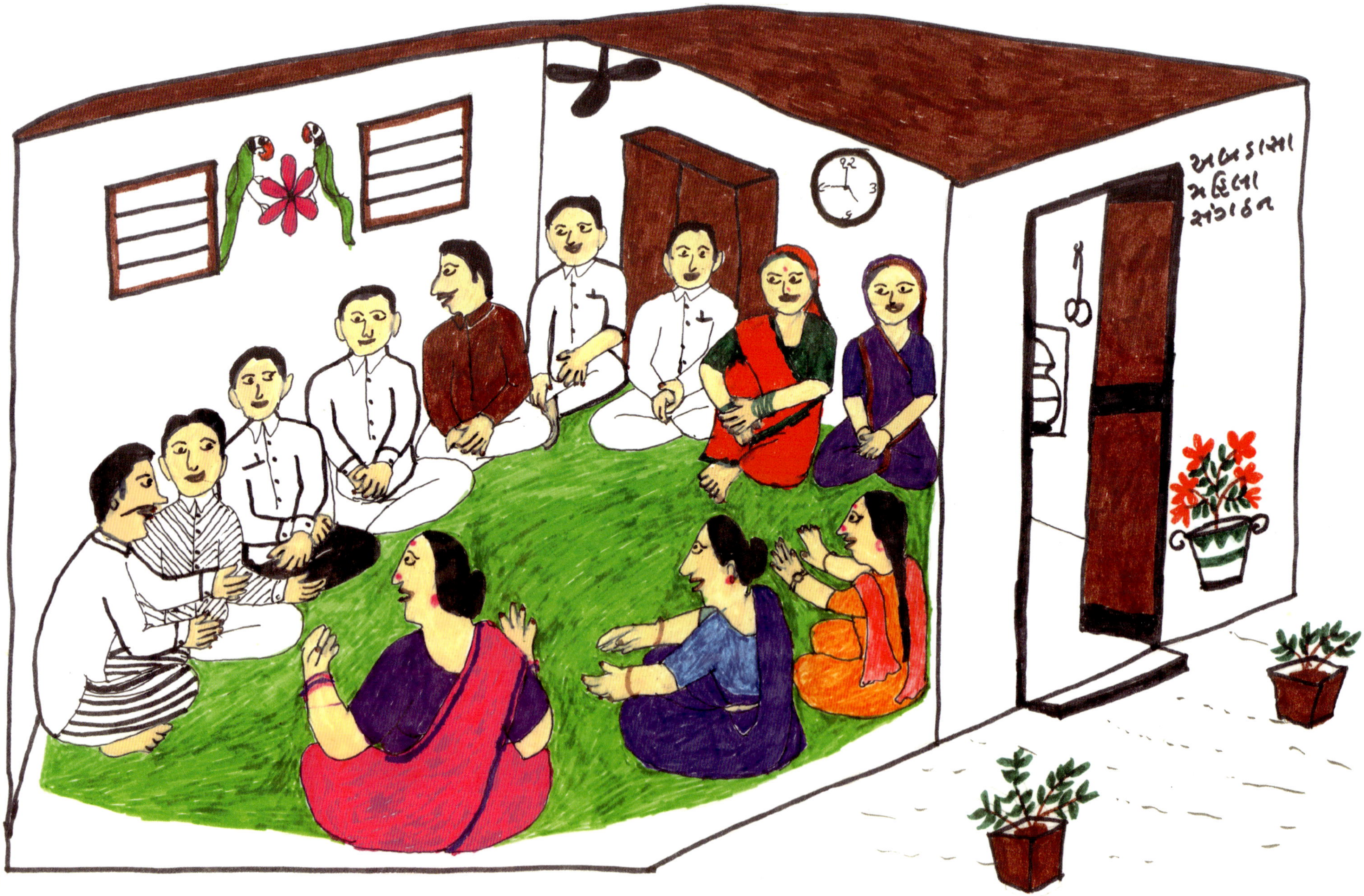
અબડાસા
મહિલા
સંગઠન

SHARING POWER

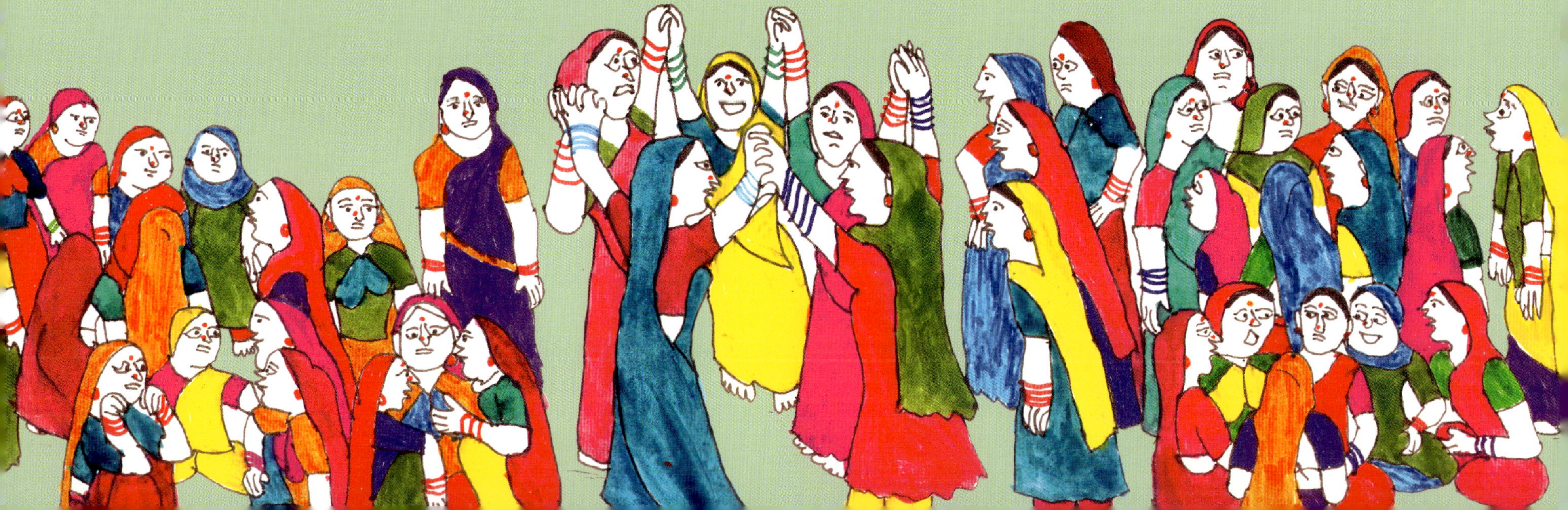

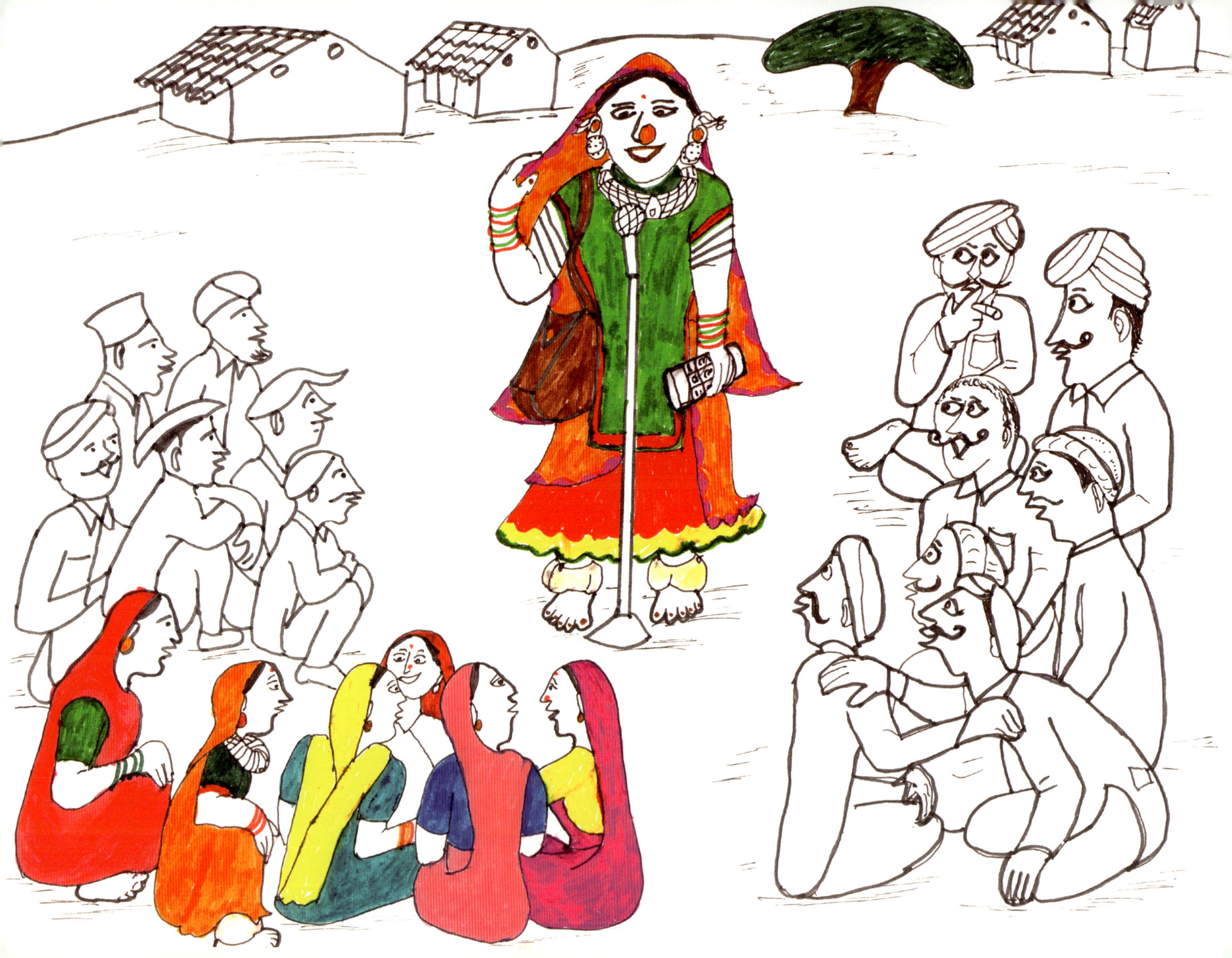

Our gram sabhas today resound more vibrantly with the voices of women than do those grand halls of our parliament!

Midway through our journey thousands of women now had earned the right to power, but barely knew what it meant. And not all of us who did were elected in the panchayats!

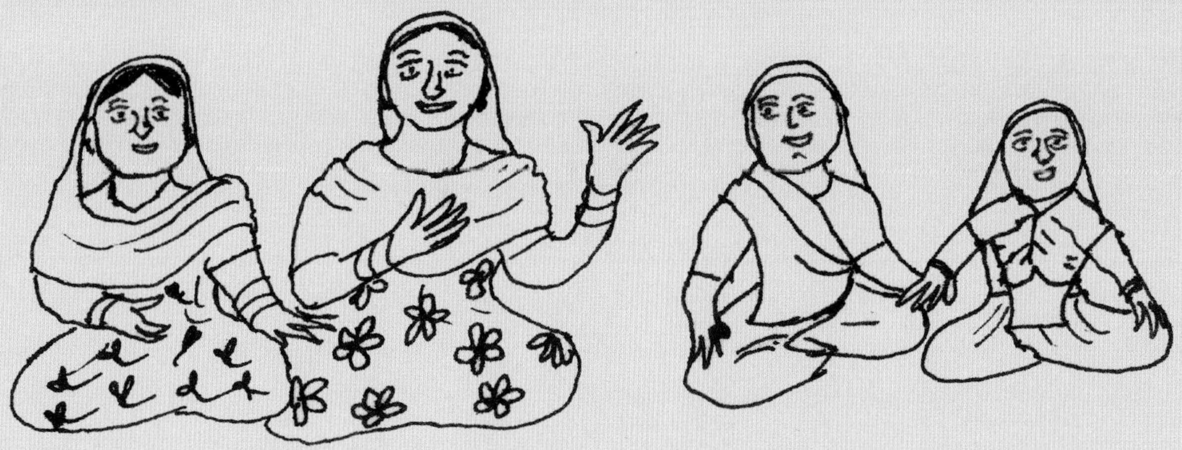

But this transition was swifter than the first half of our ongoing voyage – there was no stopping us once the law reserving 33 per cent of elected posts for women was in place.

For many of us, our lives in the panchayats went from complete absence, to mute presence; from secretly listening in on proceedings to first participating from the fringes; from standing around in bewilderment to confidently presenting plans and then asserting ourselves.

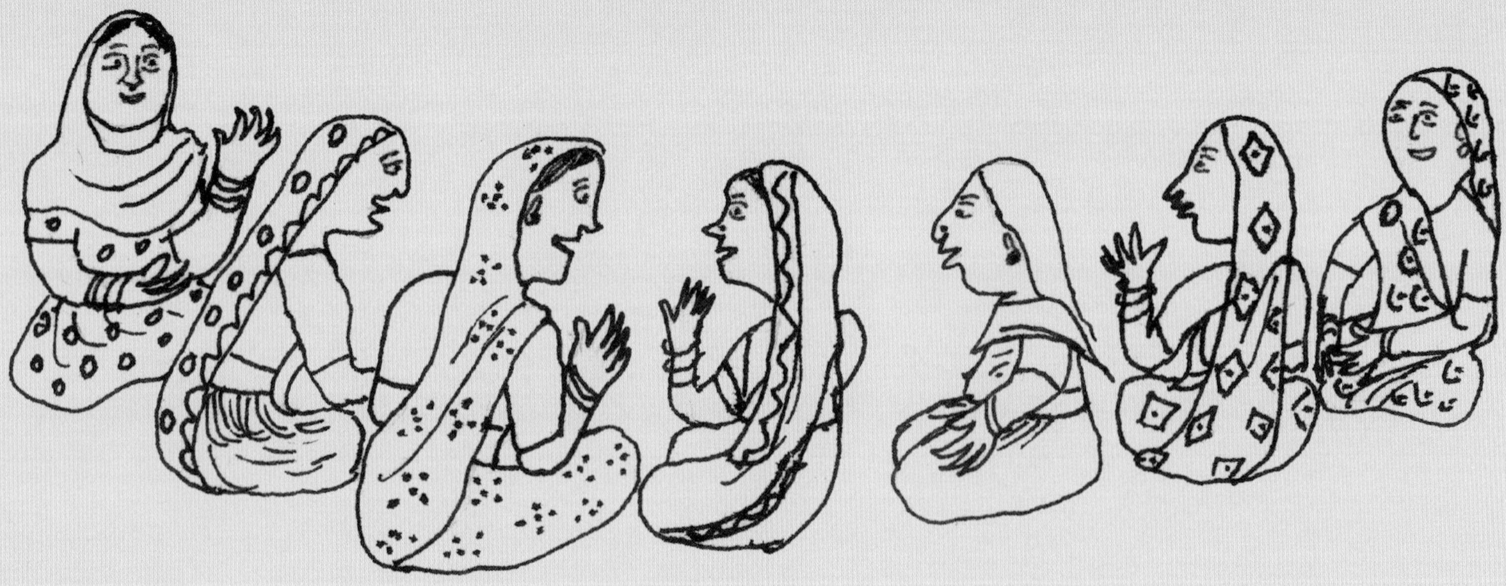

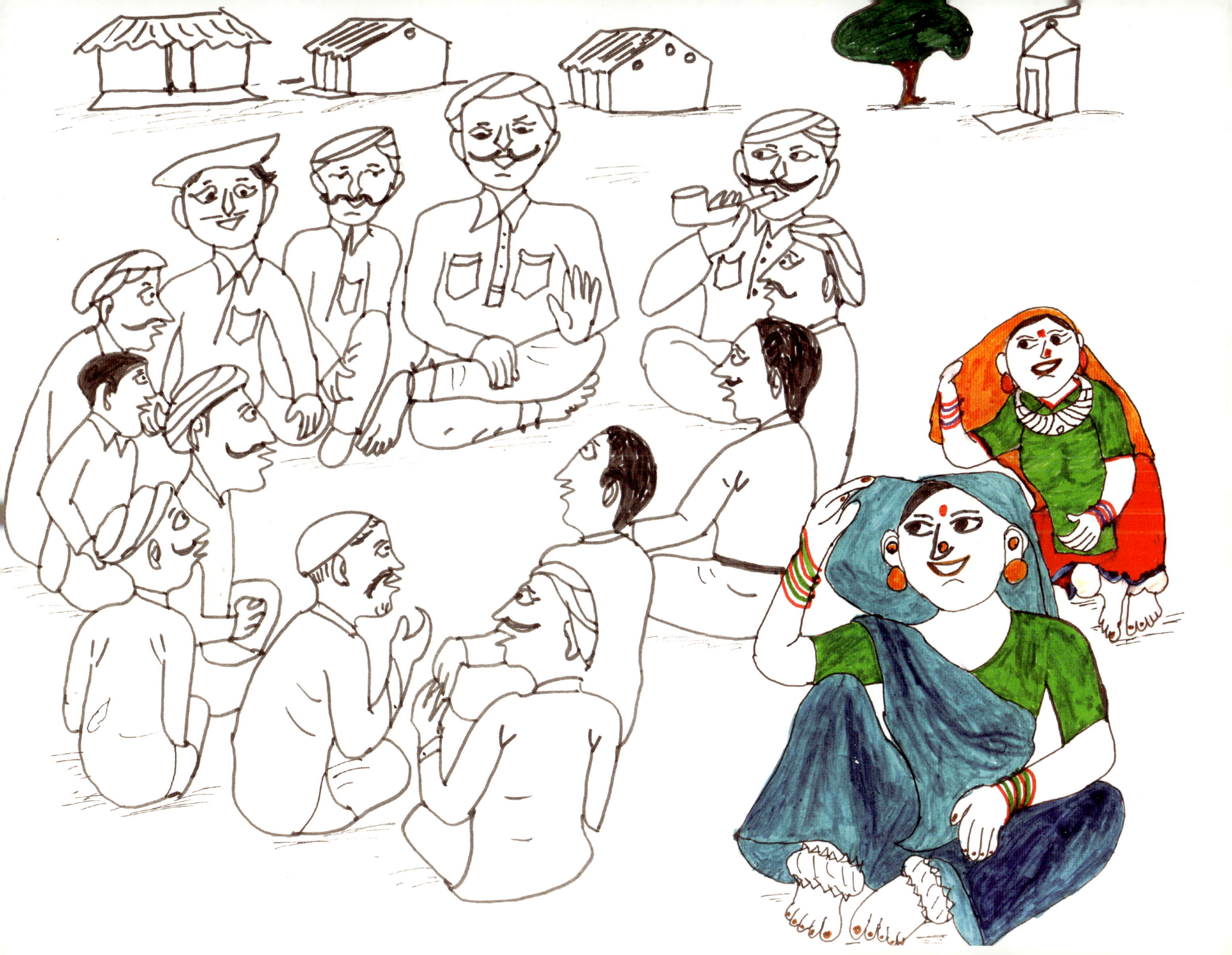

And through it all, we wondered:

Will we wear this power more lightly than men?

Will we succeed in nourishing it differently?

Will we succeed in transforming it?

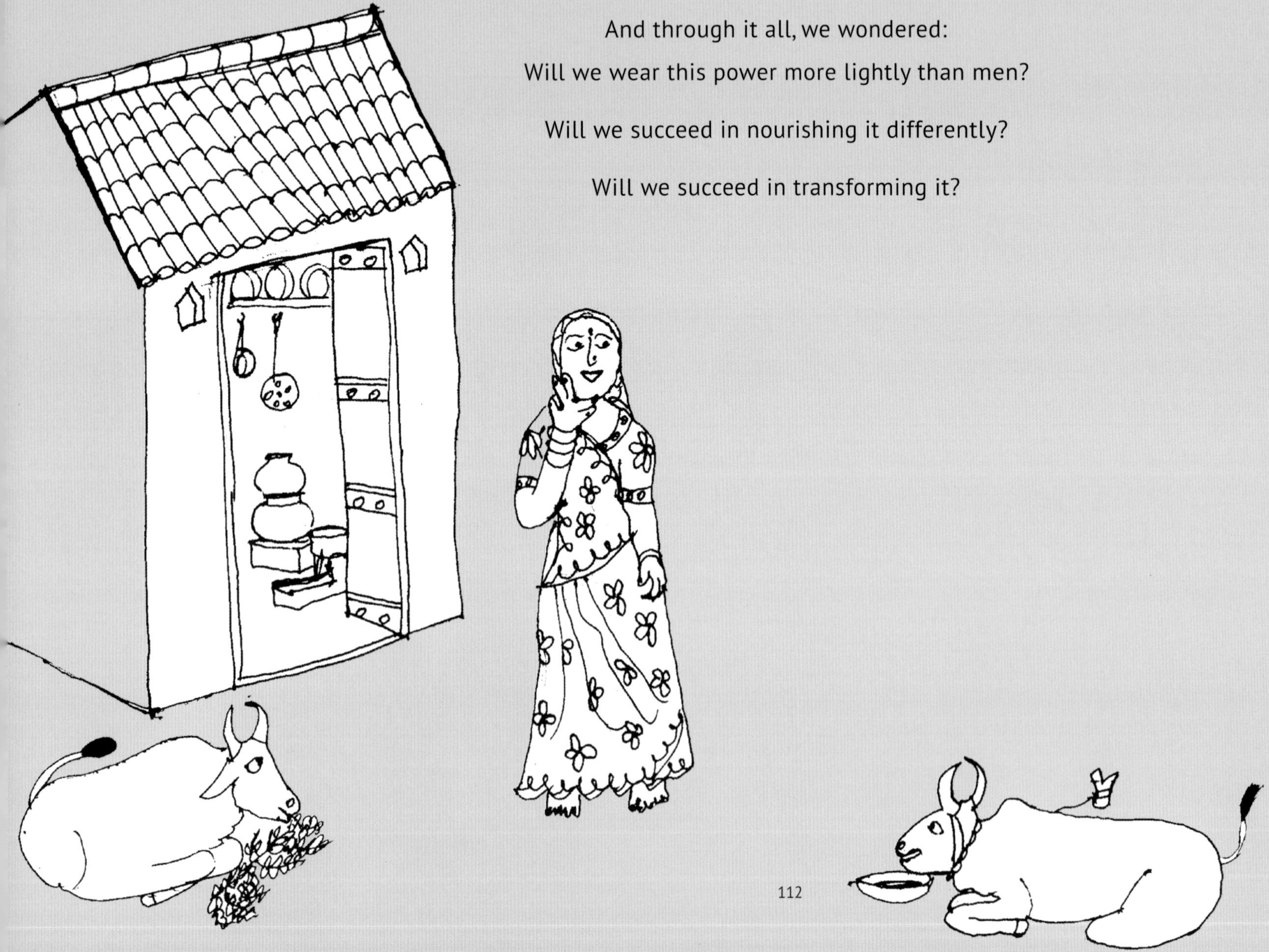

RIDING THE AIRWAVES

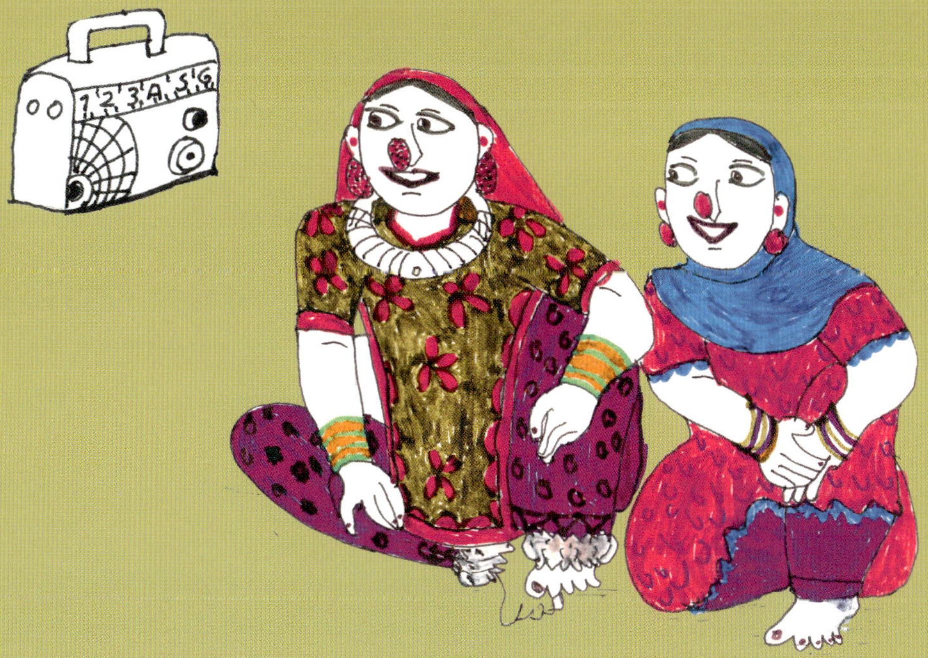

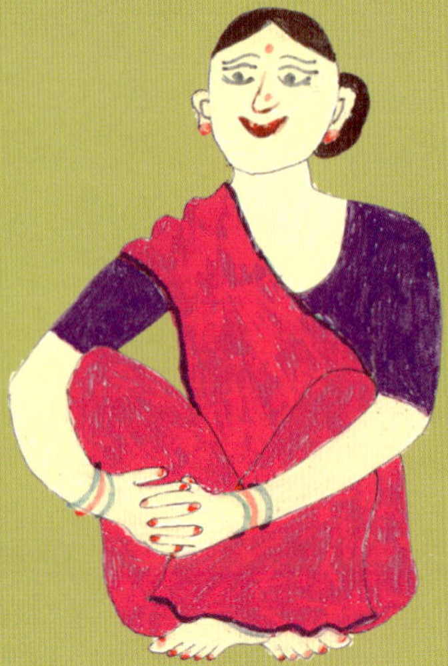

Just as we took the reins of power, we made the media our own.

We began with words and paper, but soon, the radio was made ours too. We rode on the airwaves with our stories, lending her our scripted voices, and then sitting before her on Thursday nights, to receive them back in the hushed and appreciative silence of our courtyards filled with listeners.

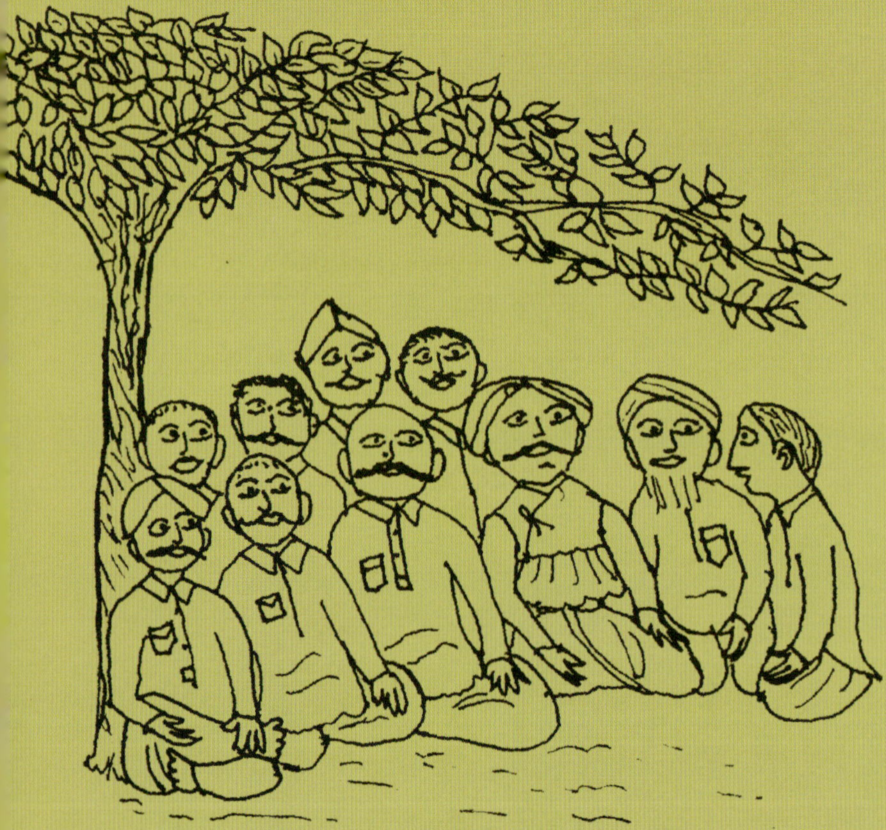

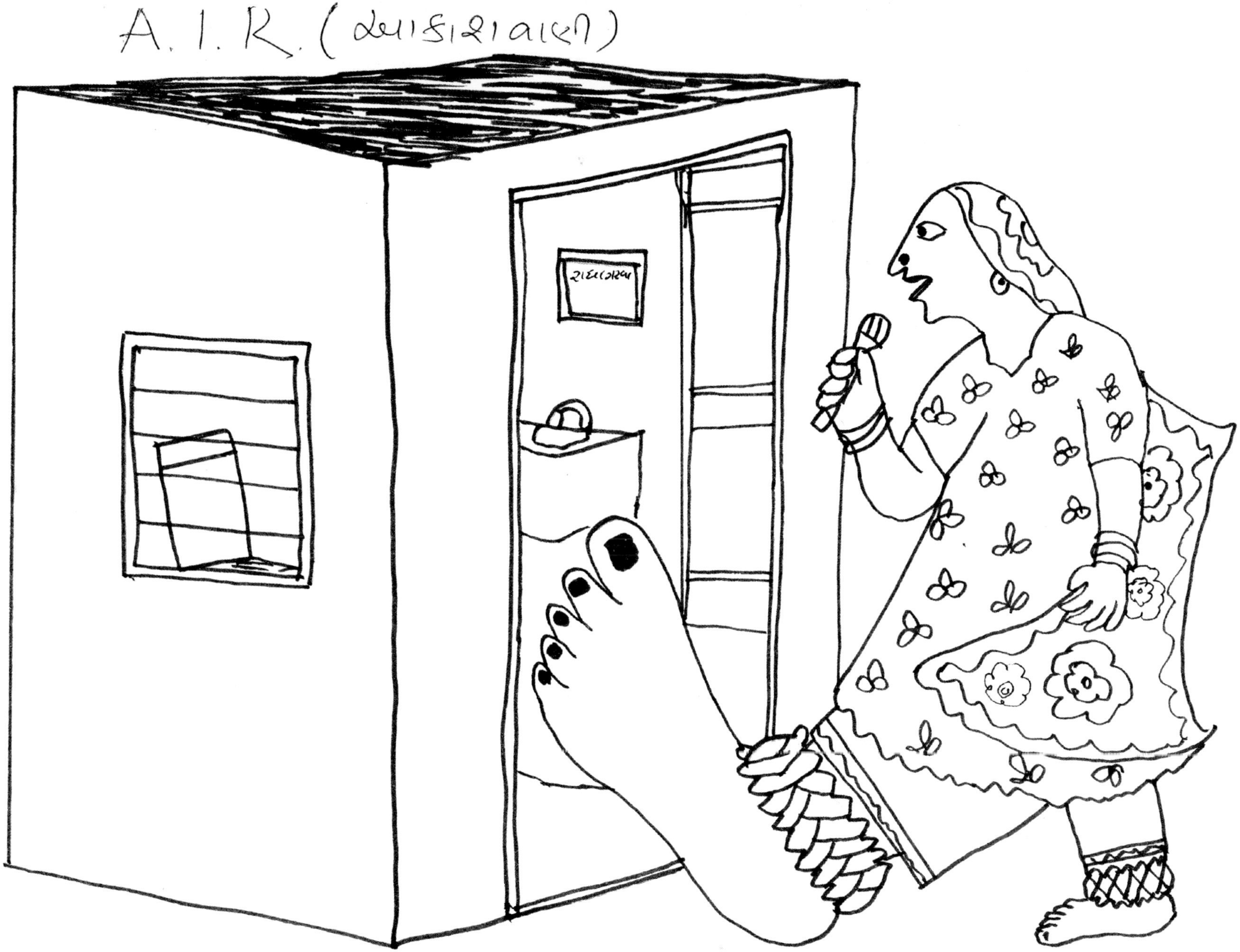
A.I.R. (આકાશવાણી)

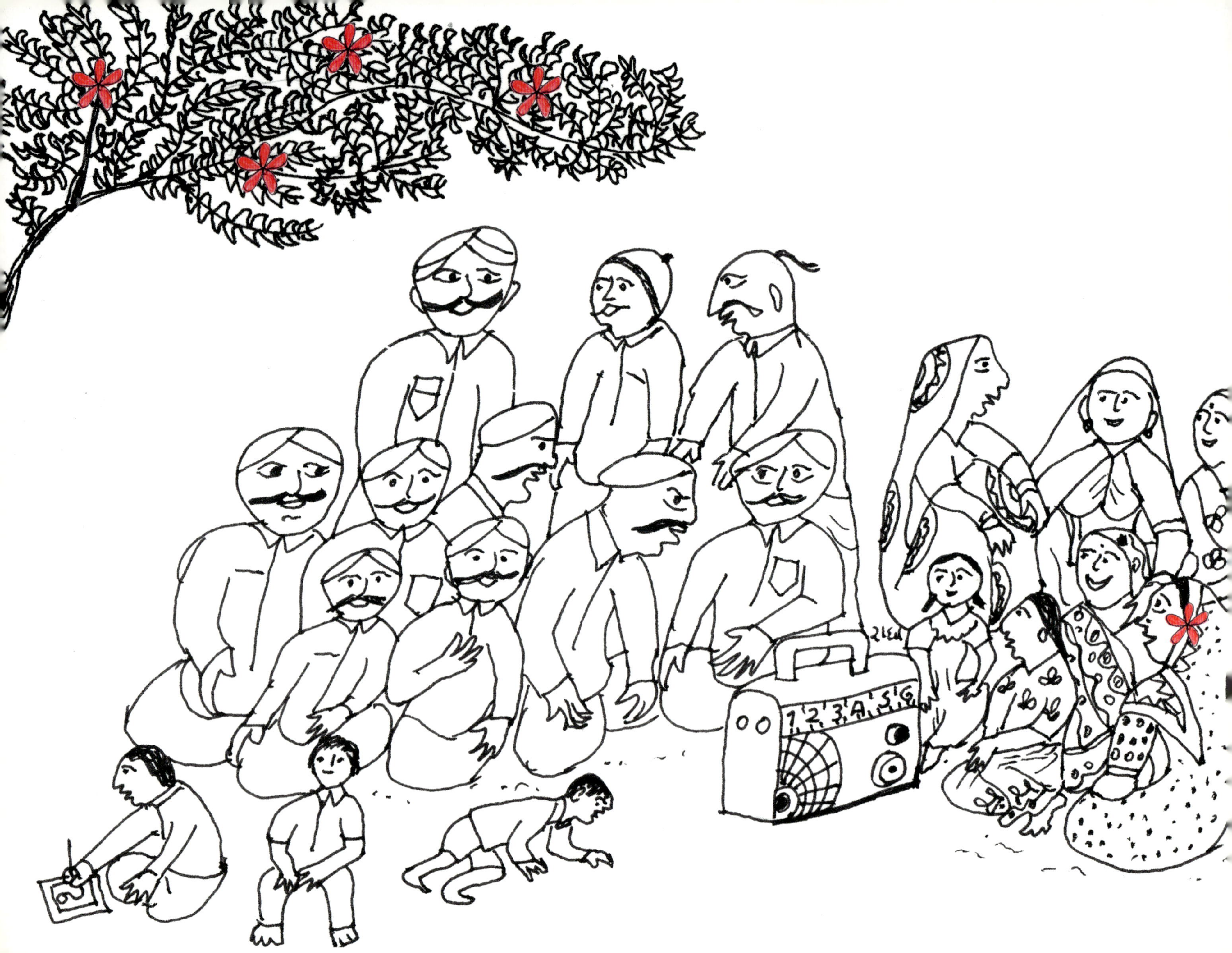
1 2 3 A S G

We had many tales to tell, scooped out of our ordinary and extraordinary lives; and there were many many listeners who discovered that these were their stories, too!

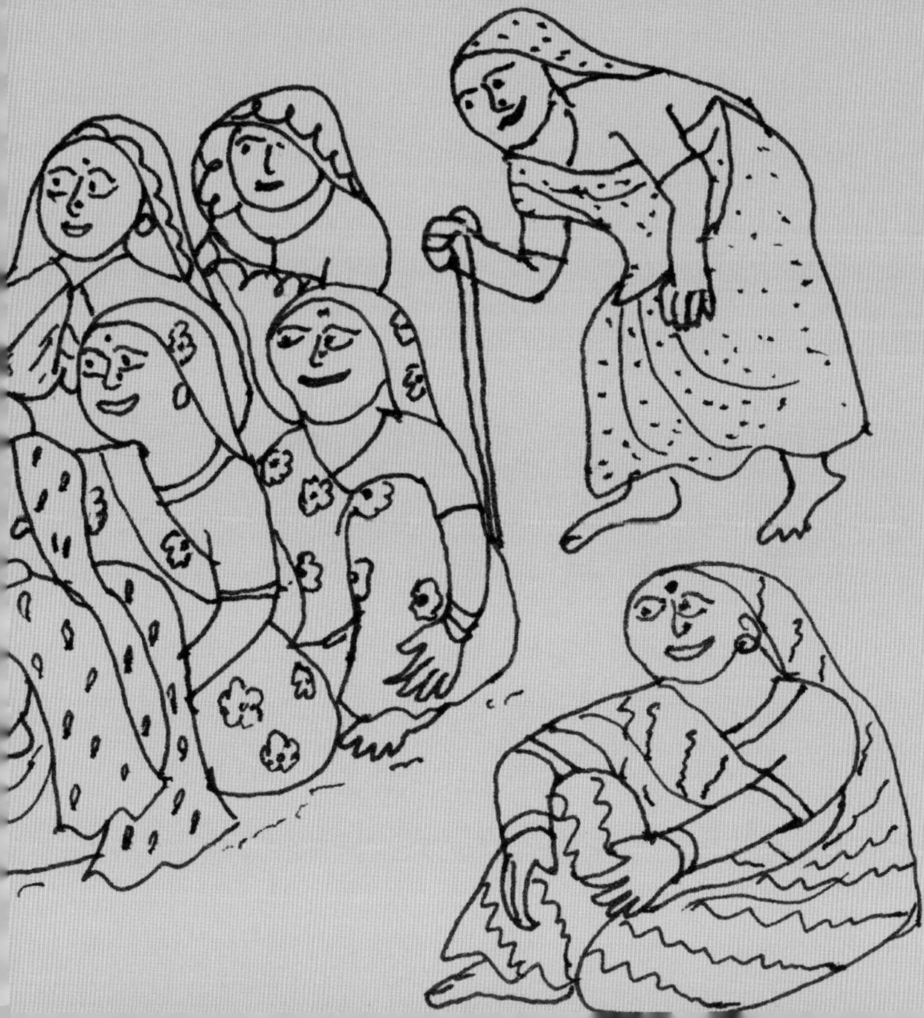

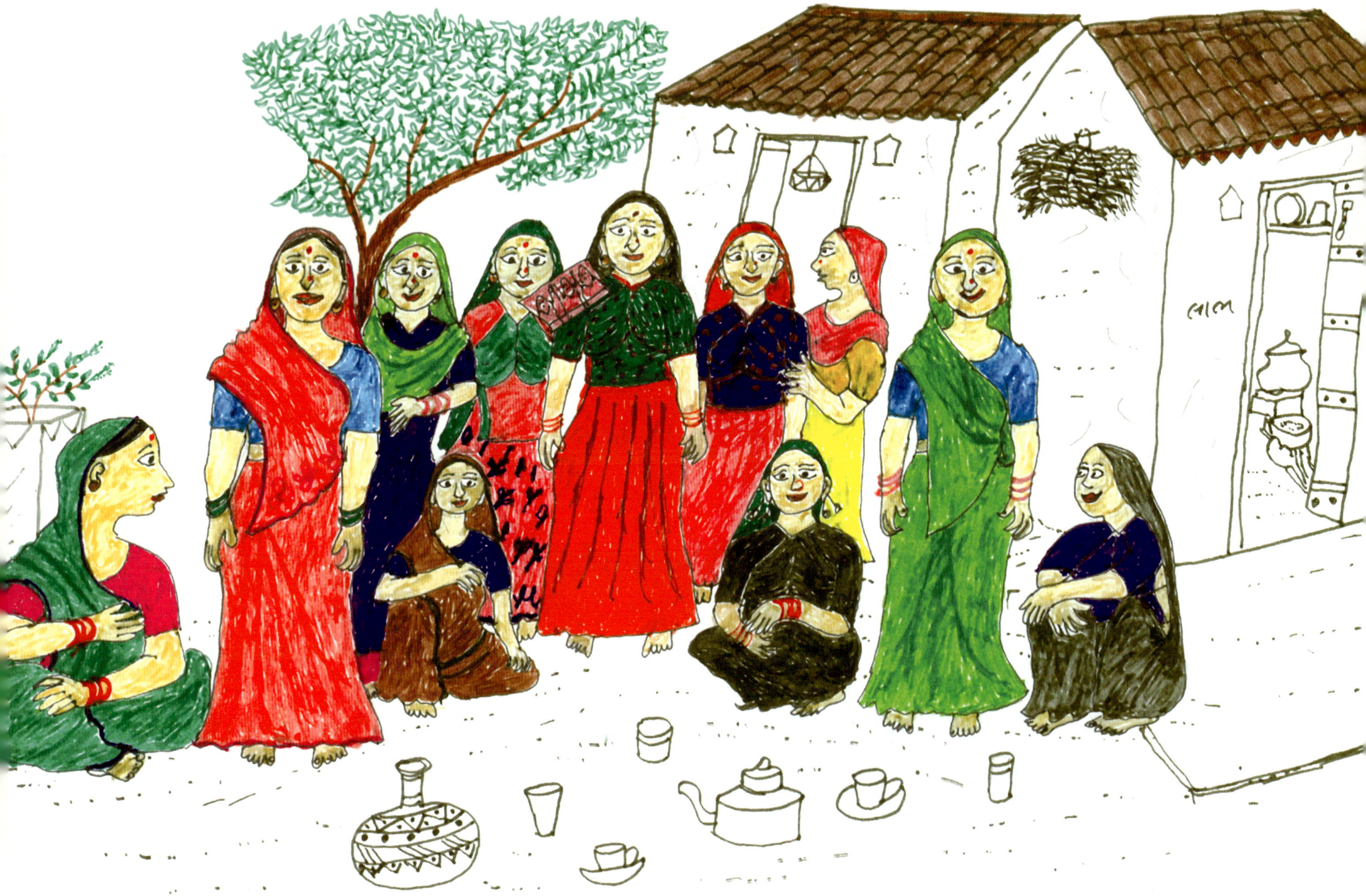

DEALING WITH THE DEMONS OF 'DEVELOPMENT'

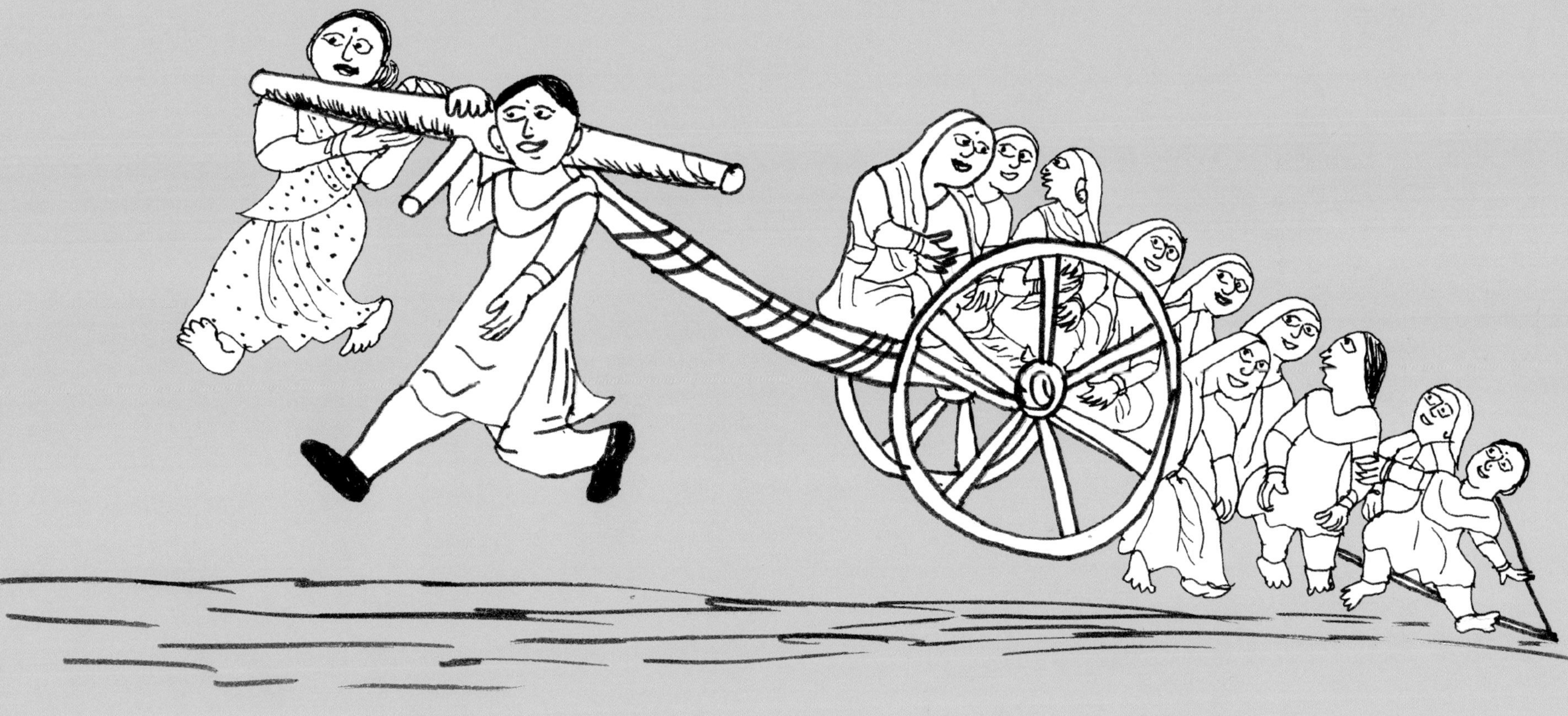

દેવી.

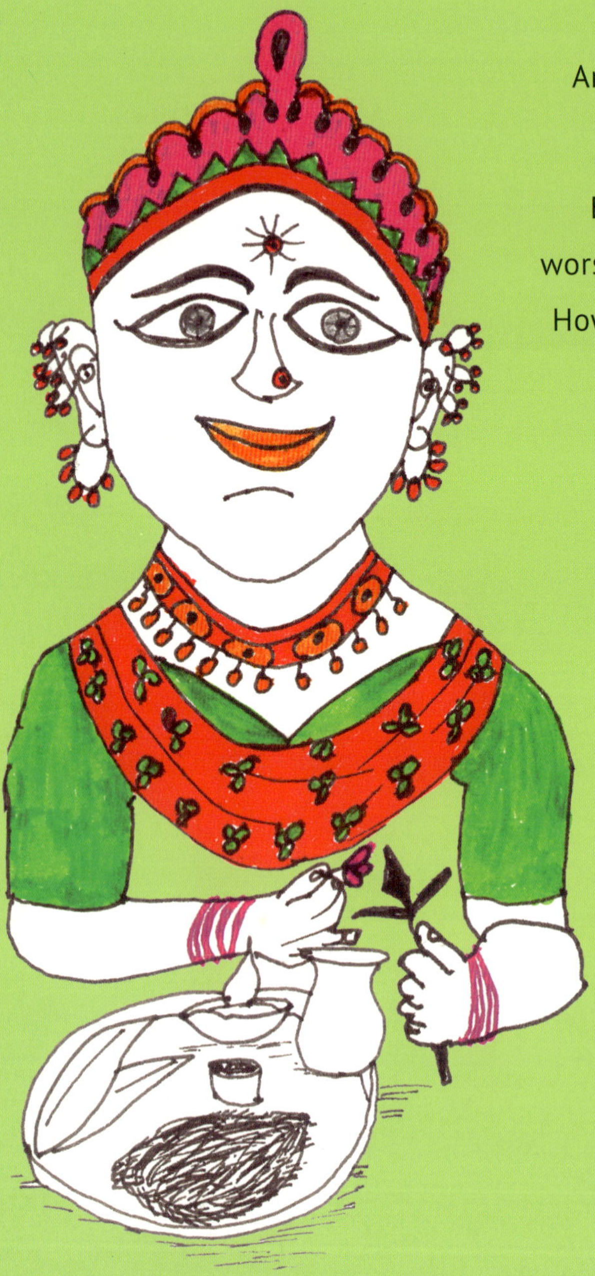

And yet, the problems have not gone away. With every success comes a setback, with every gain a new challenge.

Every day in our our bazaars we find sparkling new devis to worship, while in our homes we muffle the cry of the newborn girl. How many more goddesses will our society give birth to, to wash away the sins of our dead girl foetuses?

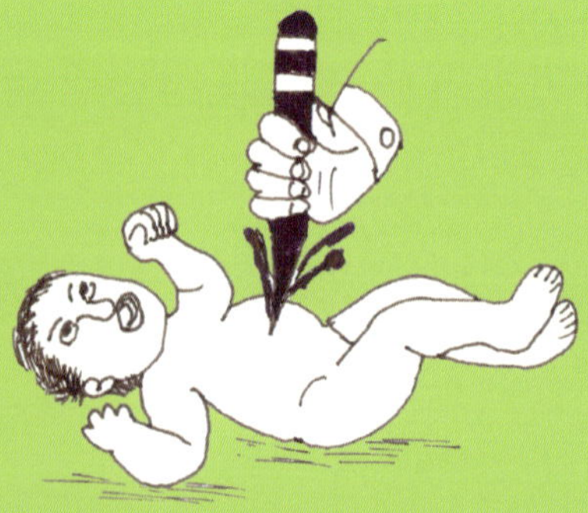

We had grown used to thinking of ourselves as poor, and yet we farmed richly. Multiple crops mingled and mixed as we shared our seeds, our knowledge and breeds. Together, we nurtured our soil, we shared our food.

But now, we farm poorly and spend richly. Our seeds are bought, our grains are bought, our farms grow alike with single crops, and we have little to share.

Surely this was not the development we had been waiting for?

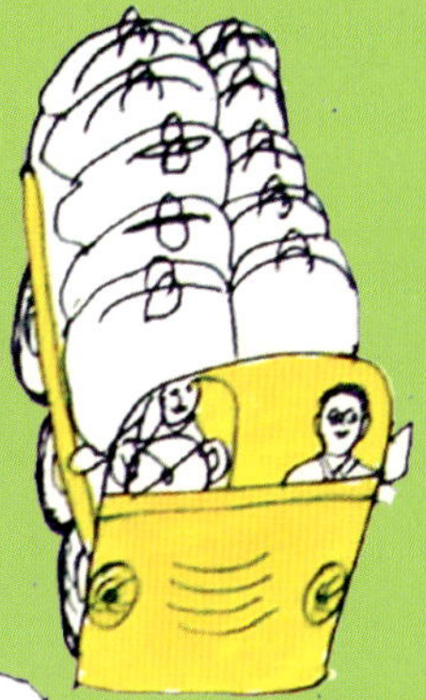

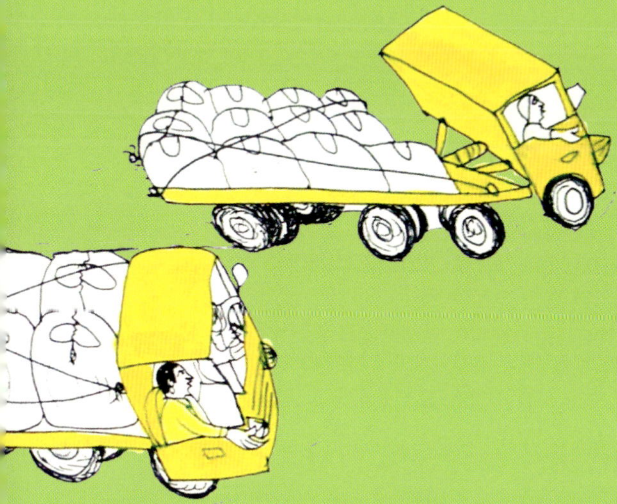

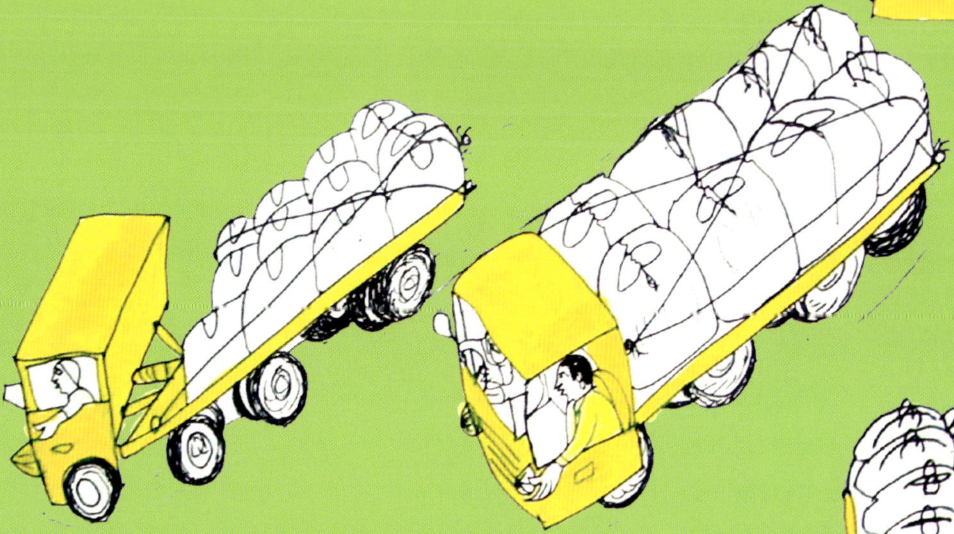

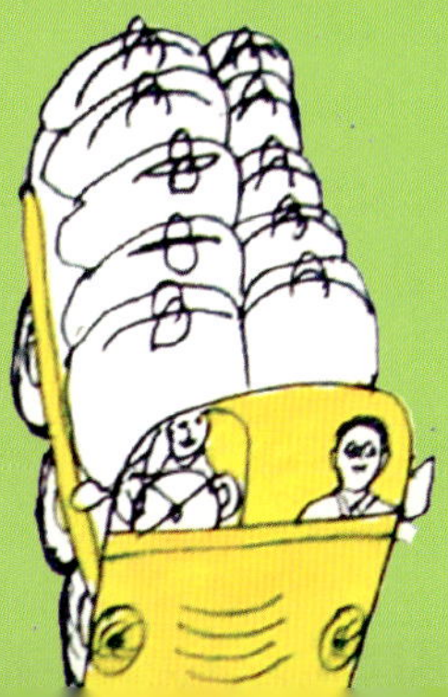

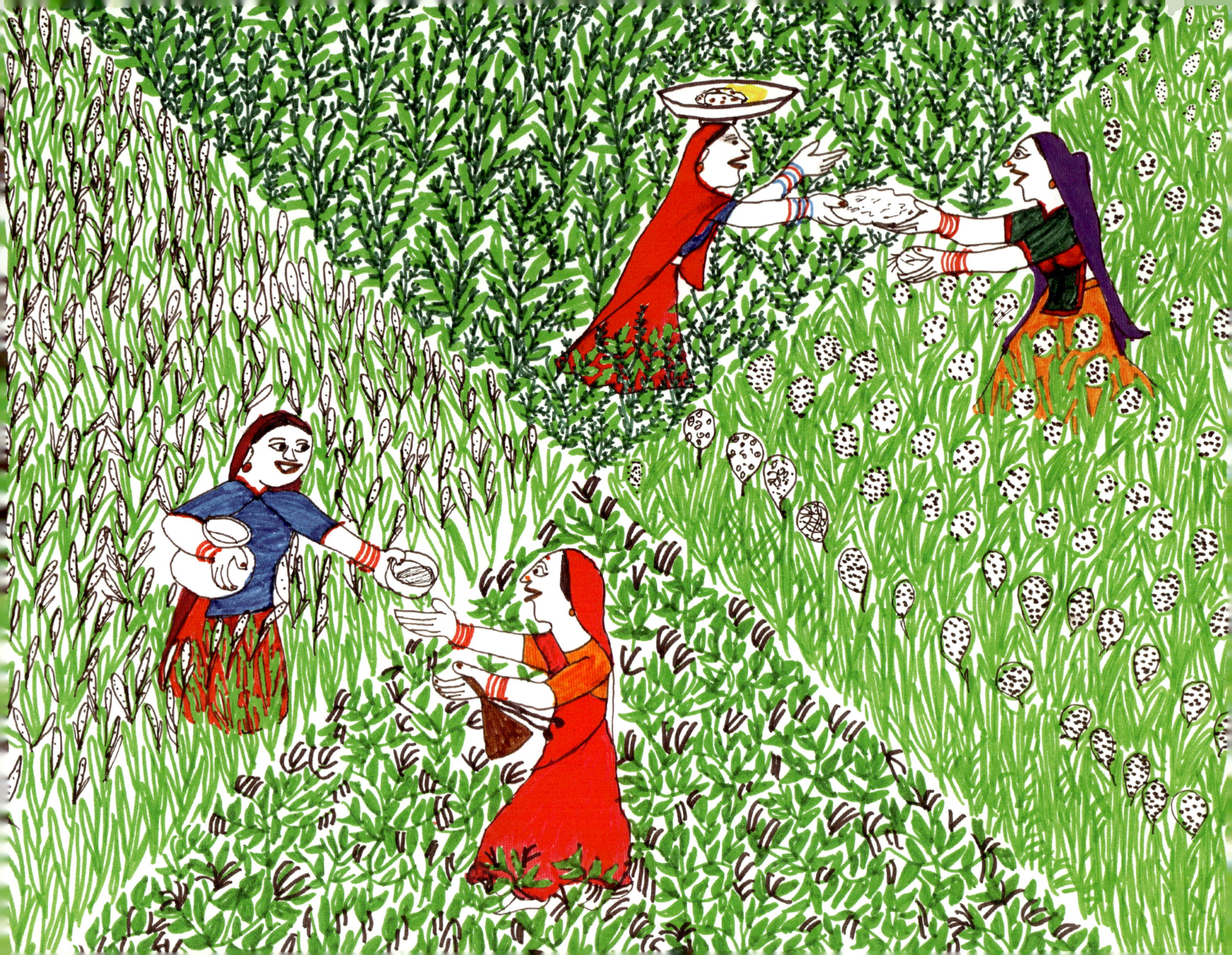

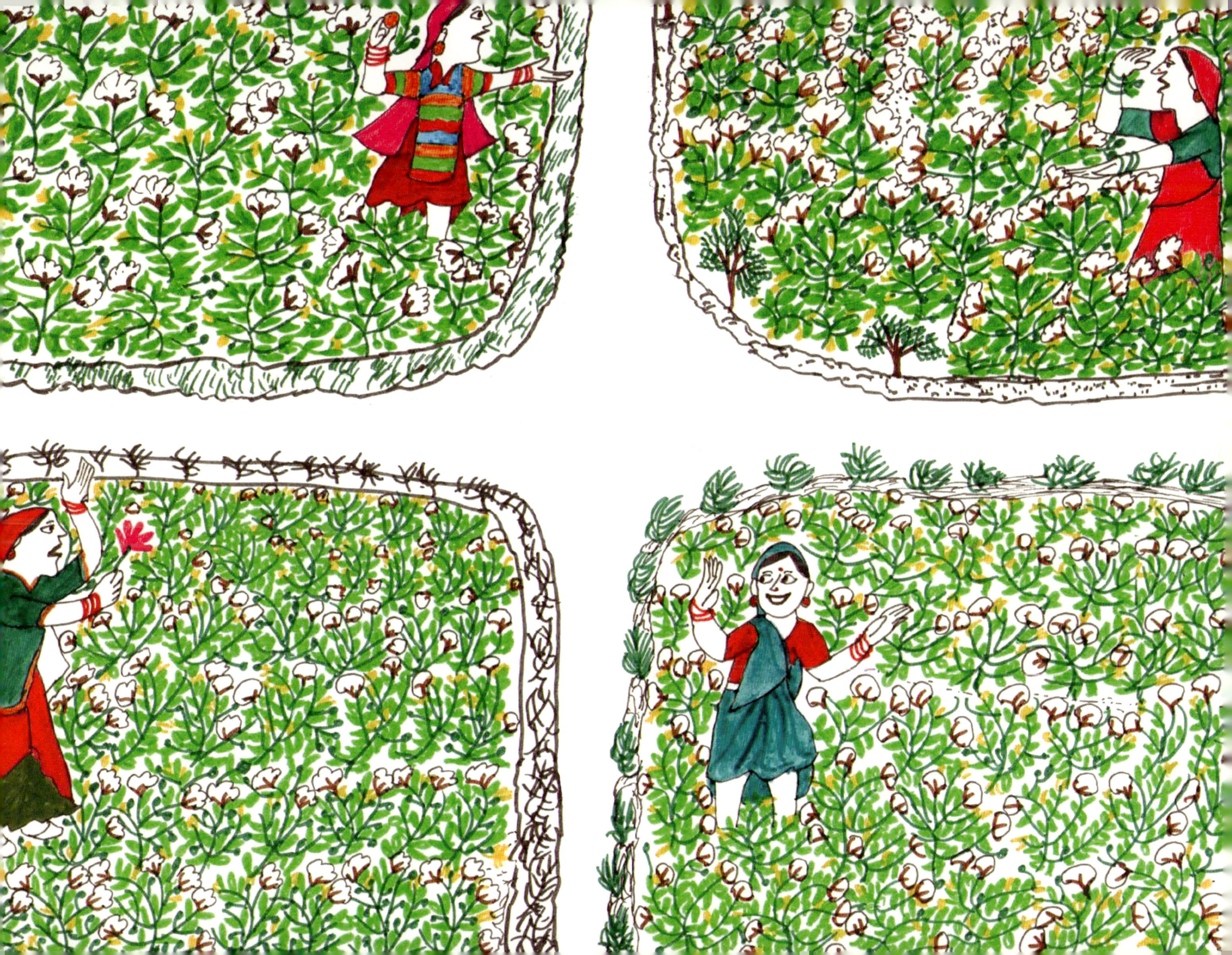

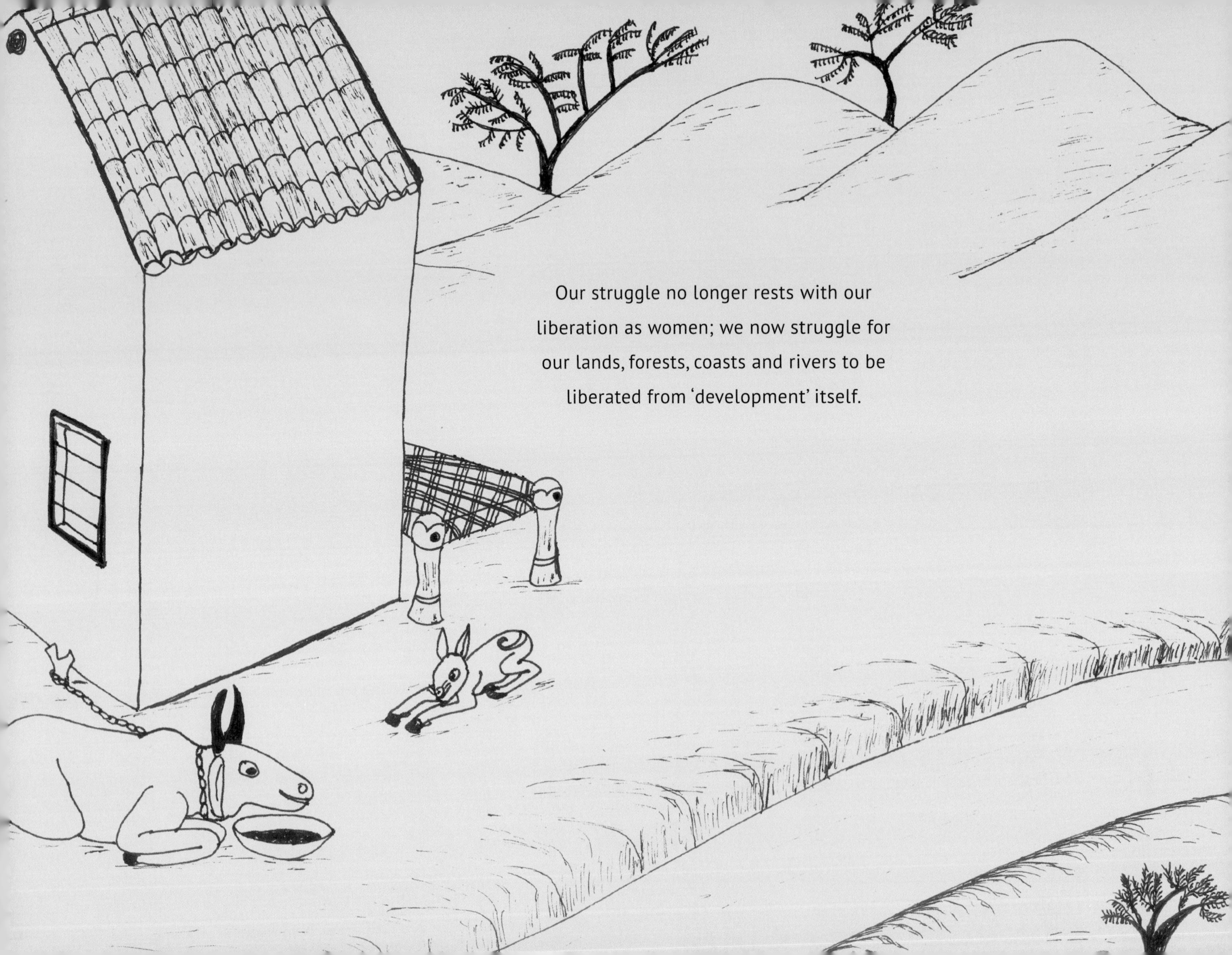

Our struggle no longer rests with our liberation as women; we now struggle for our lands, forests, coasts and rivers to be liberated from 'development' itself.

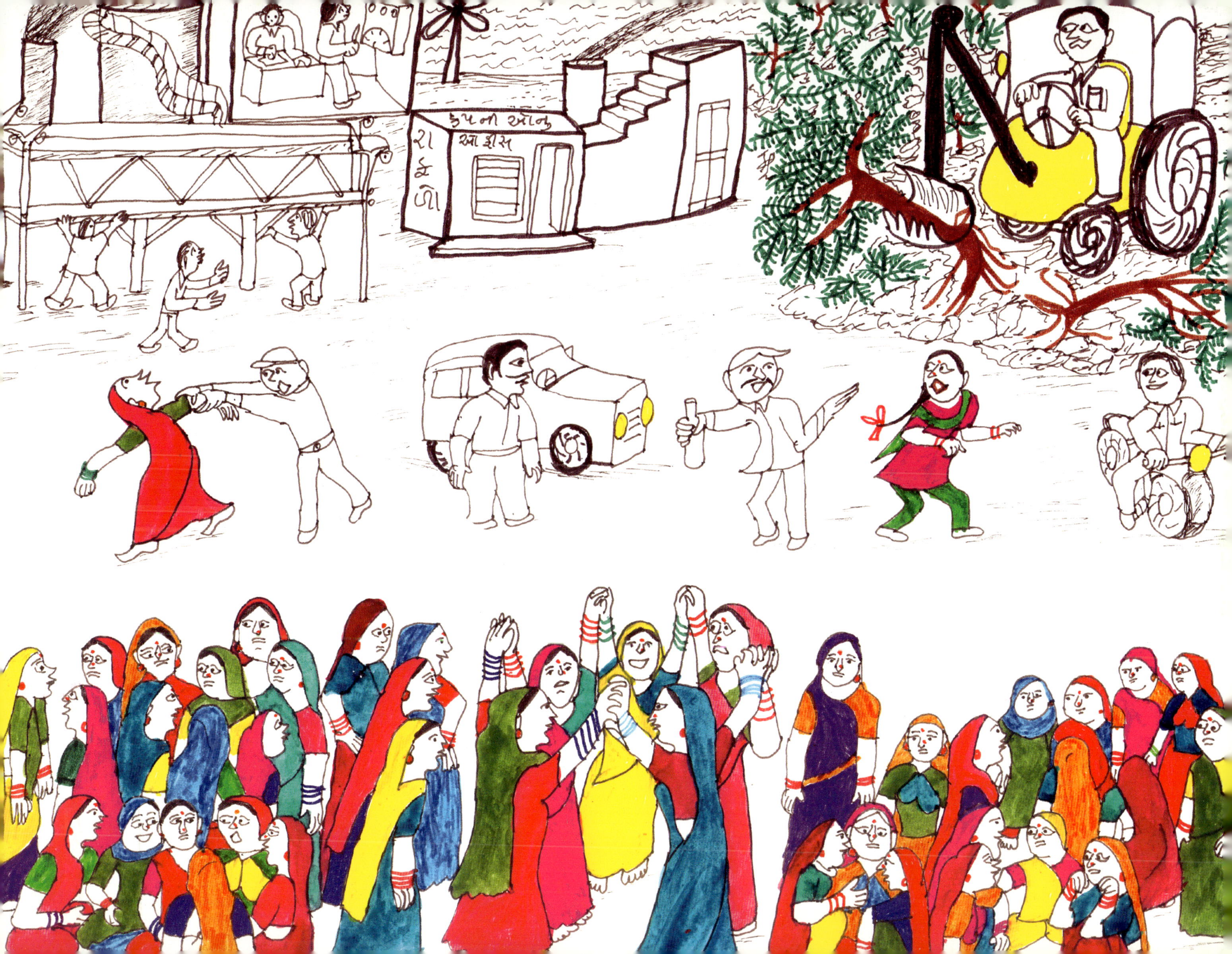

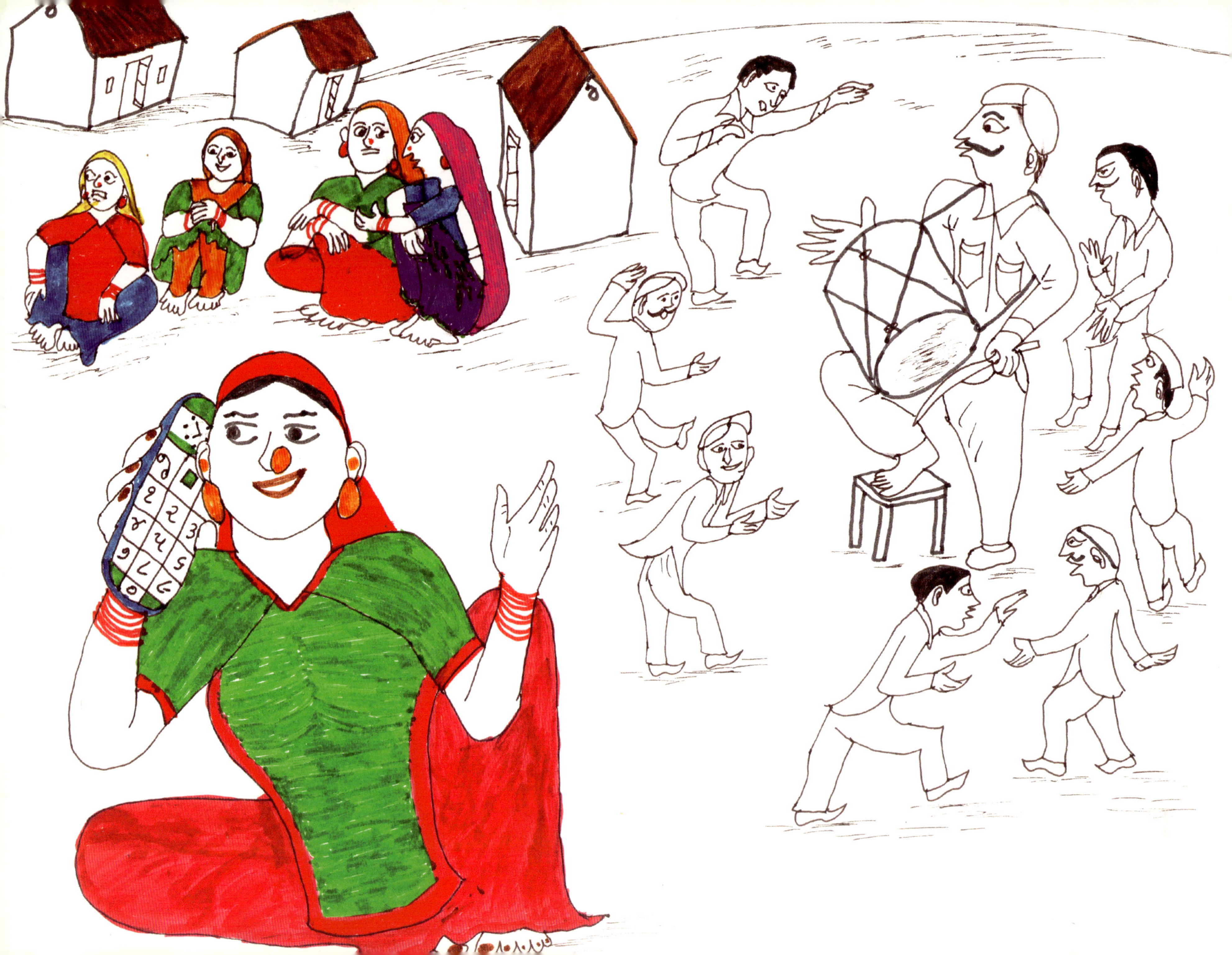

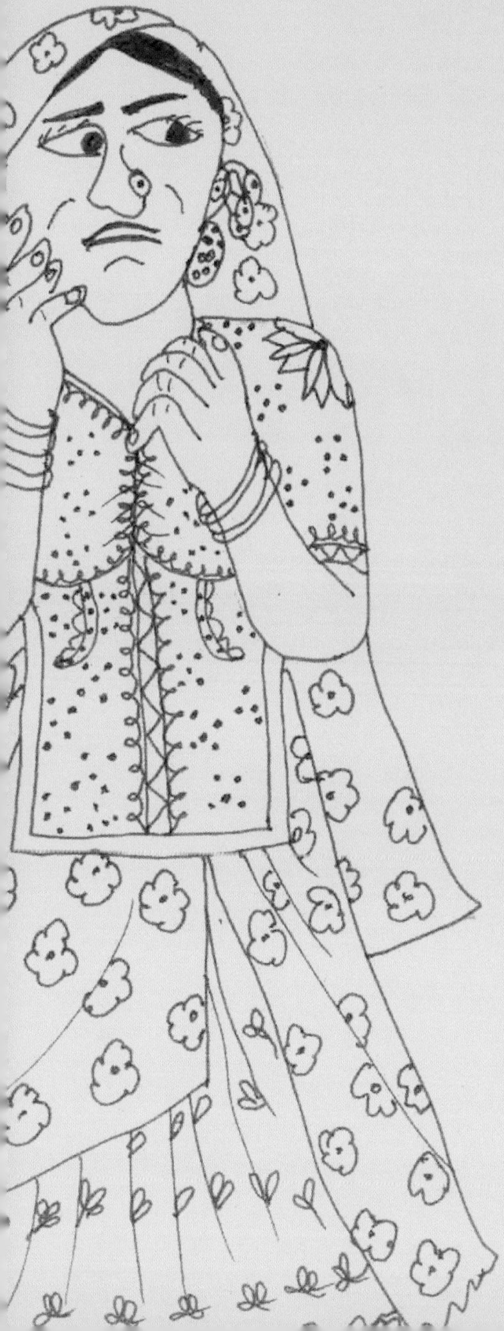

"Listen Kanta,
My songs have faded, and dances stilled.
I am told that my mobile can ring,
but in the wedding tonight I cannot sing.
They tell me you and I must not look alike,
that sisters we cannot be and
a veil must now shroud all that I like."

"Oh Fatima,
I miss our walk to Hajipir.
And the bhajans we sang for our beloved Pir.
They now want to draw lines between your god and mine.
And have me believe that my faith has a better shine".

Over the years, we overcame our fears, but now find that we live in a world more fearful. We stretched our arms to grasp the world, but this world now seems to shrink into narrow lanes where little demons live and breathe without love and ease.

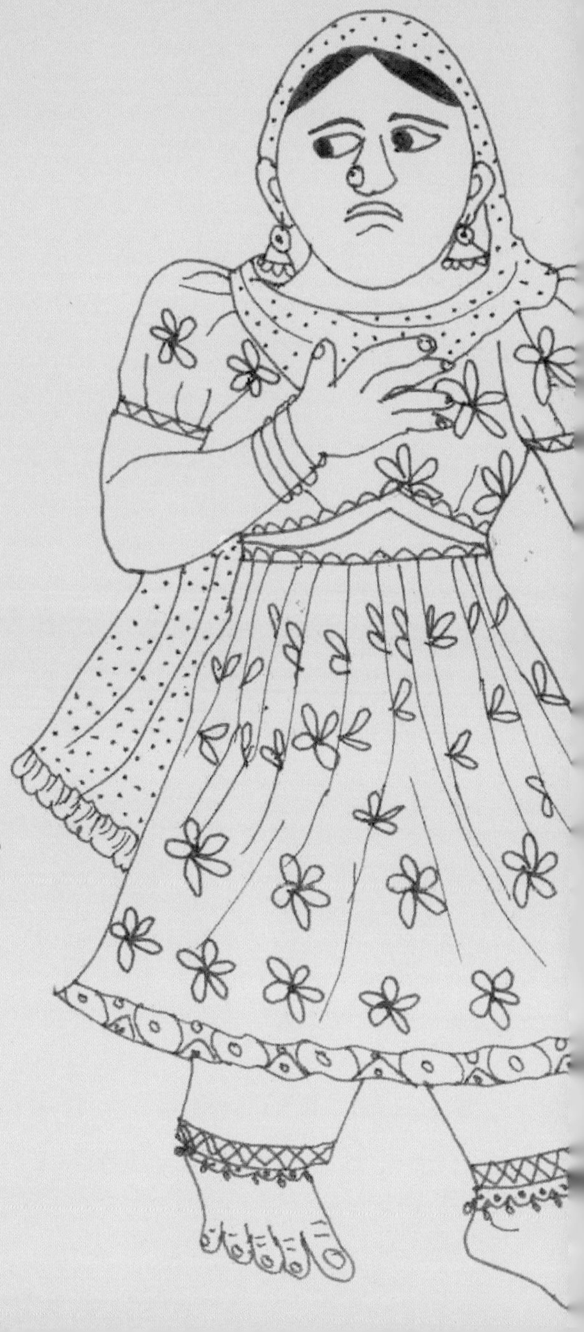

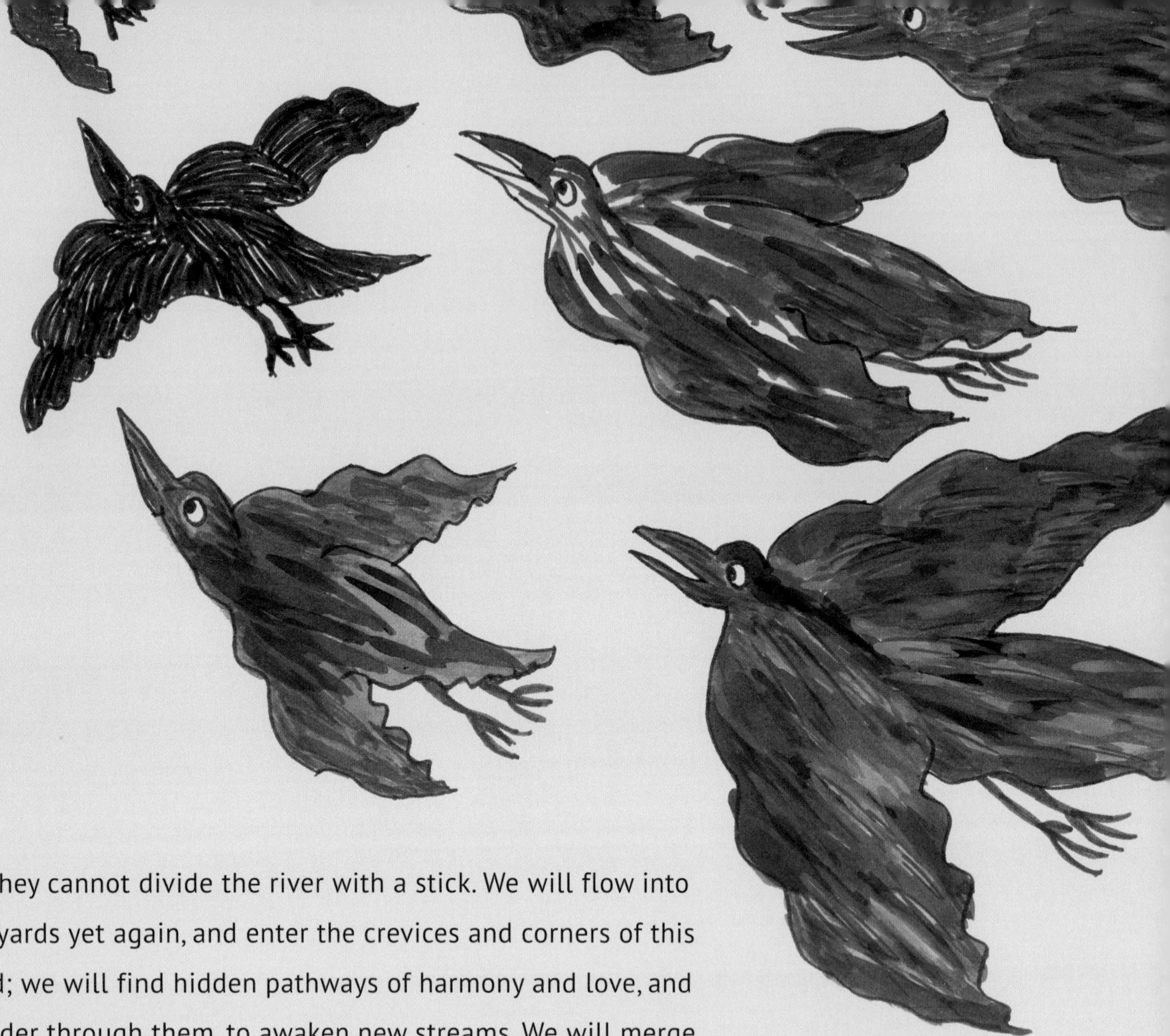

But they cannot divide the river with a stick. We will flow into courtyards yet again, and enter the crevices and corners of this world; we will find hidden pathways of harmony and love, and meander through them, to awaken new streams. We will merge identities, to create new ones, and with her shadow hugging us, we will fly and flow, with the crane.

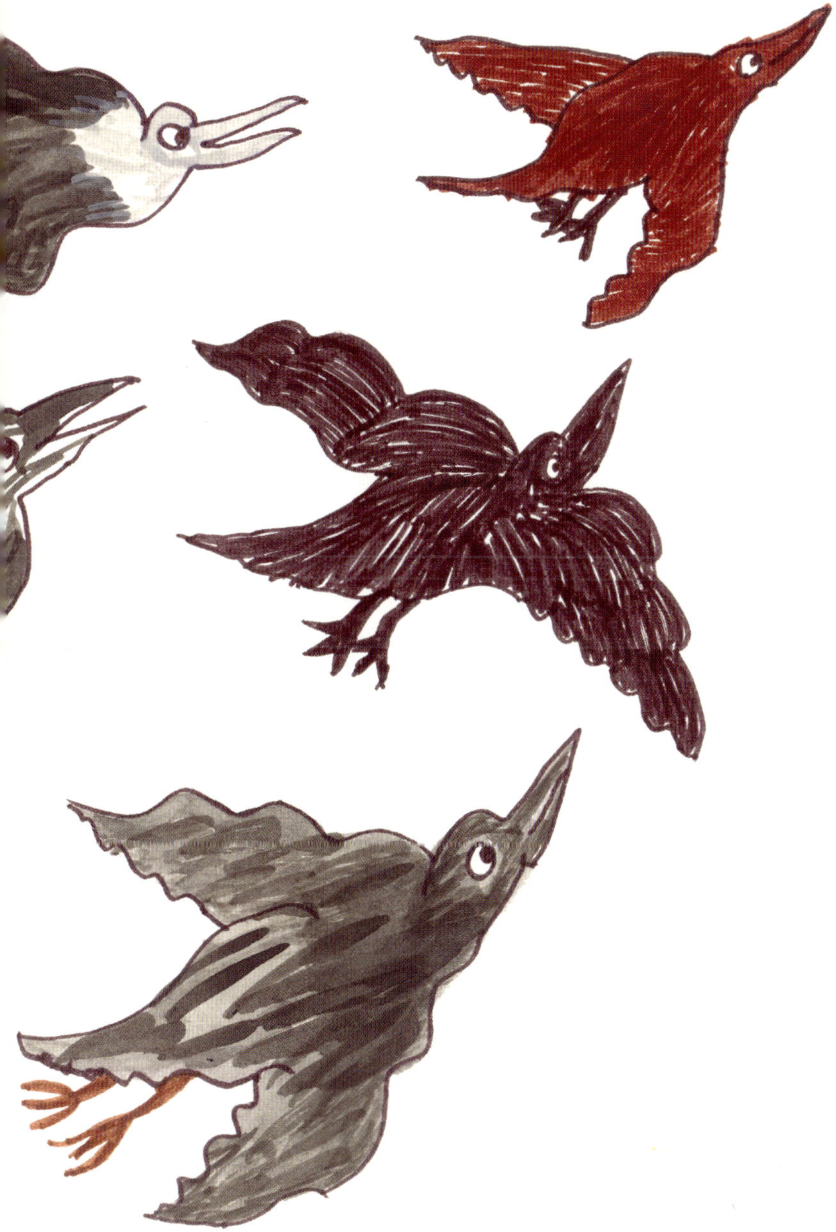

AFTERWORD

The Colours of Life

KALPANA SHARMA

The landscape is bleached of colour – there's some brown, some black and some dark green. Kutch is the largest district in India, stretching out over 45,652 sq km. Its vastness includes desert lands that are spread across the boundary into Pakistan, 352 km of coastline as well as mangrove swamps, grasslands and salt lands that shimmer between the sea and the coast.

Yet the lives of the women of Kutch are anything but devoid of colour. You can see that in the evocative drawings of Radhaben Garva that are the focus of this book. You see it in the bright, vibrant colours that mark the clothes of the many different communities and castes that inhabit this semi-arid land. And you 'hear' it in the stories that women tell you as you sit with them in a circle of equals.

So when Devalben, wearing a green choli, black ghagra and striking red odhni tells you that she can now walk into a police station and demand that her complaint be registered, you have to wonder: when did this happen? How did women, living in rural India, where vast areas are still bereft of basic services like water, sanitation, health and education, begin to believe that those they feared in the past would now listen to them? When did these entrenched power equations begin to change?

Devalben, who has found the confidence to deal with the law, is only one among the millions of women across India who are doing things that their mothers never believed women could, or even should, do. She represents a quiet, almost imperceptible process of change that has taken place over the last two and a half decades in the lives of women in many parts of rural India; changes in their perception of who they are; of their place in society; of their entitlements and of their right to fight for them. She is also one of a growing number of women who are leading the way to socio-political transformations, participating in advocacy, and coming up with new and innovative ways to express their demands for change.

This is a groundbreaking shift in a society where women believed that theirs was a secondary status to that of men. In urban India, the change is more visible. In rural India, you might have to look for it. On the surface, it would appear that little has changed. Women still carry the entire burden of household chores and unpaid work outside. They remain the

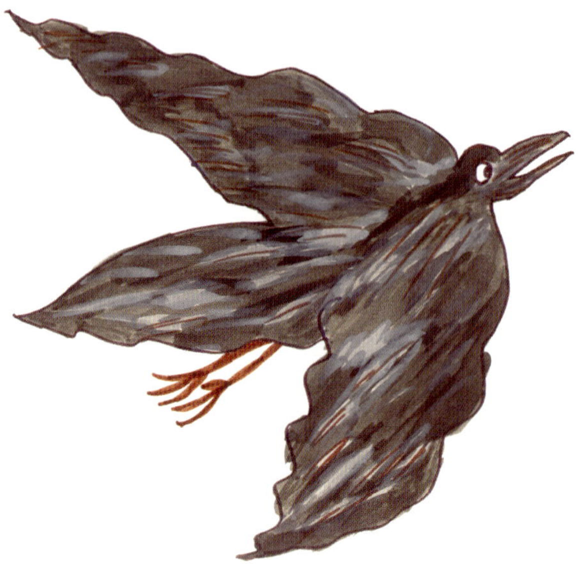

principal carers for children and the elderly. They are more often than not denied even the rights they have to inherit or own land and property. They are pulled out of school to look after younger siblings. They are married before their young bodies can deal with childbearing. And many die because their undernourished and young bodies cannot survive a pregnancy in places where emergency medical intervention is still a dream.

While their status within the household is determined by embedded patriarchy, outside the home they are often the targets of violence triggered by caste, by ethnicity, by religion. When such clashes occur, and they are increasing in their frequency across India, it is principally the women who pay the price. They are targets of sexual violence, their families are displaced and they must build their lives anew, while living with the constant insecurity of renewed bouts of such violence occurring, often without any warning.

Against these realities, women's movements in India have fought individually, or as coalitions, to assert women's rights to equity and justice. From national campaigns for changes in laws to working with rural women's collectives on issues of livelihood, health, education, and the environment, these women's movements have been responsible for a perceptible shift in thinking and attitudes towards women in the government and in society.

Since the 1980s, successive governments, irrespective of their political orientation, have reiterated their commitment to women's equality, even if some of this has remained in the realm of rhetoric. They have institutionalized programmes for "women's welfare" that address women's specific needs for healthcare and incentives to ensure that girls are educated. A National Women's Commission now exists, thanks to the pressure from women's groups, and its role is to be responsive to any incident concerning women anywhere in India. The Constitution has been amended to reserve seats for women in panchayats and nagarpalikas and the law to mirror this provision in parliament and state assemblies is pending.

In response to campaigns by women's groups, important provisions of the criminal justice system have been changed. For instance, women cannot be summoned to a police station after sunset and before sunrise; women police must be present when a woman is interrogated; in some cities police stations managed entirely by women police have been set up. New laws have been introduced, such as the Domestic Violence Act and the law on sexual harassment and existing laws such as those on dowry or rape have been strengthened.

Yet even as these positive steps have taken place because of the pressure generated from below by the women's movement, there are counter trends that are liberating women in some ways but also increasing the burden on them by making them more vulnerable to violence both within their homes and communities and outside.

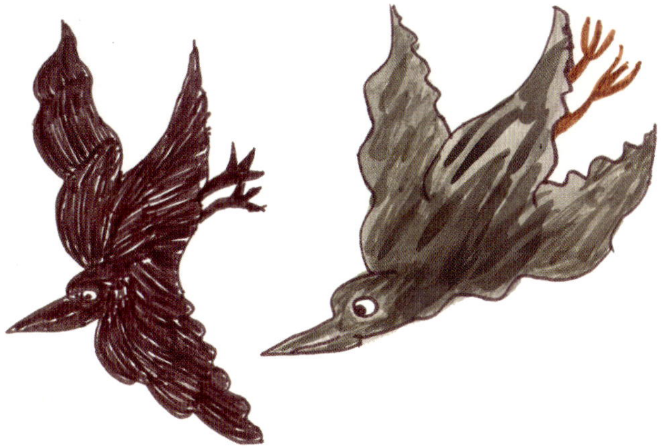

Dramatic Changes

Since the 1990s, India has seen dramatic changes with the economy opening up to global capital and markets. This has resulted in new opportunities for some but also loss of livelihood for many others. Rising literacy levels have opened up possibilities for many young people, including young women, yet the fruits of formal learning are often out of reach if you are poor or of a lower caste or belong to a religious minority or if you are a woman. Young women, led to believe that with education they can conquer the world, soon realise that tradition forecloses the limits of that world.

The growth and spread of satellite television has also contributed to change. Knowledge is now not restricted to those who can read. The power of the audiovisual is available to all. Thus the women of Idinthakarai opposing the nuclear power plant in Kudankulam in Tamil Nadu's Tirunelveli district might not know geography, or be able to mark Fukushima on a map, but they have seen the images of the havoc caused by the earthquake in Japan in 2011 and the explosion at the nuclear power plant that was considered to be safe. That image is now embedded in their understanding of what constitutes a dangerous technology. And they will not be convinced that having a plant using such technology in their backyard should not concern them. They are worried and they are determined to stop it. And to do so they have fasted, protested, shouted slogans, taken out marches and even immersed themselves in the sea to register their opposition – not for a day, or a week, but for well over a year.

The mobile phone has been another significant tool for change in rural areas. It has given individuals, including women, a tremendous feeling of freedom and power. Many of the older women would never have imagined that in their lifetime they would be able to communicate directly with people. And yet, here they are, speaking freely and confidently on mobile phones even as their young granddaughters do the same.

At the same time some traditions, including those resisting the birth of daughters have become more entrenched with modern technology facilitating sex selection. While satellite television has been an important vehicle for spreading information, some television programmes have reinforced regressive values, particularly towards women.

The downside of rapid economic growth has been an increase in disparities with only a small percentage benefitting from secure jobs while the vast majority of workers are forced to lead an insecure existence in the informal economy that affords no job security or rights. This has also compelled more women to step out of their homes to undertake wage labour. While their homes were not necessarily free of violence, they are now exposed to other forms of violence in the workplace and public spaces. Despite laws granting women equal rights on many

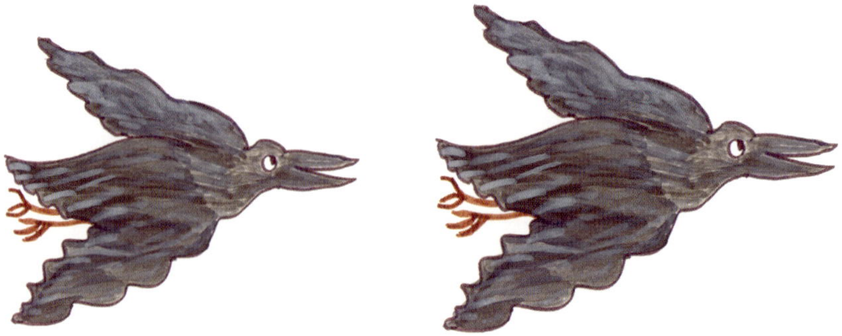

fronts, the bedrock of a patriarchal mindset that refuses to accept gender equality remains virtually untouched.

How has all this affected the lives of rural women? Radhaben's drawings in this book tell the story of the women of Kutch. But they also represent a larger picture, that of women in India, particularly rural women. They tell you how women get together and form collectives and have arrived at a non-hierarchical way of conducting their business. There are circles, not rectangles, no heads and tails but equals. They speak of violence and oppression in the home but also the joys of discovery – of the outside world, of the power of the collective, of simply being together as women. These drawings provide us with a "jhalak", as we would say in Hindi, a little taste of the immense variety that is at the heart of women's movements in India, urban or rural.

The contemporary women's movement in India cannot be called one movement because it consists of many movements with different approaches and strategies. Yet they have come together on a national level and successfully galvanized support for changes in laws that impinge on the lives of all women and fought for the enactment of new laws. They have taken up issues that revolved around women's work, their right to inheritance, their safety in public places and within their homes, their health, the way they are portrayed in the media etc.

At the international level too women belonging to these women's movements have been significant participants in campaigns leading to the recognition of women's rights as human rights, of women's reproductive health and rights as the mainstay of public health programmes, of the imperative of a gender perspective on environmental issues including the current attention to global warming and climate change, of women's work – most often unpaid – as something that must be part of national accounting systems, and many more.

The strength of women's movements in India has been their plurality of thought and views as well as the range of skills they possess. This essential diversity in the women's movements has emerged because of the complex and disparate conditions of women in India depending on whether they live in cities or villages, are from the better-off states or the poorer and more remote states, whether they belong to the long-oppressed lower castes or to a minority religion, or whether they are trapped in traditions that seclude women.

Beginnings

What do rights, empowerment, even justice mean to women who live on the edge of abject poverty, whose daily survival concerns overwhelm all else, who have no energy at the end of

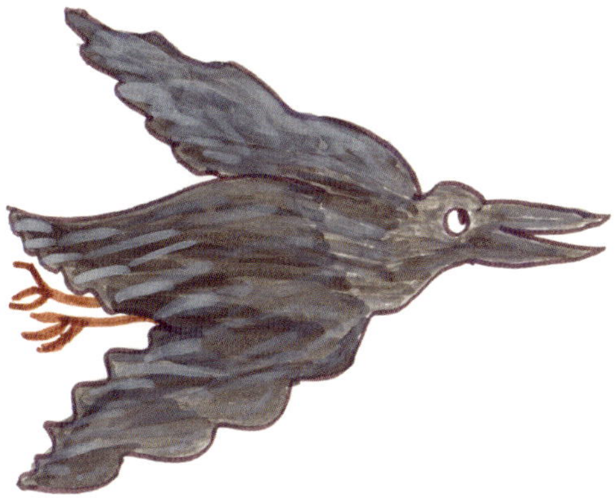

a day of back-breaking work in the field, on a work site or at home to think about the next day, the next week, the next year – the future? Where do you begin a conversation about justice and rights?

These were some of the questions that the three women who initiated the Kutch Mahila Vikas Sangathan (KMVS) in 1989 faced. Their journey, at a time when other similar movements were taking tentative steps elsewhere, illustrates the search for answers to these questions.

The initiators of KMVS decided that they needed to listen to the women in rural Kutch. They tried to understand the lives of these women. At that stage, they did not have a clear idea of where this would lead but they were convinced that women and their concerns should remain at the centre of whatever emerged.

The women they spoke to were suspicious. What did they want? Why had they come? Were they from the police? Had they come to take them away? Despite a lifetime of aggressive conditioning, these women were fearful.

In time, the women understood that the "outsiders" wanted nothing more than to learn. And learn they did. They saw what the women had to contend with. The harsh environment outside loaded their already burdened lives. They spent 3-4 hours collecting water every single day. The men had to leave them for months looking for grazing lands for the cattle. The one crop that the dry earth could yield often never materialized.

It is under these circumstances that women took to the embroidery for which Kutch is famous. Their poverty restricted the number of garments they owned. So they patched up old clothes with colourful embellishments. Those clothes beyond repair were recrafted into something else. Young girls and older women, daughters and mothers, daughters-in-law and mothers-in-law sat together transforming old into new. For the girls, a trunk full of embroidered garments and quilts were a pre-requisite to marriage. The longer you took, the longer you waited to get married.

Meghuben Rabari is a large Rabari woman with mournful eyes but a ready smile. I met her along with other women from the Saiyare Je Sangathan, one of KMVS' women's collectives in the Nakhatrana block in Kutch. This is how she explained what happened:

> Earlier our world was our village. Men would go out. Women would look after the cattle. The logic of embroidery was to patch old clothes and patch them in such a way that they wouldn't look old. Today things have changed. We get everything in the market. Apart from *Ma Baap*, we can buy anything in the market!

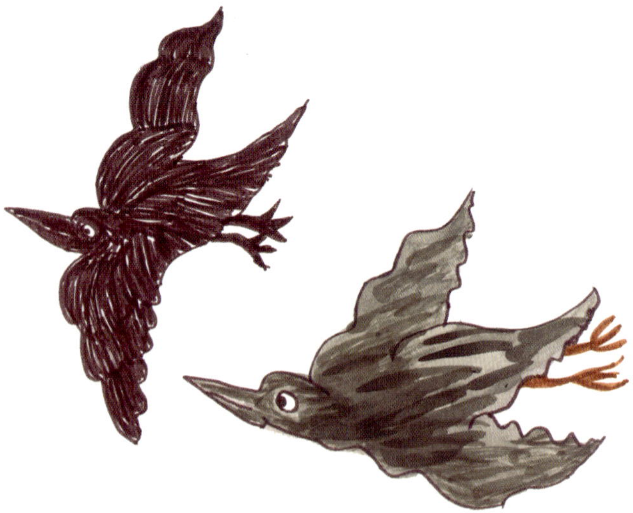

What was born out of necessity soon became a source of income. As Kutch opened up to tourists, the women realized that there was a monetary value to their work. Outsiders were interested. They were willing to pay handsomely for a piece of the intricate embroidered cloth.

Middlemen also caught on to this chance to make some money. And they quickly stepped in. They persuaded the women, who were desperate to earn any money they could during the drought years, to sell their work for a song. In turn, they resold these pieces at many times more to shops outside Kutch.

But once the women had come together as a collective, they understood the exploitation. And they worked out ways to get a fair price for their work. Today those initial steps have grown into an independent producer company of rural women artisans called *Qasab* that markets the work of these Kutchi women.

The process of moving from individual women who embroidered in their homes to a producers' collective was significant because it made the women understand their position in society, their lack of power over resources and how their work was not recognized. It would be easy today to merely admire the handiwork of Kutchi women and forget that behind it lies the story of real empowerment, a term that has become so commonplace as to lose meaning. Not just in Kutch but in many other parts of India, this process of change amongst rural women had begun to take place through interventions by groups like the Mahila Samakhya in Gujarat, UP and Karnataka and the Women's Development Programme in Rajasthan. These interventions were making rural women recognize their own worth. They had begun to understand the real reasons for their oppression and were finding ways to overcome the embedded patriarchal structures that had confined them to particular roles.

This story also exemplifies processes that define the women's movement. It illustrates how movements of rural women emerge and grow. The beginning is not necessarily a predictable one. Women decide their priority. By understanding this, and working with them, other areas of concern are talked about and addressed. These areas could include environmental concerns, livelihood challenges or dealing with sexual violence, inside and outside their homes.

ASSERTION, AFFIRMATION, NEGOTIATION

Radhaben's drawings refer to the inspiration that they drew from the women in Garhwal, living in the foothills of the Himalayas, a long way from the dry landscape of Kutch. Here life

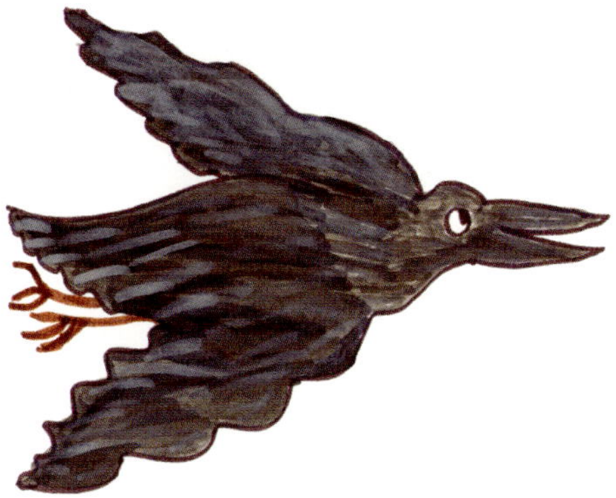

and livelihood depend on the forests covering the hillsides, the water streams that flow and the soil that remains intact because of the vegetative cover. Like the women in Kutch, these women too are often left on their own as their men migrate to cities looking for work.

Before laws had been formulated to protect forests from the axe of the logger, it was the women who guaranteed that forests remained untouched. They knew that without forests, their daily task of gathering firewood would become even more stressful than it already was. Without forests, the water that came down during the rains would run off without percolating and replenishing the underground aquifers and streams. Without forests, there would be no fodder for their cattle. Thus saving forests was like saving themselves. And they did this by the unique method of hugging the trees and daring the loggers to come and cut the trees. So the Chipko movement of the late 1970s was a women's movement that inspired many other women to fight to save the natural resources that sustained their lives.

Radhaben also refers to the women of Nellore district, Andhra Pradesh, who destroyed liquor shops as they saw alcoholism as the biggest burden women had to bear. These women were being taught functional literacy. What they learnt from it was that they could take charge of their lives, and they could act rather than be victims. The Andhra anti-liquor movement inspired women in many other parts of India including the women in Kutch.

In Gujarat, even though officially liquor is banned, it continues to be brewed, sold and consumed, often with the connivance of the local police. The women's collectives of KMVS have evolved different strategies to deal with the problem. It has not gone away. In fact each time they have been able to stem it, it has resurfaced a couple of years later, more aggressively, in newer pockets. The liquor is still brewed and sold, often inside their villages. But now the men have to sneak off to drink in case one of these women catches them.

Promoting Kutchi embroidery, hugging trees or destroying liquor dens does not fall into one of the usual categories of what are viewed as feminist or women's movements. Yet whether it is livelihood, environment, or violence, the centrality of women setting the agenda is what emerges as the common element in all these movements. For instance, forests, or the grazing lands on which so many in Kutch depend, can be saved in other ways. You can have laws that 'protect' forests. You can ban diversion of grasslands – the so-called "common" lands that are the lifeline for millions of people living in semi-arid regions like Kutch and Rajasthan. You can create livelihood options for craftspeople by centralizing marketing. You can officially ban liquor and hope that this will reduce the incidence of domestic violence that often appears to be linked to alcoholism. Yet such actions do not necessarily produce solutions that make a lasting difference. Laws do not save forests or grasslands, as we well know, prohibition does not restrict liquor or reduce violence and marketing companies do not give a fair deal to the craftsperson.

The Poor Woman's Burden

Water is another issue that is close to the heart of poor women everywhere in India. Women spend hours looking for water, fighting for it, and collecting and storing it. In Kutch, where drought is an annual visitor, you cannot escape the water crisis. With practically zero annual precipitation, where will the water come from, how will the open wells be replenished, how will communities living on a single crop survive, how will millions of cattle that form the source of livelihood for a good part of the population, find any fodder?

In the four years before KMVS began working in Kutch, the district faced one of the worst droughts. The government's response was to set up drought relief works where people would be paid partly in cash and partly in grain. Before long, this became entirely cash payment. But none of the work being done under these programmes contributed to permanent resources that would equip communities to withstand drought. This was drought relief, not drought proofing.

In their conversations with women, KMVS discovered that environmental issues were one of their primary concerns — land, water, fodder. Their land was getting degraded, there was no water and they desperately needed fodder for their cattle. It is possible that if the men had been asked first, they would have set out different priorities. Yet, because it was clear that women must remain at the centre of any strategy or decisions, it was the women who led the way. And by doing so, they quietly yet firmly stood the strong patriarchal culture that had governed all decisions thus far, on its head.

Hakima, popularly known as Haku Masi, is a Theba Muslim. She is an impressive presence, always smiling, displaying a set of teeth that have turned black with the regular use of black *manjan*. She is one of the oldest, and certainly one of the liveliest members of the Saiyare Je Sangathan in Nakhatrana.

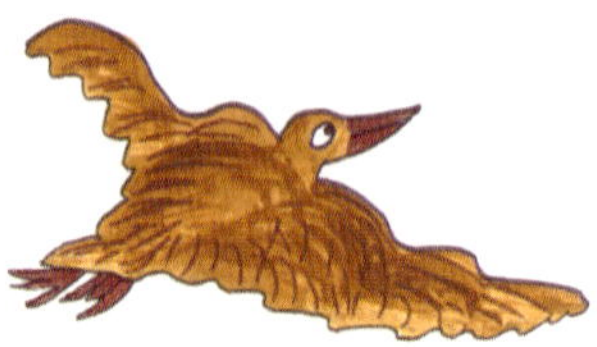

She says that in her village of Dador in Nakhatrana block, drinking water was their main concern. There only well was outside the village limit. Women had to walk the distance carrying heavy pots of water. Sahjeevan, an environmental group that worked with KMVS, devised a system of cluster distribution. Pipes were laid from the well to three 200-litre tanks in three different locations and water was pumped twice a day. Three women from each community were given the responsibility of collecting Rs 3 per person per month. For the first

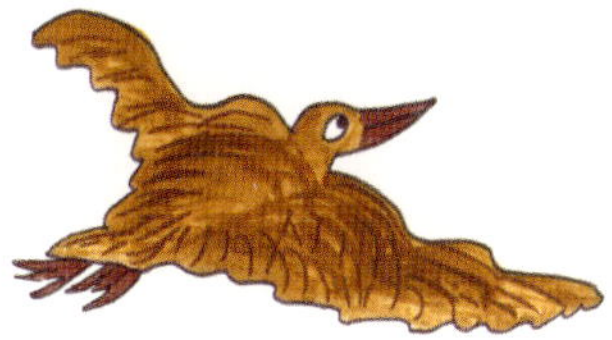

time, a solar pump was used to extract the water. As a result, 530 families living in the village benefitted. This effort might seem small in the vastness of a district like Kutch, but it exemplifies the spirit behind the women's movement – participatory, equitable and democratic. Since 2001, more than 200 villages across Kutch and Gujarat have adopted this approach for water restoration programmes and projects.

There are similar stories from other parts of the country where the women have taken the lead to find a solution to water shortage. In the process, others in the community have recognized and accepted the importance of women in leadership positions. This has not been easy. The women are the first to admit that often only the older women could take up the leadership while the younger women still had battles to fight within their homes. But an important precedent was being set as more women like Haku Masi began to be central to devising solutions for the entire community.

Difficult Choices

The choices, however, are not just about listening to women. When poor women express a concern, it is often one that the government has already heard, or at least pretended to do so. In a country like India, in the name of the poor, there are schemes and programmes that cover everything. Anyone wanting to do something for poor women can easily get absorbed in just ensuring that these programmes are implemented or take on the delivery of government programmes.

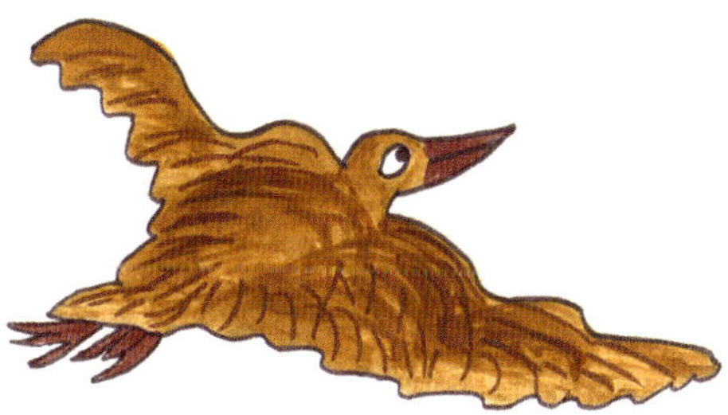

Groups like KMVS and others working with rural women have had to make choices. Do you try to ensure that the women you work with get the benefits to which they are entitled? Do you do this by taking over and delivering services on behalf of the government? Or do you inform the women of the government's promises and let them organize themselves to get these entitlements? Choices made have varied, depending on the region in which women's groups have worked.

Even programmes like Mahila Samakhya, which was funded entirely by the government but functioned virtually as a non-governmental body, moved beyond delivery of services to giving women the confidence to intervene. The women's collectives formed under the Mahila Samakhya programme in UP, Gujarat and Karnataka were similar in many ways to the Sangathans of the KMVS. And some of the outcomes were not very different. For instance, one of the lasting legacies of the Mahila Samakhya in Gujarat is the Nari Adalat, a women's court that came up in one district but has been adopted elsewhere. These structured yet informal courts have helped women resolve problems that would otherwise have meant either years in litigation, or silence because they were too afraid to approach the formal system. Apart from from sexual and domestic violence, these adalats have also taken in inheritance issues, appropriation of land, rights to equal wages and displacement.

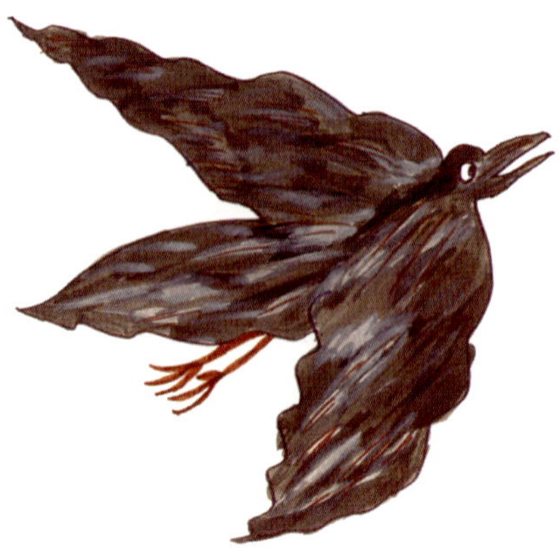

Women's Health and Wealth

Women's health and reproductive rights have been important issues addressed by the women's movement in India. This has meant articulating the concept that women have a right over their own bodies and should be able to decide when to have children, how many to have, when to stop, how to stop and the right to choose a sexual partner. Also that women's health does not only comprise problems linked to reproduction, and these other aspects too should be addressed instead of being treated as secondary or unimportant. These concepts emerged as women saw that under the excuse of 'population control' and 'population explosion' – based on a Malthusian understanding of the dangers of a rapidly increasing population – women were being targeted with invasive technologies in contraception as well as forced sterilization even as their basic health needs were being neglected.

Sterilization became especially important for poor women. The inadequate healthcare infrastructure in most parts of rural India has contributed to the high rate of maternal mortality. Women who developed complications during childbirth were unable to access emergency care. In any case, even routine ailments often went unaddressed as women were socialized to keep their own health concerns as the lowest priority. Not surprisingly, when asked, women spoke of health and particularly pregnancy and childbirth as a major concern.

In Kutch too, as in many other parts of India, the health infrastructure is poor. Primary Health Centres are often ill equipped with personnel and medical equipment. People suffer from basic health challenges such as malnutrition as well as tuberculosis and malaria. In addition women face several gynaecological problems such as prolapsed uteruses, anaemia, pelvic inflammatory diseases. Many develop poor eyesight and back problems because of the nature of their work, particularly those involved in embroidery.

The women from the Ujjas Mahila Sangathan, one of the older collectives formed through KMVS in Kutch, suggested that training women as traditional midwives would be an appropriate intervention into women's health. What began as an intervention to train women as midwives soon went beyond that. Women were trained to collect blood samples and prepare slides that could be sent to a lab for tests. This was crucial in an area where

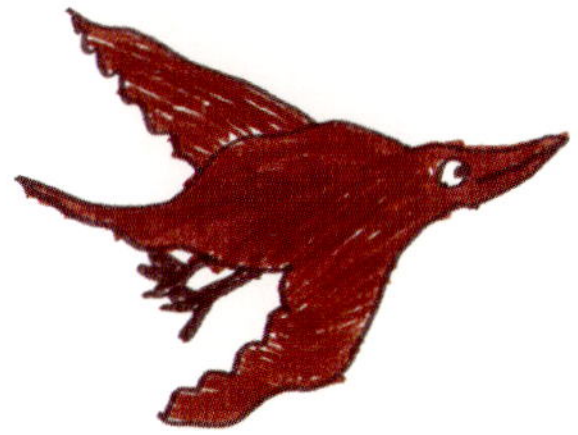

malaria is rampant but people had no way to confirm that they had contracted it. The women were also trained to detect preliminary signs of cancer of the breasts, and more recently, cervical cancer.

Women forged alliances with philanthropic hospitals, professional gynaecologists and the State health departments to regularize antenatal care, access to primary healthcare and gynaecological surgeries due to prolapsed uteruses and cancer of reproductive organs. In fact, trained midwives and women members have done extensive work on educating, preventing and providing for women with prolapsed uteruses – a condition that affects one of every eight women.

Today, irrespective of whether there is an efficient public health service available, there are women trained to meet the immediate health needs of these communities. They have not replaced the government system that includes trained village health workers but compliments it. Women's collectives are also well placed to monitor the functioning of government facilities and put the necessary pressure to make them more effective. Apart from providing a service, this intervention has given the women greater confidence in their own abilities and raised their status in their villages.

The Sangathans also conducted campaigns to create general awareness about health and surveys to assess health needs. This gave them a clearer idea of the kind of problems women and men face in the absence of a good healthcare system. Women were taught to understand their bodies, something that is rarely addressed in most Indian societies. It was a process that transformed the way women viewed themselves. The approach was not just delivering a service but equipping people with knowledge about their own bodies and health.

Related but separate was the issue of women's control over economic resources. In a society where women have little or no control over money, where do you begin? KMVS began by initiating women-led informal taluka banks akin to the savings and credit movement that was finding an enthusiastic response amongst rural women elsewhere in the country. Bringing women together to save, to learn how to access credit, how to set-up small enterprises was part of a larger effort to make women understand the power of a collective, and how through this they could negotiate and get their entitlements. The very process of operating informal banks, and then challenging the ways in which the formal banks as well as the usurious private moneylenders operate gave women an enormous sense of their own power. Although many self-help groups in other parts of India have been sucked into the microfinance strategy of the bigger banks and the state, thereby depriving them of their autonomy and often reducing them to even greater dependence, not all have fallen into the trap. Certainly, the women in

Kutch who have expanded their savings and credit collectives remained outside this and have continued to grow.

The World Outside

Yet even as these rural women's movements chipped away at structures and belief systems that restricted women's autonomy, there were other processes at play that impacted rural communities in many parts of India. These processes were entwined in the vision of development articulated by those who believed that rapid economic growth, the injection of foreign capital and large-scale privatization of industries and natural resources would automatically transform the lives of the poorest people in India.

What this optimistic story that was sold to the public did not acknowledge was that the price for this rapid growth would be paid inordinately by the people at the very bottom of the economic structure, especially rural communities. All over India, rural communities as well as the adivasis who have lived in harmony with nature in India's forests, have borne the brunt of displacement as infrastructure – dams, ports, roads and highways, industries, power plants – swallow up their lands and destroy the natural resource base on which they survive. As in the Chipko movement, you find in many parts of the country that it is the women who are the most determined opponents of what they see as destructive development – projects that give back no benefits either to the people they displace or the natural resources they destroy.

The lives of the fishing communities living along India's coastline exemplify the kind of pressures this so-called 'development' is placing on the shoulders of those dependent on the natural environment. Kutch has a 350 km coastline, which provides sustenance through artisanal and motorized fishing to over 10,000 fishing households, the majority belonging to the Wagher community. As a rule, these communities have homes in villages away from the coast but spend eight months of the year living in temporary shelters near the coast in what are called "bundhers".

The men go out and fish, the women sort and dry the fish. The men then sell the fish to merchants. In most cases, the merchants give an advance that pays for the fuel for the boats. In return, the fisherman has to sell all his catch to that particular merchant. As a result, the fisherman cannot negotiate a higher or better price. But in the absence of working capital, most fishing families have no option but to follow this system.

In the last decade, particularly after the 2001 earthquake in Kutch which killed an estimated 20,000 people and destroyed 400,000 houses, the State gave special incentives to

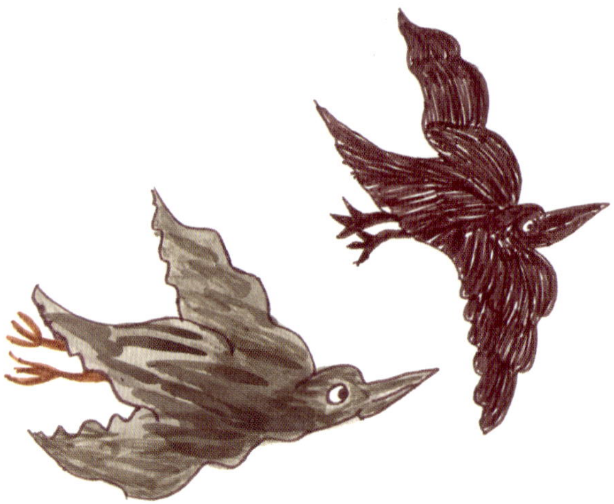

industries to expand in Kutch. Land is plentiful in this district. Most of it is under government control. As a result, in the last seven years, the rate of industrialization in Kutch district has been one of the fastest in the world. A direct consequence of this was urbanization with many villages being swallowed up by nearby towns. Inevitably, the demographic composition of many parts of Kutch has changed as industries have drawn in people from other parts of India. Another consequence was levels of land and water pollution this region had never witnessed before.

The Kutch coastline hosts mangrove swamps that are repositories of a vast range of biodiversity. They are also breeding spaces for amphibian species. The *cheria* plant provides fodder for cattle and camels and firewood for domestic cooking fuel. The construction of ports, jetties and other abutments into the sea without considering how these alter tidal patterns has begun to affect mangroves. The latter flourish when there is a mix of saline seawater and fresh river water. If access to one is cut off, the mangrove ceases to exist. This is already beginning to happen along the coast.

Inevitably, the people to bear the brunt of the destruction of the mangroves and the increasing industrialization are the fishing communities who live along the Kutch coast. Apart from industries, the State has also allowed private capital to cordon off large parcels of land for special economic zones (SEZ). Some of these SEZs are blocking access to the coast to several fishing communities.

Take the fishing community of Bhadreshwar who live for the most part of the year in Randh Bundher. The women from the Randh Bundher, who are active in the Ujjas Mahila Sangathan, found one day that an airstrip being built for an SEZ had blocked their access to the beach. All these years they could come and go as they pleased. Suddenly, they had to plead with a private security guard to let them pass.

They discussed this in the Sangathan and decided that the best course of action was to offer a dharna before the office of the mamlatdar. Says Amina Masi, one of the leaders of the Sangathan:

> We sat for 35 days in a dharna in front of the Mamlatdar office, over 500 of us, mostly women. We also held a rally in Bhuj and one in Mundra. The story of our struggle was also broadcast through the community radio. As a result, fisherfolk in south Gujarat heard and offered their solidarity. Today, although the road has not been completely opened up, we are allowed to pass and do not have to constantly seek the permission of the guards from Adani to access our homes near the sea.

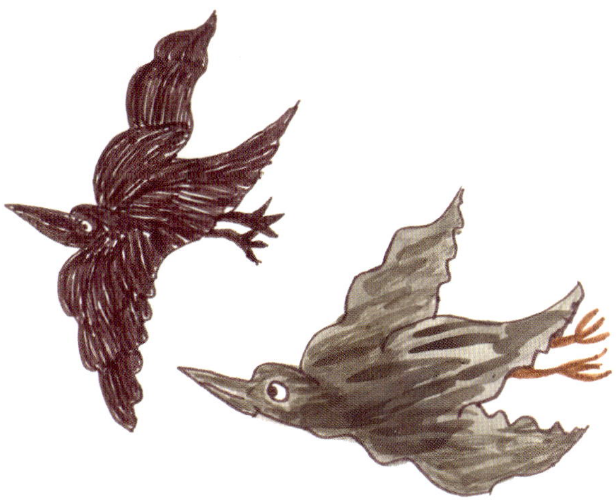

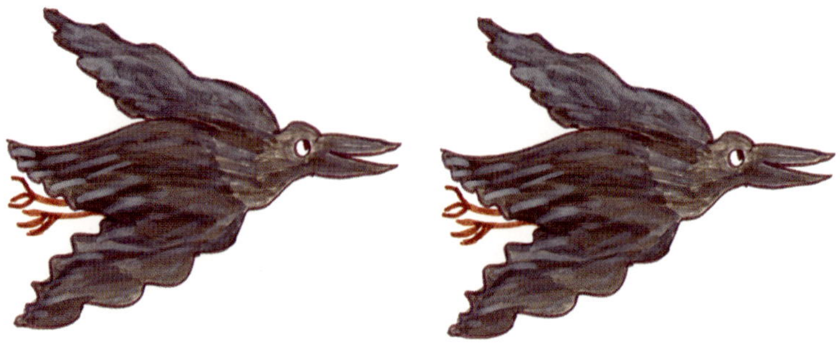

Collective action has also made a difference to the earnings of the fisherfolk. The women say that five years ago they formed a collective and negotiated with two or three traders. They felt the local traders had exploited them. They were better placed to bargain because a non-governmental organization advanced them a revolving fund. As part of the process of setting up a new system for marketing their fish, they first conducted a survey to assess the extent of indebtedness. With this information they went back to the community and resolved that a collective business model made sense.

What began initially as an intervention into their livelihood issues has now fanned out into all kinds of other activities. For instance, the Sangathan women now ensure that the children are vaccinated. They have identified women who can be trained as traditional midwives, and they have also managed to get mobile medical clinics to visit their settlements. Given that they spend two thirds of the year in these temporary shelters, these interventions have made a substantial difference to the quality of life of the community as a whole.

However, other developments in the region are scarring the environment and impacting their lives. There is a perceptible reduction in the fish catch because the spawning grounds for the fish have been adversely affected by the destruction and cutting of mangroves. The women also complained that while earlier they could go freely to collect firewood from these mangroves, now they are afraid to do so because the "company men" are hanging around.

The demographic changes in the towns and areas around these new developments are having a direct impact on women and their sense of safety in the public space. Traditionally, there are many communities in Kutch where the women would not step out. All the 'outside' tasks, so to speak, were left to the men. This has changed considerably in the last two decades in Kutch as in other parts of the country. For instance, communities like the Rabaris, who could survive on what they earned from their cattle, are now forced to work in the towns as domestics. The women say they do not like to wash other people's dishes and clothes and are particularly upset that their daughters, who end up living in towns after marriage, must do this so that the family earns enough. Yet they have no option.

A Violent World

This 'exposure' to the outside world, and the changing demographics of the towns, has also brought with it sexual violence. And women hold alcoholism as the principal reason for the increase in domestic violence. There are also generational clashes in families with young people defying custom. When girls are educated, they carry with them certain expectations of what

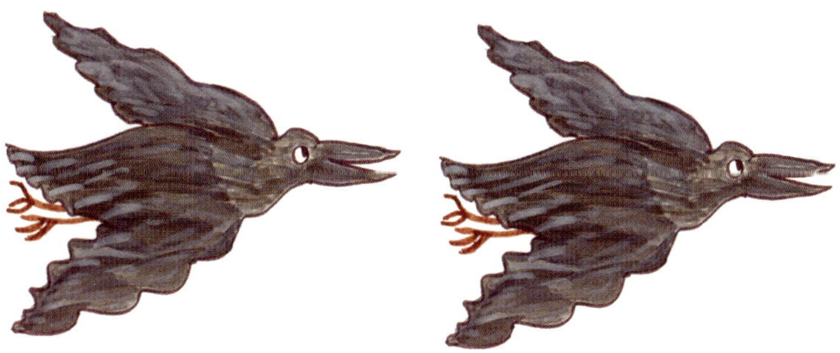

life would be in the future, a life different from that of their mothers. But once married, they quickly learn the bitter truth, that the promise of freedom and autonomy is ephemeral, that the traditional system of 'service' to the husband and his family continues to hold sway despite changes in the outside world. All these changes are contributing to friction and violence within households.

Women who suffer violence in any of these circumstances would rarely go to the police to report. The consequences for them would be too dire within their homes. In any case, the majority of rural women are afraid to enter a police station to report a crime or a violation. The story in Kutch is no different from that which prevails in most rural areas in India. Police stations are notoriously unfriendly to poor people and more particularly to women. It is easy for a poor person to get so intimidated by the very sight of a police station, that they would prefer to avoid it rather than turning to it for help.

So how do you break this barrier? One way is to provide information to women on the law, on their rights as citizens, as women, and basically demystify the criminal justice system. The Nari Adalats did that in Gujarat through Mahila Samakhya. They and other similar structures helped bring out in the open issues that would otherwise have remained locked behind the four walls of the home and most often at the cost of the women who had to survive the violent consequences. As a result, there is marked increase in the reporting of domestic violence.

The intervention of KMVS in this area of women and the law is different and innovative. In 1996-97, the organization handpicked 20-25 women who were seen as emerging leaders and gave them paralegal training. This was done in a formal and structured manner so that at the end of the training, the women would have a working knowledge of the laws that affect their lives, they would know the routine that the police must follow when someone goes to complain, they would know what had to be done in the event of a rape complaint, or a complaint about domestic violence. At the end of the training, the women were issued identity cards and called "Police Mitra" or friends of the police.

KMVS also ran socio-legal counselling centres where women would feel less inhibited to come than going to a police station. They ran awareness campaigns by going from village to village with audio commentaries and sticking handwritten posters everywhere to inform people about these centres.

The problems that they came across were neither new nor unusual. There were many cases of unnatural deaths of women. Women were also exploited as there were few men in their villages, the majority having migrated to Mumbai in search of work.

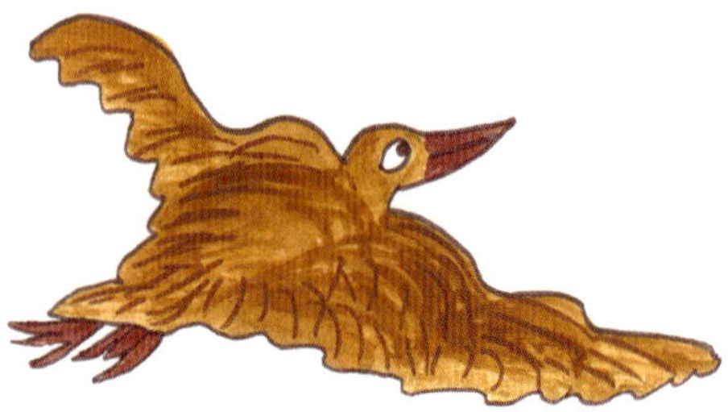

When you speak to the Sangathan women, they will tell you many stories of how this training equipped them to intervene and help women. "Sometimes we have to sit in the police station till 10 at night to get the FIR registered," says Devalben. Another says, "Now the police call us. Earlier they made fun of us. If there is a new PSI (police sub-inspector), we invite him here and introduce ourselves."

Says Devalben, "In a rape case, we didn't know what to do. Police would say, where's the proof this is a rape and ask us to take the woman to the doctor. The doctor would say this is a police case." The police would give the women the run around. Now they say this does not happen.

By the mid-1990s, despite the centres in two blocks the Sangathans found there were too many cases for them to handle. That is when the idea of a helpline that would work within the existing system came up.

Hallo Sakhi is now a well-established helpline for violence against women. Although the police have a helpline (1091), the Sangathan women realized that the helpline was ineffectual because you had to call it from a landline. These days, few people have landlines or fixed telephones. Yet almost everyone, including women, has mobile phones. Clearly a helpline must be one that can be dialled from a mobile phone. So simple, so obvious, and yet it needed the common sense of women invested in doing something effective to help other women to come up with such a solution.

Inaugurated in 2010, Hallo Sakhi registered over 800 cases in the first two years. Most of these cases were of domestic violence. There were also many complaints about alcoholism that led to violence in the homes.

What these interventions, like the helpline or nari adalats suggest is that changing laws, or introducing effective laws is not enough to make a difference to the lives of women. Despite these laws, there is growing incidence of violence as recorded by the National Crimes Record Bureau and the conviction rate remains abysmally low. For every crime that is reported, many more remain unreported precisely for the reasons that the Sangathan felt the need to set up alternative structures.

If you train women how to use and access the law, there is a greater chance of making the law work for them instead of sitting back and hoping that the existing system, which has failed them so far, will suddenly spin into effective action. But more than just delivering justice – that of course is not guaranteed and is a long drawn-out process that depends on innumerable imponderables – this process strengthens the hands of women, it gives them knowledge

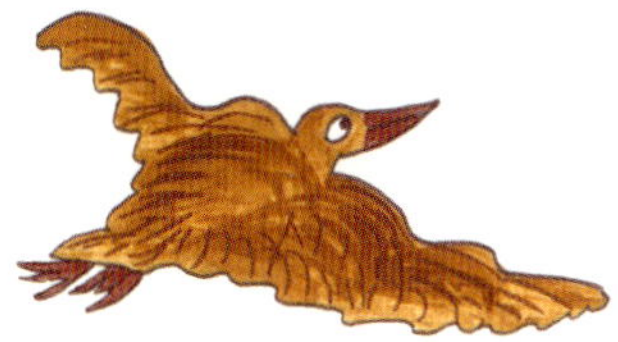

and the confidence to persist rather than giving up. In a classical sense, this kind of 'empowerment' is real.

One need not romanticize these interventions. They are necessarily limited. They reach a limited constituency. But in the absence of other, more effective, interventions, they are important because they make a difference to the lives of women. This 'difference' consists of the growth in confidence to be able to talk about a problem in an open forum, to seek assistance, and to know that keeping quiet is not the only option open to them. Even if these interventions are still not tackling areas that remain hidden, a wedge has been stuck in the door. It cannot be closed now.

Women at the Centre

This narrative has focussed primarily on the work of KMVS, which has grown from three members to 15,000 members in seven grassroots organizations, not because it is the only one working with rural women. There are many other similar organizations doing remarkable work to build the confidence and belief of rural women that they count, that they can transform their lives and their circumstances. KMVS dominates this narrative because its journey reflects many of the opportunities, challenges and limitations that so many other similar groups have faced.

It is clear from the many areas that KMVS has tackled – which also include savings and credit, training women members of panchayats as well as community radio – that the core commitment to women and their rights has undergirded all their activities. In that sense, this and other such efforts, even if they appear on the surface to be about programmes that 'help' poor women, are all a part of the growing base of rural women's movements.

Can such movements really be classified as women's movements just because women are the main participants?

Srilatha Batliwala, writing in "Changing their world: Concepts and Practices of Women's Movements" (AWID, 2008) describes feminism this way:

> Feminism stands for the power to, not power over – we struggle to change the practice of power both within our own structures and movements as well as in the social, economic and political institutions we engage. This has created a set of feminist ethics which, although they vary in different parts of the world, contain some common principles at the core: creating less vertical and more horizontal, participatory and democratic power and decision-making structures, greater

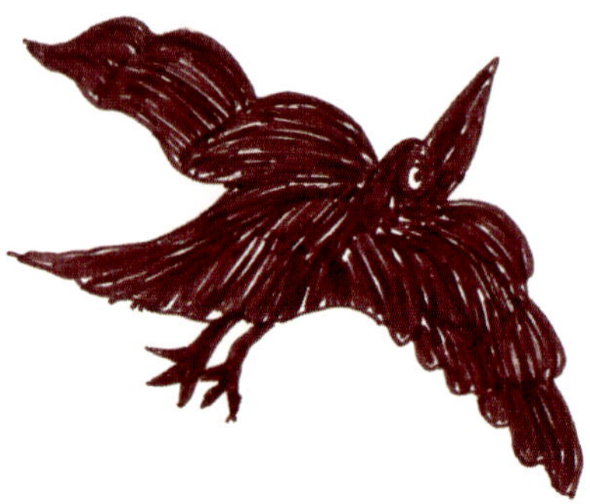

transparency and openness about internal and external processes and finances, ensuring a voice and role for all key stakeholders, internal and external, and building a sense of solidarity/sorority/inclusion, a strong sense of accountability to our constituents and to the larger movements we are linked to, creating flexible, gender-sensitive internal policies and practices based on respect for different capacities, and generally, pursuing non-violent strategies of action. These ethics underlie the struggle, in most feminist movements and organizations, to create feminist ways of working.

The way some of the rural women's movements have developed and grown reflect Batliwala's articulation of feminist ethics, particularly in the horizontal, participatory and democratic ways of decision-making. Here is something that formal democratic institutions need to emulate – where in the name of people such rigid hierarchies have been created that ordinary people, particularly women, feel completely excluded.

In their diversity and depth, women's movements since the late 1970s have demonstrated their abilities to work separately and collectively. Some engage directly with what are seen as "women's issues" – violence within and outside the home, safety, and legal rights. Others have approached it differently, particularly when the work involves poor women. Here livelihood, environment and social justice become essential components. The other issues are byproducts of addressing what are seen as the larger problems that affect both men and women, although not in the same measure.

What is also clear from the different narratives emerging from rural women's movements is that the way women begin to get organized varies greatly from region to region. Sometimes the trigger is an environmental concern, sometimes a desire for functional literacy, sometimes ways to save money and access credit, and at other times the urgent need for healthcare. But ultimately all these move in the direction where women feel most vulnerable – their lack of power within their homes, within their communities and as 'citizens' of a free country.

Batliwala speaks of changing the practice of power. Yet even the government's efforts to ensure one third – now one half – of seats in panchayats has not necessarily done this in rural areas. The sarpanch pati (called 'SP' in Kutch) is a reality in most parts of India. The women are in the front but the men run the show for the most part. Yet today, the very fact that the women can access political power has given them a little more elbowroom in their homes. At the same time, this has also opened them up to much more pressure and not necessarily given them the power to stand up against the patriarchal structure that remains in place.

The Kutchi women I have written about are transformed human beings when they are with the other women in their collective. They laugh, they joke, they express opinions. The

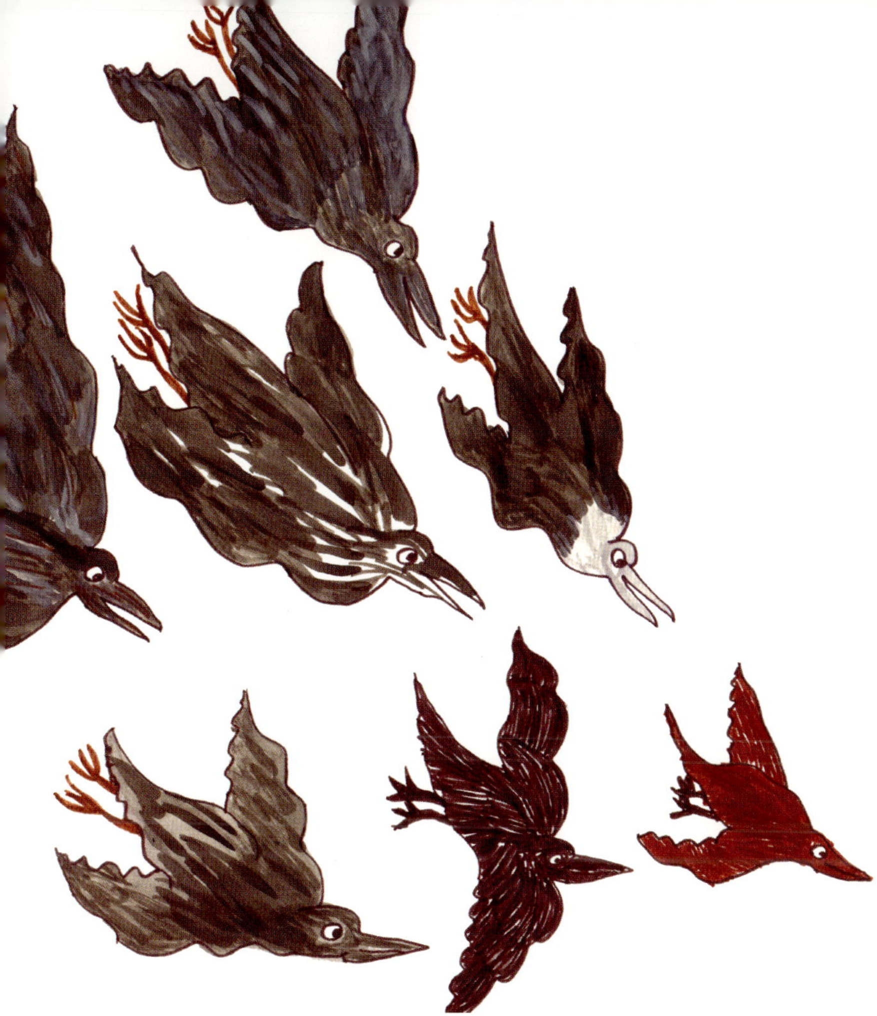

older ones now feel free to travel outside Kutch and have come back even more confident. But behind them are other women, their daughters or their daughters-in-law who would not be in a position to make such choices, to attend meetings, to travel. So even as some things have changed, much remains the same.

Yet, what is significant is that role models have been created and new precedents have been set. If we view these alongside other changes in the country such as growing literacy and the revolution in communication, it is evident that the process of change cannot be reversed. Ultimately one hopes that the walls of patriarchy will at least be dented.

Yet many challenges remain. For instance, while many rural women now feel that they can have a say in village affairs through gram sabhas and panchayats, or as members of collectives, they have not been able to alter the power structures within their families. Does this mean they are less 'empowered'?

This question should be posed differently from the perspective of poor women. For them the primary burdens are access to basic services – water, sanitation, electricity, cooking fuel, health – and secure shelter and livelihood. Then comes safety, within and outside the house, and access to some avenue to get justice. For some women, especially those caught within communal or caste clashes, the latter will take on a greater priority. But the changes, even if incremental, cannot be discounted. Perhaps in some cases social and power hierarchies will never change, at least not in this generation. Perhaps what is happening is setting in motion changes that will manifest themselves a generation down. Perhaps, if conservatism continues to grow as is evident even in parts of India that are doing well economically, even these gains made will be reversed.

What we need to recognize is that in the course of just two decades, rural women in India have taken giant strides. From being trapped in unpaid work within or outside the house, rural women can be seen handling bank accounts, speaking on mobile phones, talking confidently to the police and district officials, fighting to get their daughters educated, travelling outside their homes and villages to learn about other women and their problems, getting elected to panchayats and shrugging off the label of being just proxies for men, forming unions and negotiating for better wages, demanding and getting better services from the government, and even becoming community reporters wielding microphones and recorders as they document the lives of their sisters.

By any measure this is at least a minor revolution, a process that cannot be reversed. That is good enough for us to celebrate.

Kutch Mahila Vikas Sangathan (KMVS) was founded in 1989 as a rural women's collective in Kutch district, Gujarat and has evolved to be a network of organizations led, managed and governed by rural women in the district. KMVS has been a pioneer in fostering the social, political, economic, environmental and cultural leadership of vulnerable women, raising their consciousness and capacities to address gender inequities in their lives, and engender transformative agendas in their homes, villages, and communites. KMVS's efforts to empower women have drawn from, mirrored and contributed to the larger women's movement which played itself across the geography of India in the late eighties.

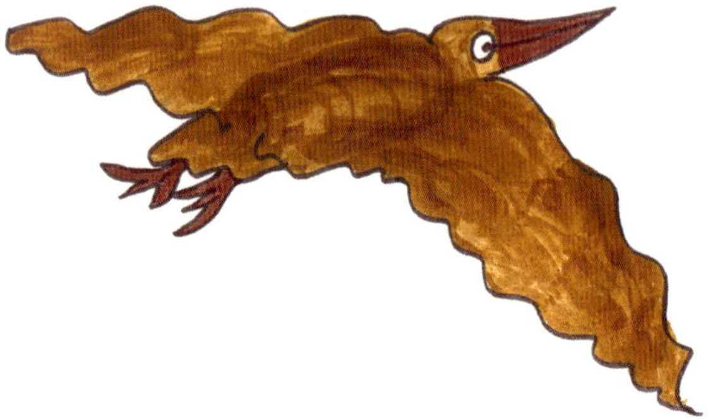